STILL COUNTING THE DEAD

FRANCES HARRISON was educated at Trinity Hall, Cambridge, and at SOAS and Imperial College in London. For many years she worked as a foreign correspondent for the BBC, posted in South Asia, South East Asia and Iran. From 2000 to 2004 she was the resident BBC correspondent in Sri Lanka. She has worked at Amnesty International as Head of News and while writing this book was a visiting research fellow at Oxford University.

Still Counting the Dead

Survivors of Sri Lanka's Hidden War

FRANCES HARRISON

Portobello
BOOKS

Published by Portobello Books 2012

Portobello Books
12 Addison Avenue
London
W11 4QR

A CIP catalogue record is available from the British Library.

9 8 7 6 5 4 3 2 1

ISBN 978 1 84627 469 5

www.portobellobooks.com

Typeset by Lindsay Nash.
Printed and bound by CPI Group (UK) Ltd, Croydon, CR0 4YY.

Burning

Those lives go uncounted, Unaccounted.
Yet a day will come
Where history will speak
That which no celluloid spoke…

Bones
Broken
Disfigured
Deranged
Morphed
Alienated
Ripped
Destroyed
Denied
Lost
Laboured
Buried
Silenced
Snuffed

The scorched earth knows it all.

Elil Rajan, *Ullmai*, Sri Lanka:
Society of Jesus, 2006

Contents

Acknowledgements

First and foremost, I would like to pay homage to the Sri Lankan Tamils who shared their stories with me. It was a huge leap of faith. Survivors trusted me when at their most vulnerable. Many of their names have been changed in order to safeguard family members still inside Sri Lanka.

I apologise that not all the stories I recorded are included in this book, on grounds of space. There were people who spent hours recounting horrific experiences, helping me understand better what it was like to be inside the war zone. They were invaluable and I hope they do not feel their efforts went to waste. Many cannot be named, but among them are: Dhamilvany Kumar, Mrs Javan, Jegan, Uthayan, Meena and Murugan. There was also the skeletal lady who physically shook in her chair as she told me how her sixteen-year-old nephew had been forcibly recruited by the Tigers, only to disappear without trace; I am sorry I put her through the trauma of reliving those experiences.

This book wouldn't have come into existence if Sri Lankan friends – both Sinhalese and Tamil – had not kept in touch after I left the country. Many journalists I knew from press conferences in Colombo were forced into exile in 2009, and from their experiences I grasped how much the paradise island had changed. If Pulidevan hadn't telephoned throughout the war, compelling me to take notice of what was unfolding, I am not sure I would have even thought of writing about Sri Lanka.

A great deal of people aided me in tracking down survivors. Many cannot be named, for their own security. Among colleagues, Bashana Abeywardene of Journalists for Democracy has been the most long-suffering, and Chandana Bandara of the BBC Sinhala Service kindly read a draft to check for cultural and political *faux pas*. Nirmanusan Balasandaram was generous with contacts and information; Annuuddha

Lokkuhapuarachchi, former chief photographer for Reuters in Colombo, looked for photographs for me; and Karunakharan Pathmanathan, former BBC Tamil Service reporter in Colombo, translated videos.

Special thanks go to SJ, who read some chapters and guided me in other ways. His courage is evident in his intention to return to Sri Lanka to serve his people. Many members of the Catholic Church who must remain anonymous have won my enormous respect for their commitment to human rights and truth at considerable personal cost. Sadly they are not the rising figures within the clerical establishment in Sri Lanka, but they should be.

Several people translated for me in different countries; many found it deeply upsetting. I owe them all a huge debt, especially S. Akka and her very hospitable cousin, who has supported many Tamils in trouble. Thanks also to Dr Panchakulasingam Kandiah and the budding author Malavi.

Mr S drew the map when he had far more important and life-threatening things on his mind; I sincerely hope that one day he finds his family. J and his wife in Australia showed me the wider historical perspective of the Sinhalese uprisings in the south of Sri Lanka. Special thanks also to Mr and Mrs Fernando – who personally sacrificed an enormous amount to speak out for justice for Tamils. In Australia, many dedicated people helped me go inside Villawood Detention Centre to interview asylum seekers and translate. Around the world it has been inspiring to see how many individual Tamils have taken it upon themselves to support total strangers who survived the war. Along the way kind people have fed me delicious spicy meals and waited patiently for me to finish my interviews. Thank you also to the nun who looked after me with such poise when I was visibly upset after interviewing Sister Ignatius.

Many non-Sri Lankans have helped in the production of this book, including several United Nations staff around the world who were very uncomfortable about what happened. Dixie, who has become a friend, generously read an early draft of the book and is now incorporating some of my material into his forthcoming graphic novel on the history of the Sri Lankan ethnic conflict. Vidar Helgesen, secretary-general of International IDEA, was very supportive and introduced me to his friend L, whose ambition from the start was to see Hollywood make a movie about Sri Lanka. Thanks also to former Norwegian Minister of International Development Erik Solheim, a rare politician who cares deeply about a tiny island on the other side of the world that won't win him any votes. I am also indebted to several Norwegian officials who spoke to me off the record. Nordic Norway couldn't be more different from tropical Sri Lanka, but it has shown a commendable altruism in trying to mediate peace there. Beate Arnestad, whose latest film *Silenced Voices* tracks the impact of the last phase of the war on three exiled Sri Lankan journalists, was incredibly generous with contacts and has become a fellow-traveller. Marie Colvin, tragically killed this year in Syria reporting on very similar shell attacks on civilians in Homs, was staunchly supportive of this venture. She came close to losing her life while trying to tell the Sri Lankan story; and when I first met the Tigers they quite legitimately asked me why I wasn't a proper war correspondent like Marie Colvin!

I should also thank Alan Keenan of the International Crisis Group; colleagues at Amnesty International's News Unit; Sam Zarifi, Steve Crawshaw and Yolanda Foster; Ole Solevang of Human Rights Watch; Edward Mortimer, Raj Thamotheram and Professor Craig Scott of the Sri Lanka Campaign; Jo Glanville of Index on Censorship; Peter Bowling of International Working Group; and Jacobo Quintanilla of Internews. I am also grateful to Gordon Weiss, author of *The Cage*, for his generous encouragement at the outset. Sri Lanka's leading expert on war trauma, Professor Daya Somasundaram, provided valuable insights and reading suggestions, as did N in Australia, who remained discreetly supportive.

Heartfelt apologies to former BBC colleagues still working in Sri Lanka that I didn't tell you what I was doing. I would have loved to consult you, but decided it better not to involve you in this venture, for your own safety.

I am extremely grateful to Oxford University's Department of

Politics and International Relations, and especially to Dr Sarmila Bose, whose book on the Bangladesh liberation struggle inspired me to think of writing this book in the first place.

Many others have provided invaluable support along the journey: human-rights lawyer turned author Sadakat Kadri, who instructed me in the process of book-writing; as did my brother, Professor Thomas Harrison; Phil Goodwin, who enabled me to watch my old TV stories from Sri Lanka; Emily Thornton, who received hefty doses of Sri Lankan politics after her yoga lessons; and Mark Brayne, who reassured me I wasn't doing damage to those I interviewed. Professor Ritu Birla at Toronto University kindly invited me to speak on my book at the Monk School of Global Affairs. Thanks also to Clare Arthurs in Sydney, and my father's Australian cousin Henry Harrison, who genuinely wanted to know about the 'boat people', as well as all my Iranian friends who initially didn't understand why I was writing a book about Sri Lanka and not their country – until they saw the Channel 4 *Killing Fields* film.

Philip Gwyn Jones at Portobello Books took an interest from the very beginning, and waded through embarrassingly rough drafts. He has tolerated with good grace my journalistic impatience to get the story out there as soon as possible. Vicki Harris has gone through the text with a meticulous care and patience that leaves me in awe.

A huge thank you to Christine Bacon from Ice and Fire drama productions, who didn't know me at all but read a draft at my insistence and is now working on *The Island Nation*, a stage version of some of the stories in this book.

Last but not least, I thank my family. Every time my mother read a chapter she would end up in tears. Eventually I took pity and stopped inflicting my book on her. My son, Cyrus, spent the first four years of his life in Colombo, feeling so at home that he used to tell people he was actually Sri Lankan. Now he goes to school and talks knowledgeably of war crimes. For months he's suffered while I've been distracted or absent because I was 'just trying to finish my book'. My biggest debt is to my husband and fellow-journalist, Kasra

Naji, whose eyes opened wide when I came home and told him the things I'd discovered. His expression alone told me I was onto a good story! I had to coax, bribe and cajole him into reading so many drafts that I am embarrassed. He spent days editing, annotating, querying and challenging the political balance of the text, and it's much improved as a result.

Frances Harrison
London, April 2012

For the website accompanying this book please go to
www.stillcountingthedead.com

SRI LANKA

Whole Island Overview

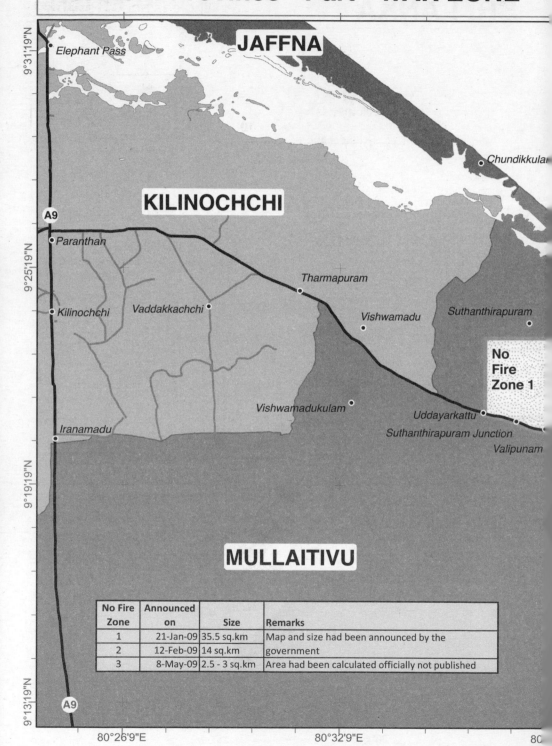

Northern Province - Part - WAR ZONE

JAFFNA

Elephant Pass

Chundikkular

KILINOCHCHI

A9

Paranthan

Tharmapuram

Kilinochchi

Vaddakkachchi

Vishwamadu

Suthanthirapuram

No Fire Zone 1

Vishwamadukulam

Uddayarkattu

Suthanthirapuram Junction

Valipunam

Iranamadu

MULLAITIVU

No Fire Zone	Announced on	Size	Remarks
1	21-Jan-09	35.5 sq.km	Map and size had been announced by the
2	12-Feb-09	14 sq.km	government
3	8-May-09	2.5 - 3 sq.km	Area had been calculated officially not published

9°31'19"N

9°25'19"N

9°19'19"N

9°13'19"N

80°26'9"E

80°32'9"E

80

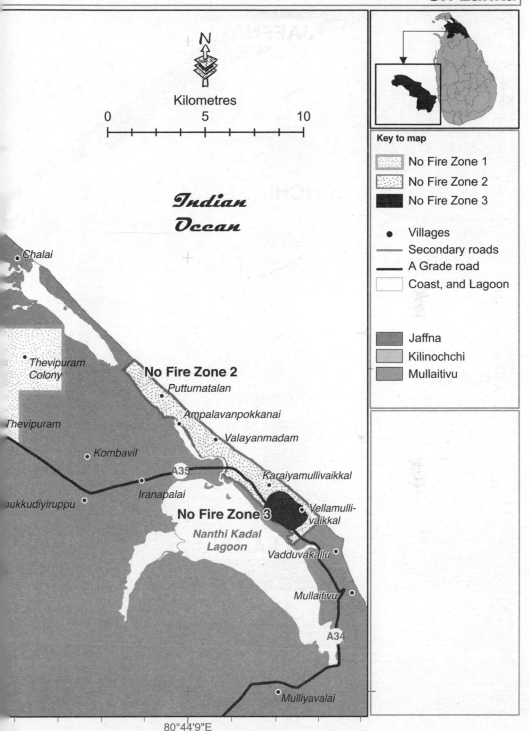

Kilinochchi & Mullaitivu - Sri Lanka

N

Kilometres

0   5   10

Indian Ocean

Chalai

Thevipuram Colony

Thevipuram

No Fire Zone 2

Puttumatalan

Ampalavanpokkanai

Kombavil

Valayanmadam

A35

Iranapalai

Karaiyamullivaikkal

ukkudiyiruppu

No Fire Zone 3

Vellamulli-vaikkal

Nanthi Kadal Lagoon

Vadduvakallu

Mullaitivu

A34

Mulliyavalai

80°44'9"E

Key to map

No Fire Zone 1
No Fire Zone 2
No Fire Zone 3

• Villages
Secondary roads
A Grade road
Coast, and Lagoon

Jaffna
Kilinochchi
Mullaitivu

Timeline

1972		Velupillai Prabhakaran forms a militant group called the Tamil New Tigers.
1976		TNT changes its name to the Liberation Tigers of Tamil Eelam (LTTE).
1977		Anti-Tamil riots.
1981		Burning-down of Jaffna Library, one of the biggest in Asia and a symbol of Tamil culture, by a pro-government Sinhalese mob.
1983		The country's worst anti-Tamil riots, in Colombo, after thirteen soldiers are killed in a Tiger ambush.
1985		Talks held between the Sri Lankan government and the LTTE for the first time in Thimpu, Bhutan.
1987		Indo–Sri Lanka pact signed between President J. R. Jayawardena and Indian Prime Minister Rajiv Gandhi. India deploys peacekeeping force to north and east Sri Lanka.
1990	MARCH	India withdraws troops due to clashes with the Tigers, who take control of Jaffna.
	JUNE	Tigers kill hundreds of policemen in eastern Sri Lanka following breakdown of talks.
1991	MAY	Rajiv Gandhi killed by a Tiger suicide bomber.
1993	MAY	President Premadasa killed by Tiger suicide cadres during a May Day rally in Colombo.

1995:	JANUARY	Government of Chandrika Kumaratunge and Tigers agree to talks.
	APRIL	Peace talks fail after Tigers blow up two navy vessels.
	DECEMBER	Jaffna recaptured by Sri Lankan Army.
1996	JANUARY	Suicide bomb attack on the Central Bank building in Colombo kills ninety-one and injures 1,400.
1998	JANUARY	Suicide bomb attack on Sri Lanka's holiest Buddhist shrine, Dhaladha Maligawa, in the central town of Kandy, kills seventeen people.
1999	DECEMBER	Tigers attempt to assassinate President Chandrika Kumaratunge.
2001	JULY	Tiger suicide attack on Colombo International Airport.
2002	FEBRUARY	Government and Tiger rebels sign a Norwegian-mediated ceasefire and a series of peace talks begins.
2003		Tigers pull out of talks. Ceasefire holds.
2004	MARCH	Renegade Tamil Tiger commander in Eastern Sri Lanka, Colonel Karuna, leads split in rebel movement.
2004	DECEMBER	More than 30,000 people are killed in the Boxing Day tsunami.
2005	NOVEMBER	Prime Minister Mahinda Rajapaksa wins presidential elections.
2006–7		Sri Lankan Army offensive begins to recapture rebel areas in eastern Sri Lanka.
2007	FEBRUARY	Fighting recommences in north of the country.
2008	JANUARY	Government pulls out of 2002 ceasefire agreement and launches massive offensive.

	APRIL	The country's most holy Catholic shrine in the rebel-held village of Madhu captured by the Sri Lankan Army.
2009	1 JANUARY	The President takes over the running of the Media Ministry.
	2 JANUARY	Tigers' main administrative town Kilinochchi captured by Sri Lankan Army.
	6 JANUARY	Attack on offices and studios of private TV station MTV in Colombo.
	8 JANUARY	Sinhalese newspaper editor Lasantha Wickremetunga assassinated after writing his own obituary.
	9 JANUARY	Sri Lankan Army captures strategic A9 highway.
	15 JANUARY	Tharmapuram captured by Sri Lankan Army.
	16 JANUARY	Final UN food convoy leaves for rebel territory.
	21 JANUARY	Government announces first 'no-fire zone' or 'safe zone' for civilians.
	25 JANUARY	Mullaitivu captured by Sri Lankan Army.
	28 JANUARY	Vishwamadu captured by Sri Lankan Army.
	12 FEBRUARY	Second 'no-fire' or 'safe' zone for civilians announced by Sri Lankan Army.
	9 MARCH	Tamil Tiger commander Colonel Karuna, who defected to government in 2004, is made Minister for National Integration and Reconciliation.
	5 APRIL	Puthukkudiyiruppu (PTK) captured by Sri Lankan Army.
	21 APRIL	Puttumatalan captured by Sri Lankan Army; tens of thousands of civilians pour out of war zone.

	13 APRIL	Sri Lanka officially drops Norway as a peace facilitator.
	16 APRIL	President Rajapaksa makes a surprise visit to the town of Kilinochchi, now held by the army.
	8 MAY	Third no-fire zone announced by Sri Lankan government.
	14 MAY	Vellamullivaikkal captured by Sri Lankan Army.
	18 MAY	The last village under rebel control, Karaiyamullivaikkal, captured by Sri Lankan Army.
	AUGUST	Tiger arms dealer and international spokesman known as 'KP' captured in Malaysia. He now works with the Sri Lankan government.
2010	JANUARY	Incumbent Mahinda Rajapaksa wins presidential election by a big margin but the outcome is rejected by his main rival, General Sarath Fonseka.
	FEBRUARY	General Fonseka, the army commander who achieved victory in the country's civil war, is arrested.
	APRIL	President Rajapaksa's ruling coalition wins landslide victory in parliamentary elections.
	AUGUST	Military court finds former army chief Sarath Fonseka guilty in the first of a series of court cases.
	SEPTEMBER	Parliament approves a constitutional change allowing President Rajapaksa to seek unlimited number of terms.
2011	APRIL	UN panel of experts advising the Secretary-General, Ban Ki-moon, issues report on Sri Lankan war crimes calling for an

		international investigation. Sri Lanka calls the report biased.
	DECEMBER	The Sri Lankan government's internal inquiry, the Lessons Learnt and Reconciliation Commission, issues its report.
2012	MARCH	Weak resolution, with no mention of war crimes, passed against Sri Lanka at United Nations Human Rights Council in Geneva.

Introduction

That afternoon was pregnant with malice, the weather oppressive and sultry. A tropical storm hung in the air, waiting to explode above the tiny strip of golden beach at the north-eastern corner of the island of Sri Lanka. It was 18 May 2009. Four Catholic priests in grubby white robes with black sashes had just come out of bunkers. They carried a white flag and held their hands in the air. Terrified, they knelt on the hot sand. They were surrounded by dozens of emaciated children in ragged T-shirts: orphans in their care, some of them in blood-soaked bandages. All were pleading for their lives with the Sri Lankan soldiers who had their guns trained on them from across the beach.

In the background, a plume of grey smoke billowed from vehicles set ablaze by the shells that had rained down. Even the palm trees on the beach that had so recently been a tropical paradise had been decapitated by the ferocious battles of the previous weeks. Now blackened stumps replaced foliage. Strewn on the ground were people's last belongings – a shoe, a water bottle, a piece of clothing; dotted around the bloated corpses that lay sprawled out in the open. The stench of decomposing flesh and burning tyres hung in the air, mixed with cordite, sweat and the tang of human fear.

The gunfire had been relentless. For days the Tamil priests and the children – some as young as six – had been waiting for a lull in the fighting so that they could surrender. The landscape was dotted with trenches reinforced with sandbags. Injured fighters and civilians were all trapped together in this, the final killing field, just a few hundred square metres in size. One of the priests had a radio telephone and used it to call a brigadier-general in the Sri Lankan Army, who advised them to raise a white flag when the soldiers approached. Twice the priests had tried to come out, but each time they'd been shot at and forced to crawl back into the bunker on their hands and knees. The day before, one man had been killed while trying to defecate.

The priests knew that the war was over, and that if they didn't surrender soon they'd be taken for rebels. All night they had heard the cries for help as the soldiers threw grenades into bunkers. The mopping-up operation was under way at the end of five months of unprecedented carnage. Miraculously, the priests and the children had survived.

More than a dozen Sri Lankan soldiers stood in full combat gear, rifles and heavy machine guns pointed at the group, ammunition belts strung across their shoulders. They'd masked their faces with black cloths to hide their identities, making them look even more like executioners. Young recruits from the south of the island, they were frenzied with fear after seeing so many of their comrades killed. For the last three days they'd faced waves of rebel suicide fighters making a futile last stand. Now they wouldn't think twice about shooting at anything that moved.

'The soldiers were like animals, they were not normal. They wanted to kill everything. They looked as if they hadn't eaten or slept for days. They were crazed with blood lust,' said one of the priests later.

'We are going to kill you,' the soldiers shouted in their language, Sinhala. 'We have orders to shoot everyone.' The tense stand-off lasted about an hour, with the kneeling priests begging to be spared in broken Sinhala. They told the soldiers that they'd already been in touch with the brigadier-general at army headquarters, who'd promised to send help. They implored them to use the telephone to check their story. The soldiers were so frightened they made a priest dial the number and then put the handset on the ground in the space between them, fearing it might be booby-trapped.

Ordered by their superior officers to accept the surrender, the soldiers instructed the group to cross over one by one; they began to strip-search them, including the clerics, even removing bandages to check underneath. One young boy had a dressing on his lower back and the soldiers pulled it off and stuck their fingers in the wound. They punched a priest in the chest for no apparent reason.

Then it was time to leave. After so many weeks of starvation, nobody had the energy to carry the injured. One badly wounded female rebel in a nearby bunker was too weak to be picked up. She told the priests to leave her and help the others who could walk. As they left, a Tamil in the group glanced back and saw a soldier pointing a rifle at the girl's forehead. Terrified, he turned around before he heard the shot ring out.[1]

They made a long march up the coastal road to an army camp, traversing a living hell, their bare feet stained with human blood. Around them fires were still burning, and limbless, decomposing corpses lay under vehicles or alongside bunkers. A priest said he personally saw thousands of dead on that journey, most of them civilians, not fighters.

'We have killed all your leaders and you are our slaves,' jeered one of the soldiers guarding the group, using broken Tamil so they'd all understand. As they trudged on, some fainted with exhaustion, including the priest who'd been punched. The people with him insisted he be given medical treatment. 'Many people have died. Why are you crying for one father? Let him die,' the soldiers said.

At one point a senior army officer came and the people got down on their knees to plead for the priest's life. By the time a medic attached a saline drip, the priest had already died. He was not alone. As the survivors were driven out of the war zone later that night they saw hundreds of naked male and female bodies lined up on the ground, illuminated by lights powered by generators. The victorious soldiers were using their mobile phones to take trophy photos of the dead rebels – some of the disturbing images that soon appeared all over the Internet. It was the digital era's equivalent of a triumphant swordsman putting his foot on the chest of a vanquished enemy.

Three hundred kilometres to the south, on the winning side, people had been dancing in the streets of the capital, Colombo. There was an eruption of joy, with car horns honking, firecrackers exploding and bystanders waving yellow Sri Lankan flags depicting a lion carrying a sword. After decades, the civil war was over. It was a victory few military analysts had thought possible.

State television had interrupted programming that day to announce that the rebel leader, Velupillai Prabhakaran, had been killed. They broadcast pictures of his bloated corpse lying on the ground in the jungle, the dead eyes staring and a handkerchief covering a bloody gash in his head. Nothing more clearly marked the end of the war than the corpse of the Tamil Tiger leader who had once been worshipped like a god by his diehard supporters.

At his peak he'd controlled a quarter of the island, commanding an army of thousands of devoted Tamil men and women who wore cyanide capsules around their necks to avoid being captured alive. They took up arms to fight for a Tamil homeland because they no longer felt safe living with the majority Sinhalese community on the crowded island; Tamils had been burned alive in the streets of the capital. They faced discrimination in employment and education and had become convinced that they would never be given a fair deal in Sri Lankan society.

From a band of a few angry young men, the Tamil Tigers developed into one of the world's most brutal insurgent groups, and one of its best-equipped, with tanks, artillery, naval and air wings, and spies and sleeper suicide bombers planted all over the island. They purchased arms in the black markets of Asia and Africa, operating legitimate shipping businesses to move weapons and raising at least £126 million a year in contributions from the Tamil diaspora.[2] When I first visited the Tigers in 2002 as the BBC correspondent in Sri Lanka, they ran a *de facto* state for Tamils in the north-east, with their own courts, police, banks and border controls.

Predominately Hindu and Christian, Tamils were the majority in the north, but the Sinhalese, who are Buddhist and Christian, formed a majority in the rest of the tiny island of twenty million people. Sri Lankan Tamil links to the sixty million fellow-Tamils who live just across the water in the southern tip of the Indian mainland made the Sinhalese insecure. 'A majority with a minority complex' is how many have described them. Initially it was India, then the diaspora populations in Canada, Europe and Australia, that funded and equipped the separatist cause.

The rebels succeeded because they were ruthless – willing to obliterate any challengers, even from their own side, and kill innocent Sinhalese civilians. Tigers drove suicide trucks packed with explosives into the heart of the capital, murdering presidents, prime ministers, ministers, MPs, office workers, and anyone who got in the way, with chilling efficiency. In one such attack in 1996 ninety-one people were killed and more than 1,000 injured, including 100 who lost their eyesight. In July 2001, the Tigers attacked the island's only international airport, knocking out half the fleet of the national carrier. The economy suffered, holding the whole nation back. Poor Sinhalese men had little choice but to join the army, only to come home disabled or in a body bag. Ordinary people lived with the constant threat of suicide bombers, terrified even to let their children walk to school. Because of the Tigers' campaigns against both the government and civilians – bombs on buses and in shopping centres, for example – everyone in the south knew someone who had narrowly missed a bomb blast.

During the decades of war, foreign tourists kept on coming to sun themselves on the southern coast. As if by unspoken agreement, the rebels never attacked holidaymakers. Europeans sipped coconut juice and stared out at the horizon of the ocean, unaware that just an hour's flight to the north people were dying in First World War-style trench warfare. No waiter or driver in the south would volunteer an opinion about the civil war, knowing it was bad for business. Look at the Sri Lanka Tourist Board website and you will see pictures of idyllic beaches, heritage sites, colourful festivals, steam trains and lush tea gardens. The only odd thing is that none of them is in the north of the island, which has, if anything, more beautiful beaches. In the north you can paddle utterly alone at midday, on miles and miles of flat sand, without seeing a single hotel. Dig a little deeper on the Tourist Board webpage and you will find that the heritage sites are all Buddhist.

You'd be surprised to know that Sri Lanka also has Hindus, Christians, Muslims and animists. The website's history section abruptly ends in 1972, just when the civil war got going. The Tourism Board simply doesn't mention four decades of Tamil separatist struggle. Denial has become a Sri Lankan habit.

Not surprising, then, that in 2009, when the brutal climax of the war arrived, tourists on winter-sun holidays were lying on Sri Lanka's southern beaches oblivious to the bloodshed that was unfolding on the opposite side of an island the size of Scotland. Tamil civilians were being bombed by the government, used as human shields by the rebels. Medics were performing amputations with no anaesthetic, and watching half their patients die. The Tigers snatched people's children to die a pointless death in jungle trenches. They said they were fighting for the Tamil people and this justified making them stay in the war zone, whether they liked it or not.

Like the tourists, the world turned a blind eye to the tens of thousands of civilian deaths that took place in the north-east of Sri Lanka in the space of just five months in 2009. A UN panel later found reports of up to 40,000 dead credible; there are signs that the final death toll could be a lot higher. At the same time that Sri Lanka's vicious war was raging, the world's attention was focused on the Israeli incursion into Gaza, where the final death toll was about 1,500.

Sri Lankans haven't been very good at counting their dead, but the UN's assumption is that at least 100,000 have perished during the four decades of civil war – roughly equivalent to the number who died in the Yugoslav wars of the 1990s.

By 2009, much of the international community had made a conscious decision to side with the Sri Lankan government and ignore the cries for intervention. A Norwegian-led peace process had failed, and many countries blamed the Tigers' intransigence. The European Union, the US, Canada and India all proscribed the Tamil Tiger rebels as a terrorist group. The Sri Lankan government found it easy to rebrand its long-running ethnic conflict as part of the global 'war on terror'. This meant that those who might have spoken out for the victims were muted in their efforts.

Sri Lanka also found new allies emboldened by the West's hypocrisy – how could Washington and London preach to others about human rights after Guantánamo Bay and Abu Ghraib? – so China, Russia, Pakistan, India and Iran were staunch in their support for the Sri Lankan government, ensuring it received enough weapons and credit. Today the same countries protect Sri Lanka from war-crimes investigations, championing its achievements in defeating terrorism.

In academic circles across the world, the winning strategy is now dangerously referred to as 'the Sri Lankan option' – a new way of crushing terrorism using brute military force rather than a political approach. It involves scorched-earth tactics, blurring the distinction between civilians and combatants, and enforcing a media blackout. Proponents tend to gloss over the indiscriminate killing of women and children, the violations of international law and the crushing of a free press. Worryingly, other countries with ethnic problems have been studying Sri Lanka's approach – the Burmese military, the Thais and the Bangladeshis, for example. When the Sri Lankan military held a three-day conference in June 2011 to teach other armies its brutal tactics, the stench of war crimes didn't stop representatives from forty countries, including the USA, attending. They hoped to learn from a country that now claims to be expert in counter-terrorism.

There is another side to the story – the human cost of 'the Sri Lankan option'. The focus of this book is on the final months of the battle between the Tigers and the Sri Lankan military. It is not a history of the whole war and does not tell of the suffering of the ordinary soldier or Sinhalese commuter living in fear of bomb blasts – that is the (entirely legitimate) subject for another book. It is an account of the victory from the perspective of the defeated. Yes, some in this book were terrorists or their sympathisers, but by no means all. This story matters because Sri Lanka is no longer just a country whose people did bad things to each other – it's an unexpected piece of the jigsaw of the discourse on global terrorism.

Nobody has told these tales before because there simply were no international journalists or aid workers in the war zone in the final months to send harrowing accounts of civilian suffering to CNN or the BBC. That was an important part of the government's strategy. Independent witnesses were deliberately excluded, to distort the writing of history. As a result, perhaps there n

ever will be an agreed account of what actually took place in those final months of war – Sri Lankan history will continue to be written differently according to your ethnic group or political bias. If Tamils and Sinhalese are ever to live together peacefully, then these accounts from survivors need to be heard and acknowledged. The bloodshed of those five months in 2009 far exceeded, in scale and trauma, anything that happened before in Sri Lanka. If the truth is not confronted, another generation of Tamils will inherit the collective trauma that fuels the desire for revenge.

On the Tamil side, too, there needs to be an honest rethinking of the unquestioning support for the rebels. The sizeable Tamil diaspora across Europe, North America and Australia funded the insurgency, driven by guilt about those they'd left behind. Deep down most knew that the Tigers were brutally abducting children to fight against their will, extorting money in the name of tax and killing dissenters, but they chose to remain silent. Denial infects both sides.

The final months of the war saw the Tamil Tiger leadership cynically control the movement of the civilian population, exposing them to the horrors of battle in the hope that the appalling images of suffering would prompt the world to intervene. It was immoral and ultimately futile. At the height of the mayhem, the rebels turned down an internationally mediated surrender plan brokered by Norway that would have stopped the killings. It could have saved thousands of lives. In the end, all the top Tiger leaders were wiped out anyway and the movement destroyed. It was just much bloodier than it needed to be.

As a journalist I cannot prove every single detail of the accounts given to me because I was not there myself. However, the patterns of the stories match each other and expand on the findings of a UN advisory panel and the reports of different human-rights groups. I have travelled the world, hearing hair-raising stories of escape; watching sleepless, suicidal, haunted people weep, shake with trauma, whisper with horror at what they had to recount. Their stories marked me indelibly. Some grown men cried before they even started to tell me their story, just at the thought of the enormity of it all; others had tears in their eyes when I, a total stranger, left them – simply because I'd shown an interest in their tragedy.

Amid the suffering, I have also heard stories of incredible bravery, self-sacrifice and generosity from ordinary people who drew on inner strength they didn't even know they possessed. There are many unsung heroes, but they would be the last to consider themselves such; rather they feel failures, because they didn't save more people.

The majority of those I have spoken to are now refugees. I sometimes wonder what strangers who pass them on the streets, dismissive of their inability to speak English or navigate local customs, would say if they knew even a fraction of what they'd been through. For many survivors this is the first time they have told their story in full. It was not a decision they took lightly. Their motivation was not revenge, or even scoring a propaganda victory. It was about making the dead count for something.

Sri Lankan Government Statements

15 SEPTEMBER 2008   'We will completely crush the LTTE, but I do not want to set a time frame for it. It can be done...I will not allow them to raise their heads again with their weapons.' – *President Mahinda Rajapaksa*[1]

12 DECEMBER 2008   'There are no good terrorists or bad terrorists. All terrorists are bad.' – *President Mahinda Rajapaksa*[2]

30 JANUARY 2009   'The war will be over very soon. We believe [the rebels] are left with only 1,000 or 500 forces at the most.' – *Keheliya Rambukwella, government spokesman for national security and defence*[3]

31 JANUARY 2009   Defence Secretary Gotabhaya Rajapaksa warns Western diplomats, foreign journalists and aid groups that they will be 'chased' out of the country if they appear to favour the rebels.[4]

4 FEBRUARY 2009   'The Tigers will be completely defeated in a few days.' – *President Mahinda Rajapaksa*[5]

6 FEBRUARY 2009   Sri Lanka says an international effort is under way to tarnish the country's image.

14 FEBRUARY 2009   'We also want to give these people dignity and privacy...This is not like visiting a zoo. These are innocent people. Why should people go and take photographs of them and exploit them to get aid donations like they did during the tsunami time? We are not here to satisfy the international community. These are our Sri Lankan brothers. We are thinking about

them.' – *the President's brother and adviser Basil Rajapaksa, on why no journalists were granted access to Manik Farm*

23 FEBRUARY 2009   'We have a job to do. We are not bothered about any truce at the moment.' – *Brigadier-General Shavendra Silva*

25 FEBRUARY 2009   'We're not going to leave any room for them to come back…The main reason for the success is from day one, we maintained a clear mission. We maintained it without ambiguity: that is to finish off the LTTE.' – *Defence Secretary Gotabhaya Rakapaksa*

3 MARCH 2009   'Our progress from now onward should be made meticulously, taking maximum precautions, keeping the civilian factor in mind at all times.' – *Lieutenant-General Sarath Fonseka*

24 MARCH 2009   The Defence Ministry says that those 'pretending to be humanitarian and aid agencies' are prolonging the conflict 'to secure their income'. It says a 'vicious coalition' that has 'been pretending to be humanitarian agencies, aid agencies, free media, civil rights movements, etc., has made the continued bloodshed on Sri Lankan soil a lucrative business'.

31 MARCH 2009   'We will not cave in to pressures from any international quarters, locally and internationally, and will not stop until the war is completely over.' – *President Mahinda Rajapaksa*

28 APRIL 2009   'We tried to have a dialogue and negotiations. That was rejected. We were then compelled to use force, the force that is the right of the State, force that is the only language that the terrorist

seemed to understand.' – *President Mahinda Rajapaksa*

30 APRIL 2009   'We can't use heavy weapons. And we can't do air attacks, because we are worried about the innocent people there. They may be Tamils. But they are citizens of this country. My heart would not allow any civilians to be killed by bullets' – *President Mahinda Rajapaksa*

7 MAY 2009   'The manner of rescuing the hostages would indeed be an example to others engaged in military operations. It may also be one of the greatest rescue operations in the world' – *President Mahinda Rajapaksa*

19 MAY 2009   'Our troops went to this operation carrying a gun in one hand, the Human Rights Charter in the other, hostages on their shoulders, and the love of their children in their hearts.' – *President Mahinda Rajapaksa*

The War the United Nations Lost

'I was so disgusted. The whole system failed. It wasn't only the UN, but the whole international community. Tens of thousands of civilians were slaughtered by the Sri Lankan government and the world just moved on. It just passed us by.'

– UN aid worker

The lanky British aid worker was sweating in his pale blue flak jacket and helmet, but it wasn't the tropical heat of northern Sri Lanka, or anxiety about the deserted road ahead. It was shame. Dixie was about to abandon people in his care, just at the moment they needed him most. He worked for the United Nations and had spent four years inside rebel territory. He and the other seven international aid workers had just been ordered out by the Sri Lankan government.

It was September 2008 and the last phase of the war was about to start: slaughter on an apocalyptic scale.

Sri Lankan soldiers were just five and a half kilometres from the rebels' *de facto* capital Kilinochchi, a sleepy farming town with inter-mittent electricity and a rural lifestyle. Tens of thousands of hungry, ragged refugees had been surging into town, desperate to escape the barrage of shells. For months the Sri Lankan Army had been relent-lessly pushing into rebel territory from both the south and the west, capturing more and more land. The Tigers had no choice but to retreat, and they forced the civilians to move with them, using them as human shields. Soon they'd all have nowhere to go except the sea.

Villagers had lost count of how many times they'd made a run for it in the middle of the night, hiding in ditches, hoping to cheat death one more time. Many started off on ancient tractors laden with doorframes, chairs, diesel cans and palm thatch, chugging through the verdant landscape of banana trees, palms and paddy fields. Then they walked, barefoot along the red dusty road that cut through the scrub jungle. Rolls of bedding, a bucket, a briefcase, a baby; everyone in the family carried something. Some had bicycles laden with mats and overnight bags into which they'd packed jewellery, school certificates and land deeds. Stick thin, they soon had just the clothes they were standing in, their reserves of energy and food supplies depleted even before the war took a new turn for the worse. Their eyes had that exhausted, traumatised look but they still managed a smile for the tall white man as they spotted him taking photos from the roadside. The mere presence of a foreign face was reassuring.

Dixie was sure the Sri Lankan government had ordered them to quit so that there would be no independent witnesses to what was coming. As the United Nations packed up and prepared to leave, half the population depended on it for their next meal. Dixie knew better than anyone else how many people were destitute, because it was his job to build shelters.

'We were leaving people under a tree with not much. They'd lost everything already. Ten displacements was the norm, and many arrived on foot. We would give them a hut. We kept finding people under mango trees; if they'd been hit by artillery in the night they just ran and jumped on the first tractor out. They had no cooking utensils. We started by handing out kits to construct shelters, and then we realised they were building them and five days later the same people were displacing. So it was pointless. We resorted to giving out three poles of wood and a bit of tarpaulin so they could construct a tent and carry it with them if they moved again.'

For a fortnight the attacks had been so frequent that Dixie spent every night in a reinforced-concrete bunker, listening to the relentless thud of advancing artillery that made the earth shake under him. That was after he'd literally been thrown out of bed at dawn by a supersonic jet dropping three bombs on the house next door. A piece of shrapnel had narrowly missed his leg, while four people were killed in the neighbouring house (which had become a rebel intelligence base without the UN realising). Clearly the Tiger spies had thought they'd be safe if they lived next to the foreigners.

Dixie had found saying goodbye to his staff agonising – the rebels banned most local Tamils working for the UN from leaving, effectively holding them or their families hostage. He'd driven around town distributing precious food and fuel to anyone he'd worked with, hoping it would keep them going in the coming months.

At first the rebels wouldn't let Dixie and his colleagues go either.[1] Tamil women in faded frocks and flip-flops and worn-out men in blue and white checked sarongs had suddenly appeared outside the UN compound, blocking the way. It was the hands waving for help he saw first: scores of disembodied brown hands poking through a gap three-quarters of the way up the big, white metal gate. 'Don't go!' they shouted, holding up home-made cardboard placards on which they'd written the same message in English, for the benefit of the foreigners. One demonstrator suggested they do no relief work if it was too dangerous, but remain to witness the war. There were many familiar faces in the crowd that sat on the road to prevent the UN lorries driving out. Mrs Javan, whose husband ran the rebel radio station, was there that day. 'We begged them not to leave,' she recalled. 'We feared we would all be killed.'

The first night they'd tried to leave, there had been a surreal dinner with the rebels. In the background the aid workers could hear incoming shells falling far too close for comfort. Waiters in white gloves had served stuffed crab and lobster while outside people went hungry. The smiling Tiger spokesman, Pulidevan, told the aid workers they couldn't leave, making it obvious the rebels had instigated the demonstration to force the UN to postpone its departure. The reason soon became clear.

In the dead of night Dixie heard the rumbling noise. He crept out of his bunker and stood in shadows on the main road, the earth vibrating under his feet as a long line of rebel artillery guns and armoured vehicles thundered out of town. It was a tactical withdrawal, using the UN presence as cover. The Tigers were pulling out all their heavy weap-onry; when they'd finished, the protests outside the UN offices stopped as if by magic and the aid workers were free to go.

The day of departure came: 16 September 2008. The robust UN lorries looked as if they came from a different planet from the over-laden, antiquated farm vehicles spluttering out diesel fumes. On one side of the road was the departing UN convoy, the epitome of sleek modern technology; on the other, fragile bicycles and carts that looked about to collapse.

Aid workers in their blue helmets paced anxiously up and down, talking to colleagues in government territory on crackly walkie-talkies. They were nervous. There was only one road out and it wasn't safe: the Tigers were on one side and the army on the other, poised to seize it. Either side could attack and then blame the other. The military said it couldn't guarantee the UN's safety, while the rebels wouldn't think twice about using UN personnel as a human shield. Being caught in the middle was gruesome, as those left behind were to discover.

Both warring parties had been informed that the UN's departure was scheduled for ten o'clock in the morning. Minutes before they were due to leave, a government fighter jet suddenly screeched in and dropped a bomb. It was very close. Jolted by the huge noise, everyone automatically ran to take shelter. 'For me it was never the sound of the bomb – it was sound of that engine. The plane swoops and goes into supersonic – it's a roar of death; I would put my hands over my ears. It gives me shivers even now to hear it,' Dixie recalls. When they emerged from the bunkers after the attack and drove out, the UN discovered the Sri Lankan Air Force had blown up a tractor. 'I don't think they wanted to hit us,' Dixie says; 'it was a clear sign to get out. It was scare tactics.'

It should have been a major diplomatic incident – an attack so close to UN staff – but the UN in New York never commented publicly. It was simply not their way to confront the Sri Lankan government.

The journey out of rebel territory was eerily quiet; normally busy junctions deserted, villages emptied of their populations. A lone Tiger stood on the edge of the road, more for decoration than defence. After an hour they reached the last rebel checkpoint; the red Tiger flag was still flying but the place had been abandoned months before. This had once been the frontier in all but name, complete with security clearance, customs and identity checks.

A few emaciated cows gazed obliviously across the barbed wire at no man's land. On the army side, Sri Lankan soldiers spent an hour frisking every aid worker and going through all their belongings and vehicles. Dixie was nervous because he'd hidden photographs of the fighting in his laptop.

Soon the aid workers were having a party, cracking open cold beers and congratulating each other on getting out safely. Dixie, who'd left close friends behind, remembers it as the most emotional time of his life. 'There was nothing to celebrate; we had left carnage behind,' he says.

In the capital city, the UN issued a statement saying it had been forced temporarily to relocate because of *its* assessment that the situation was too dangerous. It failed to mention that it had been summarily ordered out by the government.

In his traditional white tunic and signature burgundy scarf, the Sri Lankan president, Mahinda Rajapaksa, further confused the picture by saying the ban on aid workers was just 'a short-term measure', adding that the UN could go back very soon. This may have eased the conscience of the world, but was simply untrue. International organisations ended up having no access to civilians they had a duty to protect. More than 400,000 Tamils had been abandoned to an army bent on eliminating the rebels at any price. The UN's departure from rebel territory was the first step along this path and it's questionable whether they really fought hard enough to protect the people they left behind.[2] Dixie certainly didn't think so. Guilty and utterly frustrated, he resigned and started speaking out about what he'd seen, until he was told in no uncertain terms by the UN to stop.

For many Tamils trapped in rebel territory, the UN's departure in September 2008 was the turning point. Some stopped their bicycles and stared as the sturdy white UN transport lorries and jeeps with their huge radio antennae drove out of town in a cloud of dust. 'I felt abandoned by the rest of the world,' recalls English teacher Uma. 'The UN was supposed to help people in need but they left us to the mercy of aggressors.'

Every household in town had already received a letter from the rebels informing them the war was on their doorstep and ordering the able-bodied to dig bunkers. Experienced as Tamils already were in the sacrifice and suffering of war, they simply could not imagine the hell that lay ahead.

The humanitarian situation was already dire. For months nobody had been able to harvest crops or fish because of the incessant attacks. Food was running short. Lack of diesel meant transport was beginning to collapse and doctors could no longer run generators for the cold storage of blood and drugs.[3] Even material for making artificial legs for the war-wounded had run out – Dixie was haunted by the thought that they left behind 250 disabled people without prosthetic limbs.

The civilians now left to fend for themselves didn't just fear the daily bombardment by government forces. They were also at the mercy of the Tigers, who wanted their beloved children as cannon fodder. Losing your home was bad enough, but losing your young son or daughter was utterly unbearable. From 2007, the rebels had insisted every family give one boy or girl as a fighter. First they visited all the schools. Teachers recall how subdued the older students were, anticipating their forced conscription when they reached their seventeenth birthday. As war approached, schools often had a third of the class missing: abducted and sent for training in the jungle.

Later the rebels recruited village by village, combing the tranquil rural homes along the palm-fringed eastern coast, where chickens pecked around the homesteads and in the distance the huge waves crashed on the empty white beaches. Desperate to protect their children from a brutal death in trench warfare, parents would go to any lengths to hide them. One family Dixie knew buried their seventeen-year-old daughter inside an oil drum under the sand in the garden. The girl would only come out at night to wash. One day it was so hot she couldn't bear it any more and emerged during daylight hours. A jealous neighbour, whose child had already been taken by the rebels, spotted the girl and informed on the family. That night the rebels came for her. It was one of many betrayals that slowly ripped Tamil society apart. Three months later the girl was returned home, her dead body wrapped in a red Tiger flag.

Even old men were taken for a fortnight's training and then given rusty old shotguns and made to stand on the side of the main highway as home guards, to give the illusion of stability and permanence just as the road was about to fall to the army for the first time in a quarter of a century. At one stage the Tigers recruited by profession, and for two weeks nobody could get a haircut because all the barbers had been called up for compulsory military training.

Barbers, shopkeepers, schoolchildren – nobody was exempt, even UN staff. As the UN prepared to leave, the Tigers eyed up local Tamils working for the UN, commenting about how good this woman was on the computer or how well-built that man was. Humanitarian organisations repeatedly struggled to protect their people from the clutches of the rebels. A skinny twenty-one-year-old UN security guard was forcibly recruited to fight with the Tigers' naval wing. He was said to be a timid boy who couldn't even stop a stray dog entering the compound. Vigorous protests did nothing to get him back. Within a few months he too had been killed on the front line.

Without the UN there were no international aid workers or journalists inside rebel territory to provide independent reports of the war or prevent the worst abuses. A few expatriates working for the Red Cross had sporadic access to collect the seriously wounded but they maintained a long-standing policy of strict neutrality and confidentiality, refusing even today to comment on what they witnessed for fear that it might jeopardise access to war zones in the future. Over the coming months of fighting most people would be displaced at least twenty times, some forty times.

As Kilinochchi came under sustained attack the entire population moved towards the coast, out of range of the army's heavy guns – for the time being. People camped wherever they could find open space, cooking on little wood fires and sleeping under tarpaulin as the flash of shells lit up the distant sky. Amazingly there was still some semblance of civil administration: children in their white and blue uniforms went to makeshift schools, while charities handed out food rations and tried to care for orphans and the disabled. Everyday life was constantly on the move, hospitals and offices evacuating villages as the front line crept closer.

Until the end of January 2009, the United Nations still sent in occasional food convoys to sustain the civilian population. Every convoy had to be negotiated with both sides, and on several occasions the Tigers and the Sri Lankan Army cynically used the UN as cover to advance their positions militarily.[4]

Understandably lorries were checked to prevent weapons being smuggled in to the rebels, but UN international staff say they were almost strip-searched and their personal belongings opened in public, even toothpaste tubes undone, in a humiliating fashion. The Sri Lankan government told the UN what route to take, when to leave and when to return, allowing them only enough time to unload the food if they worked right through the night with no sleep.

Visits did afford a glimpse of what was happening. John Campbell, a retired Scottish army officer who travelled with a convoy as a UN security officer in December, witnessed shells landing close to his route. 'Mortars came from a direction four kilometres away which could only mean the army fired them,' he said, adamant it was not the Tigers. Red Cross officials with the UN convoy had to get on the phone and beg the military to stop shelling so they could proceed. 'They were not targeting us but they weren't being careful about where they were dropping the shells even though they knew we were there,' said Campbell. On the way out he had to stop and move a tree blocking the road: it had been broken in half by a shell. 'This was harassing fire and if we'd been passing at that time there would have been casualties. It was random and the intention was to terrorise civilians. They just fired willy-nilly,' he said.

The UN staff saw few young men of fighting age on the streets, but a lot of very frightened old women and children in a dreadful state.

Campbell was told by the UN to give an interview on the satellite phone to the BBC. Asked how the situation compared to his experience elsewhere, he said conditions in the war zone in Sri Lanka were 'as basic as Somalia'. People were living extremely uncomfortably in flimsy shelters made of old sacks, plastic sheeting and cardboard in waterlogged camps, almost entirely dependent on food aid, he explained.

His remarks sparked fury from the government in Colombo, which threatened to suspend all aid convoys to the north. Campbell was summoned to a meeting with a Sri Lankan Army general. He found the officers all dressed up in their formal uniforms, with TV cameras at the ready. Campbell refused to enter the room without a witness, a friend he'd wisely brought along. There was a stand-off where he waited for twenty minutes outside the general's office and the general's ADC tried to get him to go inside. Finally he was informed that he was banned from the war zone and the military were extremely unhappy with him. Campbell returned to the capital, sensing that his presence in the north of the country was putting himself and others at risk.

The UN called Campbell's remark about Somalia a 'regrettable personal opinion' that did not necessarily reflect its official position. He was allowed to serve out the remaining weeks of his contract, but it was not renewed. 'Effectively I lost my job for speaking out,' he says. 'I took it quite badly.'

A few weeks later the Tigers' administrative capital Kilinochchi fell to the government, and with it the main north–south highway. The rebels and the hundreds of thousands of civilians they took with them were confined to a shrinking patch of jungle, paddy fields, marshland and beach. Fighter-bombers screeched overhead; soon there was nowhere to run from the thundering shells. White-haired old ladies were so thin their bodies looked like those of children, but sapped of all vigour. They just sat on the ground, crumpled and deflated, with huge empty eyes that spoke of utter despair. By January 2009 the whole population was relying on the UN to eat.

But after one horrific journey into rebel territory the food convoys would stop.

In the early hours of 16 January, fifty-three trucks and light vehicles loaded with dry food and tents set off on the precarious four-hour journey from the garrison town of Vavuniya to Puthukkudiyiruppu in the heart of Tiger territory. The aim was to deliver essential supplies and then to try to extract the local Tamil UN staff and their families who'd been forced to remain behind. Seven international staff travelled the fifty-kilometre route with the convoy into the diminishing rebel enclave, which was being attacked from the south, the west and the north.

As they drove along the main road inside the Tiger areas, the aid workers saw panic everywhere. Shells were falling dangerously close to civilians. Thousands of people were on the move again, heading north, unsure where safety lay this time, feeling trapped and increasingly desperate. Exhausted and frightened, they were on foot, in bullock carts and riding tractors, while stern young Tiger fighters passed them heading in the opposite direction.

In Puthukkudiyiruppu, affectionately abbreviated to PTK, the sound of incoming artillery could be heard as the Sri Lankan Army tried to hit the Tigers' mobile guns, which were playing a deadly game of cat-and-mouse, firing off rounds and then quickly moving position. Neither side worried too much about the civilians still present in the town. Scores of injured poured into the overwhelmed hospital, not just fighters but dazed, bleeding children.

For three days the UN convoy was trapped by heavy bombardment, unable to leave rebel territory. On 20 January, just as clearance came from Colombo for the convoy to start its return journey, the Tigers stopped the lorries and refused to let the 132 Tamil staff and their families through. The security situation was deteriorating so fast that it was clear this would be the last food convoy to travel inside the war zone. It was also the UN's last chance to get its local staff out. A heated discussion ensued: five of the aid workers wanted to go rather than risk their lives staying on. However, two men – a former colonel from Bangladesh who was the security officer and a young aid worker from Australia – decided to stay, hoping they could persuade the Tigers to let the local staff out.

The bulk of the convoy drove out. The remaining seven trucks moved north to the area the Sri Lankan government had just demarcated as a 'safe' or 'no-fire zone'. That morning the air force had dropped leaflets advising civilians to take shelter in the thirty-five-square-kilometre zone, adjacent to the main road. The UN workers set up a food-distribution hub on a large piece of open ground well inside the safe zone, which was already crammed with thousands of people. The two international staff used their satellite phones to transmit their location to the military while more civilians settled around the UN, assuming they'd be safe with the foreigners.

During the day, shells started landing occasionally, but by night-time the UN staff found themselves under extremely heavy fire from cannon, mortars, and shells from multi-barrelled rocket launchers that pounded the area. The white UN vehicles were covered in dismem-bered body parts and the corpse of a baby hung from a tree. UN employees had flak jackets and helmets, and had hired labourers to dig them an earthen bunker topped with sturdy tree trunks for protection against flying shrapnel, but the Tamil civilians were in the open, totally exposed. With only tarpaulins for shelter, they stood no chance as the shells ripped them to bits. In forty-eight hours of bombardment the aid workers counted 1,000 shells falling in the field where they'd set up the food-distribution point, which was just 500 metres square.

The two UN staff 'could do little more than listen to the screams of people dying besides their campfires as artillery blasted them', wrote the former UN spokesman Gordon Weiss later. The shrill cries for help turned into moaning that gradually stopped as the injured women and children bled to death. The Bangladeshi colonel later told a UN investigation panel that it was 'nothing short of the intentional murder of civilians'. As an experienced military man, he concluded the fire came from army positions. One explosion injured a UN staff member.[5]

Every half-hour the aid workers were on the satellite phone to UN headquarters or the Sri Lankan Army, trying to get them to redirect their fire. They were adamant there were no rebel fighters in the open ground where they were located, though the rebels did fire mortar guns from positions half a kilometre away and from near the hospital.

For two nights the UN came under incessant attack. One shell landed so close to its bunker it left the inhabitants deafened for a few seconds. Climbing out of their shelter at dawn, the aid workers had to remove the torso of a seventeen-year-old girl sprawled at the entrance; they found that a third of the labourers they'd employed to dig their bunker were dead. The men photographed and documented evidence of the slaughter before they fled, lucky to be alive. UN headquarters had managed to negotiate a pause in the fighting for them to drive out.

'It was a set of a war film,' the Bangladeshi colonel said afterwards; 'trees were snapped in half, and some were still burning. There were burning vehicles all along the road, and bodies everywhere, torn open, lying together with farm animals.'[6]

Ironically, when they drove through areas of rebel territory that had not been declared part of the 'no-fire zone', the UN found them untouched in spite of a heavy Tiger presence and far fewer civilians.

One UN official privately concluded that the government had declared a safe zone only to concentrate civilians in one place so as to kill as many as possible. It was a view the UN hierarchy did not share. Even though it now had first-hand testimony and photographic evidence of war crimes, in public it issued only bland statements urging better treatment of civilians by both sides. Bullied by the Sri Lankan government, the UN continued with its carefully worded, even-handed pronouncements as the war became yet more bloody.

Tamils abandoned in the war zone still placed their faith in the United Nations, hoping the organisation would intervene and stop the madness. They were to be sorely disappointed.

As the Tigers retreated, the Sri Lankan government declared two further 'safe zones', both of which were to prove equally *un*safe. Under bombardment, tens of thousands of civilians were herded towards a tiny coastal spit where they were penned in and attacked. Those who tried to escape risked being shot in the back or the legs by the rebels. Both the army and the Tigers claimed to be saving the Tamil people, but thought nothing of recklessly endangering them.

It was a world in which death was so omnipresent that few expected to walk out alive. Mothers cowered in ditches, covering the eyes of their starving children to shield them from the sight of their friends being blown to pieces. Distraught families sifted through corpses and body parts to find their loved ones. Worse still, some were forced to abandon the injured by the side of the road because they were too badly maimed to run for their lives. People lived with the din of crashing explosions and the cacophony of high-pitched screams. All this time the Sri Lankan government claimed to be operating a 'zero civilian casualty policy' – a ridiculous assertion that was repeated regularly between February and May 2009 even as thousands and thousands of civilians were slaughtered. The UN and many Western diplomats knew it was a lie but remained silent.

With no access to the war zone, the UN set up a task force to collate casualty figures by telephone from the capital.[7] Without taking into account the casualties in the last week of the war when many people died, the task force estimated that 7,721 people were killed and 18,479 injured.[8] This figure is by necessity an extremely conservative count, because every incident had to be verified by three sources, including a UN employee, and if it might have been double-counted it was not recorded.

Nobody knows how many thousands died in the final week. A UN spokesman declared it a bloodbath, only to face fierce protests from the Sri Lankan government. UN experts analysed detailed satellite imagery to estimate shifting population numbers. We know from leaked embassy cables that the UN came to a very rough estimate of between 7,000 and 17,000 people who went missing in the last week, presumed dead.[9]

On 10 May, a Catholic priest still trapped inside the war zone with civilians wrote to the Pope claiming there had been 7,000 casualties the previous night alone:

I a priest of the diocese of Jaffna am prompted to write this open letter to Your Holiness after a night of terror and horror, the worst of the daily ordeal meted out by the Sri Lankan Security forces on the innocent Tamil civilians huddled in the so called 'no fire zone' of about three square kilometres. Last night's toll of the dead is 3,118 and of the injured more than 4,000. It was a barrage of artillery, mortar and multi-barrel shelling and cluster bombs, weapons which the Sri Lankan Government denies using on the civilians in the no fire zone. The cries of woes and agony of the babies and children, the women and elderly fill the air that was polluted by poisonous and unhealthy gases, and pierced the hearts of fathers and mothers, of elders and peasants, of old men and women of all walks of life. I am not unaware that this letter would arouse the wrath of the Sri Lankan government which will resort to revenge by killing me.[10]

This priest later disappeared without trace, after being seen by many surrendering to the army.

The UN never made public even its conservative death count. Diplomats in Colombo were briefed with the numbers, but when they leaked the UN in New York said it couldn't confirm them. 'Lots of people in the UN were very upset,' said one agency head afterwards. 'There had been months of considerable effort triangulating each report and the number was fairly solidly verified.' The French newspaper *Le Monde* alleged that the UN hierarchy deliberately played down casualty reports – something the organisation denied. The paper reported that the Secretary-General's special representative, Vijay Nambiar, told staff in Sri Lanka the UN should 'keep a low profile' and play a 'sustaining role' that was 'compatible with the government'.[11]

A panel of independent experts commissioned by the United Nations later concluded that 'the decision not to provide specific figures made the issue of civilian casualties less newsworthy', blaming pressure from the Sri Lankan government and the UN's fear of losing access.

One UN official described the statistics he collected as merely a snapshot, adding that he'd be staggered if the final death toll didn't exceed 30,000. He pointed out that there were twenty to thirty heavy shell attacks a day, but on average the UN only received reports from three. His warnings of a massacre were ignored. The experts for the UN concluded later that the overall casualties were extremely high and a death toll of 40,000 couldn't be ruled out.

Some say the numbers could be even higher. Estimates have been calculated based on subtracting the number of survivors from population statistics before the war. The death toll could be 55,000 if the population figure for January 2009, given by a senior Tamil civil servant, is used. A Tamil Catholic bishop did the sums using the government's own population data for late 2008 and found 146,679 people unaccounted for. Even if this is adjusted for UN population figures there would appear to be well over 100,000 people missing as a result of the final stage of the war. The bishop had hoped the government would explain why he was wrong in his calculations, but in place of an explanation he received only death threats.

The figures speak for themselves – the world watched silently as thousands and thousands of innocent civilians, held against their will in the war zone, were killed by a government that actually claimed it was rescuing them. American Embassy cables released by WikiLeaks show the diplomatic community had a pretty shrewd idea that civilians were being pounded by heavy weapons and thousands were dying, but no government spoke out.

Arguably the failure of the United Nations merely reflected the indifference of its member states, who were happy to see another terrorist group defeated. Many blame China – the largest arms seller to Sri Lanka and its biggest aid donor by 2008. Beijing remains openly supportive of Sri Lanka's right to defend itself against internal threats, even at the cost of human rights. Other countries backed Sri Lanka, including Israel, Iran, India, Pakistan and even the Maldives, whose president at the time was a former Amnesty International prisoner of conscience. Today the same countries shield Colombo from any action on war crimes.

Most Western diplomats in Colombo did not oppose the war. The decision to proscribe the Tigers as terrorists meant they supported the war aim. Politicians in Europe and the United States spoke of human rights but indirectly backed the Sri Lankan military by selling weapons or providing training.

According to leaked diplomatic cables, Britain's foreign secretary at the time, David Miliband, spent 60 per cent of his days working on Sri Lanka in the spring of 2009 in order to woo Tamil votes for the upcoming parliamentary elections.[12] The Sri Lankan government can't have taken Miliband's efforts very seriously, knowing that Britain had been quite happily selling weapons to its military throughout the ceasefire and the build-up to war. It's not widely known, but from 2001 to 2008 the UK issued more arms-export licences for Sri Lanka than any other nation in Europe, selling items such as semi-automatic pistols, components for combat aircrafts, armoured vehicles, small-arms ammunition, military sonar detection, grenades and military communications equipment.[13] The then Shadow Defence Secretary, Liam Fox, was also busy visiting Sri Lanka in March 2009, to discuss investment and reconstruction in the north, at a time when appalling crimes were being committed.[14]

Sri Lanka needed money to buy all these weapons. At the end of April 2009, when the war was at its fiercest, the UN Security Council saw no reason to delay a £1.2 billion International Monetary Fund loan to Sri Lanka, effectively underpinning an economy depleted by frequent arms purchases.[15]

The failure of the United Nations to protect Tamil civilians was symptomatic of the indifference of the world as a whole.

Even when the guns fell silent, in late May 2009, the killing did not stop – only the counting of bodies. After the war 282,000 traumatised

Tamil survivors were interned against their will in a giant refugee camp called Manik Farm. It was built and run with UN aid and international money, to the tune of £440,000 a day.[16] Overnight it became the second largest city in Sri Lanka and the world's largest refugee camp. All around the site were huge posters of the Sri Lankan President and his two brothers. 'Nasty, absolutely horrible and horrendous' was how one UN agency head described the camp. Ban Ki-moon, the UN Secretary-General, himself described conditions as worse than anything he'd seen in Goma and Darfur.[17] The UN controversially decided it was better to be involved, because otherwise the refugees – roughly a third of whom were wounded – might be even worse off.[18] In an odd compromise, UN agencies refused to invest in more comfortable and permanent cement structures for fear the refugees would be interned for years. A USAID team which saw refugees at the end of April reported even then that the number of amputees was staggering. They said open defecation was rampant, there were festering wounds, and malnutrition was evident.[19]

Even the UN's own local staff were detained in the camp, which was heavily guarded. It was a deeply disturbing sight: huddled four or five rows deep were ragged, emaciated women and children peering through barbed wire – images reminiscent of the detention camps for Bosnian Muslims more than a decade earlier. Armed soldiers from the conquering army roamed at will through the interminable rows of white UNHCR tents and tin sheds. Two UN drivers were arrested and tortured by the Sri Lankan authorities. Reports of rape and disappearance started to trickle out of the camp from the few local charities allowed access. Protection workers from the UN had to struggle to get in. 'The government didn't want people in there asking questions about what happened in the war and what was going on in the camps,' explained one aid worker. 'It was extremely frustrating; we couldn't do anything,' said another UN employee, who watched the suspected combatants being separated at the checkpoint and taken away from their families.

One day an international aid worker in Colombo received a distress call from one of the Tamils who'd worked for the UN. The distraught man said the army had rounded up pretty young Tamil women and girls from the refugee camp to go and cook and clean for Sinhalese construction workers outside. His wife had been put on the bus. When she returned a few days later, she and all the other women had been gang-raped. The UN wasn't even protecting its own staff, let alone the hundreds of thousands of civilians who felt utterly betrayed.

Matthi, a disabled Tamil asylum seeker in detention in Australia, told me he'd lost all confidence in the organisation: 'The United Nations should never have left us in the first place. Then at the end they should have come so we could have surrendered to them instead of the government. They could have sent ships. They were selfish and I have no faith in them. At the right time they simply didn't do what they had to do.'

Aid Worker Expulsions 2008–9

OCTOBER 2008   Italian aid worker for Dutch relief agency
                      ZOA expelled after challenging the
                      government order to quit rebel territory.

DECEMBER 2008   John Campbell of World Food Programme
                      forced to leave.
                      Nobert Ropers, head of the Berghof
                      Foundation for Conflict Studies, asked to leave
                      Sri Lanka.[1]
                      The British head of Solidar, a consortium of
                      NGOs, ordered to leave within seven days.

MAY 2009   Gordon Weiss, UN spokesman, threatened with
                      expulsion for describing the last three weeks of
                      war as a 'bloodbath'.
                      A British employee of Norwegian NGO Forut
                      stopped from re-entering Sri Lanka.
                      Two internationals, including a Briton,
                      working for Care International forced to leave
                      after their visas were not extended.

JUNE 2009   Head of Forut Ranvei Tvetenes deported
                      for refusing to hoist a Sri Lankan flag on her
                      office, which she felt violated its neutrality.

JULY 2009   International Committee of the Red Cross
                      asked to close two offices.
                      Peter McKay of the UN Office for Project
                      Services expelled after working on collecting
                      casualty statistics from sources inside the war
                      zone.

SEPTEMBER 2009   UNICEF spokesman James Elder expelled
                        after speaking about children going through an
                        'unimaginable hell' in the war zone.

After the war, visas were not renewed for dozens of foreign aid workers. New rules prevented them staying in Sri Lanka for more than three years. As a result *The Times* reported that 'A Briton working for the Norwegian Refugee Council, an Ethiopian working for the Save the Children Fund, and three foreign members of staff for ASB, a German NGO', as well as Care International staff, were forced to leave Sri Lanka.[2]

APRIL 2009   Swedish Foreign Minister Carl Bildt refused a
                        visa for Sri Lanka.
JUNE 2009   Canadian MP Bob Rae denied entry at the
                        airport and deported.

The Journalist

Lokeesan was escaping a strip of golden sand, a tropical beach transformed into a place of random slaughter. Six foot tall, with an unkempt beard and long, dishevelled hair, the twenty-seven-year-old carried his father in his arms like a child. He hardly noticed the bullets flying overhead and the corpses underfoot as he walked. Most of all he remembers being consumed with thirst that scorching April afternoon in 2009 – a dreadful, overriding craving to drink.

In just a few months, the Tamil Tiger administration that governed Lokeesan's whole life had disintegrated. Once thought of as invincible, the rebel force kept retreating in the face of the Sri Lankan Army. They're accused of forcing hundreds of thousands of people to come with them to a tiny strip of beach as a human bulwark – something Lokeesan disputes. There was nowhere to run: the sea was on one side and the army on all others. It was a scene of carnage, dead civilians still clutching white flags, fresh bomb craters around the hospital building, the sound of shells falling behind them amid the palm trees. Choking grey smoke hung in the air.

On the way Lokeesan passed a small tent where an old man lay, crying softly because he had nobody to carry him to safety. People ran for their lives in such a hurry that the elderly and injured were abandoned.

After months of looming defeat, the end came very suddenly. The rebels lost the middle section of the last tiny spit of land they controlled. Tens of thousands of frightened, war-weary Tamils had no choice but to surrender to the army – they were surrounded and cut off. Lokeesan, his mother, father and girlfriend had delayed leaving, but sunset was approaching and in the dark it would become even more dangerous. They didn't want to be the last ones left on the beach when the soldiers came to mop up. The only way out was to wade through the freshwater lagoon that separated them from the army.

As he stepped into the gently rippling water, his father slung across his shoulder, Lokeesan thought he could at last have a drink. Then he saw corpses floating in the water – the dead bodies of two women. It struck him that he was now walking among the dead. He resisted for some time and then he succumbed to his craving for water, any water. 'It was the most horrible thing – not because it was so disgusting, but because I had sunk so low. For six months I had been stepping over dead bodies, but finally I was drinking water with bodies in it.'

Years later, sipping bottled mineral water on a black-leather armchair in Berlin, Lokeesan has tears in his eyes, remembering a time when he drank water polluted by corpses. With short-cropped hair, a neatly starched shirt and dark blue jeans, it's hard to imagine this restrained and polite young man in such desperate torment. He's tall and athletic-looking, but has a gentleness in the careful, considerate way he moves around others: a watchfulness that comes of being a professional observer. He recounts his story with poise and precision, but his dark, anguished eyes betray his inner feelings.

It was Lokeesan's job to report on other people's horror, but he has plenty of his own. As a journalist for a pro-rebel news site, Tamilnet, he gazed at thousands of dead bodies, normally through the viewfinder of his camera. He observed people take their last breath, the life going out of them before his very eyes. He saw children's brains exposed by shattered skulls, he heard the desolate screams of their mothers and inhaled the stench of death. He witnessed the aftermath of hundreds of attacks in the final months – running for his life, depositing his family in a safe place and then retracing his steps to document the butchery.

Lokeesan was one of the very few surviving eye-witnesses who actively sought out and recorded other people's tragedies. He watched hundreds of thousands of trapped Tamils being herded into a diminishing tract of land. Rockets, mortars and bombs drove them towards the sea, where they were penned up in squalid encampments with no food. After decades of conflict, these people were good at surviving immense hardship, but the last few months stripped everyone down to a kind of numb, primal terror. Death could strike at any moment, inexplicably obliterating some and not others, leaving searing grief in its wake. There was no pattern, no logic and no limit, just a lot of blood and loss.

At first Lokeesan recorded videos of the savagery he found, using his laptop and portable satellite dish to send them to his head office, based in Norway, a country with a long association with Sri Lanka as aid donor and peace mediator. But after a while he realised that the images were too horrific to be used. He started sending black-and-white photographs instead, deliberately toning down the graphic slaughter and destruction.

Lokeesan's work was read online around the world by diplomats, journalists and the Tamil diaspora. It was not appreciated, however, by the Sri Lankan Army, which checked his reports every morning, and must often have been choking with rage at what they read. They loathed Tamilnet, calling it terrorist propaganda, furious that the international media quoted Lokeesan's casualty figures to balance those of the Sri Lankan military. That was because, unlike all the rest of the media, Tamilnet actually had a reporter on the ground. He didn't criticise the Tigers, but he did try to tell the world what it was like to be trapped in a place where death rained down from the skies. Like many a journalist, he thought he could influence the outcome of events. He believed that, if people knew what was going on, they would try to stop it.

'The world knew so many Tamils were suffering there – they were practically there looking at the war on the satellite pictures – but they did nothing,' he says, adding sadly, 'If Reuters or the BBC had been there it would have stopped, but not my organisation.'

The first time Lokeesan had a deep sense of foreboding was the day Dixie and the rest of the United Nations evacuated rebel territory in September 2008. The shells and bombs had reached Kilinochchi, and the government ordered all the international aid workers to leave, just when hundreds of thousands of people most needed their help. Fearing for his future, the young reporter stood in the red dust at the edge of the road as the convoy of white four-wheel-drive jeeps sped past. He caught a glimpse of the aid workers' familiar faces under helmets and flak jackets and wondered how much worse the war could get. Already half the population had been made homeless; ragged, traumatised farmers and shopkeepers were now camping under trees. Lokeesan had seen the injured in the district hospital run for their lives during air attacks, ripping off the intravenous tubes still attached to fluid bags on stands. Even with the UN present, ambulances and school buses had been attacked.

'People felt hurt and upset. None of us really imagined that they would abandon us there. There was nobody left from outside to act as a witness. I still believe that one of the biggest reasons for all the killings was that the United Nations left. No organisation could report on what was going on. If they'd stayed, there would have been far fewer shell attacks,' he says.

There was also nobody to protest when the rebels forcibly took more and more teenage boys and girls to fight for the Tamil cause, even when it was clear it was a lost one. Any semblance of civil administration started to collapse with the departure of the UN. Lokeesan's boss told me he needed a special letter from the Tigers in order to be able to move about in the rebel zone when reporting; otherwise roaming recruitment teams might snatch him and send him off to the front line.

As the Sri Lankan Army shelled its way deeper into rebel territory, civilians fled along the coastal road – a bumpy, potholed minor route that snaked up the stunning eastern seaboard with its long, palm-fringed beaches and flat, marshy lagoons. Inland the road ran through farming villages nestled in shady coconut groves, with irrigation tanks and fruit trees. Normally, aside from the birds and animals, the only sound would be the odd passing motorbike, a carpenter hammering, or the Hindu temple playing cassettes of devotional songs. By January 2009 that peaceful, rural life was a thing of the past. Screaming rent the air, all the voices at different pitches. There was wailing, shrieking, shouting, weeping and howling all at once from several directions, much of it from bewildered, shaken children calling for their mothers.

Like everyone else, Lokeesan and his family fled through a succession of hamlets, hoping each one would bring safety. Every time they moved, Lokeesan would construct a bunker, erect a tent and unpack their dwindling stock of possessions, unsure how long they could stay, while he carried on sending reports. Unusually heavy monsoon rains added to the misery. Months of downpour caused flooding, quickly filling the bunkers with dirty water. Ponds and lakes overflowed and cattle were washed away; farmers lost even more of their meagre belongings.

The route to safety was packed with people fleeing on foot, squeezed in around the vehicles. Vintage tractors lumbered noisily down the road, which was now a small stream in places because of the flooding, the water churning to a muddy orange colour. Trucks looked as if they were transporting someone's junk rather than the essentials for life. They were laden with salvaged roof beams and mangled sheets of corrugated iron, and most had a big rusty diesel can and a bicycle perched on the back. Brown bullocks, more accustomed to pulling ploughs, found themselves lugging carts full of their owners' last worldly goods, including palm thatch from the roofing of rural huts. In January the road came under relentless attacks every day. The shells splintered trees, set vehicles on fire and scattered human and cattle body parts indiscriminately.

After one attack in January, Lokeesan counted 300 corpses before he gave up, too shaken by the hysterical children screaming for their dead parents. Many more people were killed inside their vehicles while trying to flee, but he didn't count them. He took photos and videos, but when he was a few kilometres away he collapsed in tears.

The images stored in his memory are nightmarish – like the grieving mother clasping a dead baby to her chest, blood gushing from the child; or the corpses tied on top of piles of possessions on the backs of bicycles, dripping blood as they went. Families were reluctant to abandon their dead, but they couldn't stop and bury bodies when under heavy bombardment. They found any way of taking their loved ones somewhere quiet enough to dig them a hasty, unmarked grave.

Lokeesan felt relieved that he didn't have small children. 'I saw parents forced to watch their children starve. It was something no human being can bear.' It was impossible for parents to keep young children cooped up in bunkers twenty-four hours a day; they would try to escape as soon as their mother wasn't looking. 'When a child was running around outside, a bomb would fall and the mother would run towards it to protect her child and be killed as well. It was mostly mothers and children who died there.' People feared being separated from their loved ones even for a few minutes because of the very real prospect only one of them would die, leaving the other to suffer grief in addition to the powerful cocktail of fear, shock, physical hardship, hunger and chronic exhaustion they already had to endure.

Lokeesan would leave his parents and girlfriend in their bunker while he went off to do his work as a journalist. He told his girlfriend, who was twenty-five at the time, that if anything happened to him she should look after his parents. While travelling he often saw old people alone and abandoned and it haunted him to think the same fate could await his own mother and father. Unsure whether he'd come back alive, they would wait for him every day before eating their daily meal of rice porridge. 'They never said, "Don't do it," but they couldn't eat without me there because they were so anxious all the time; it was as if they were on pause until I returned,' he explains.

The first thing Lokeesan would do when he came back to his tent was recharge his phone and camera using a solar power pack. It was a signal to his parents that he meant to go out and report again the next day. They never discussed what he was doing or the risks he took.

He had countless near-misses. In late January, he was on his way to Uddayarkattu Hospital to check the casualties. He couldn't decide where to park his motorbike, picking one spot and then another. Minutes later, more than twenty shells landed in the hospital compound, around the area and on the main road, where he'd been just about to park. Another day he was photographing people fleeing the bombardment when a shell landed just thirty metres from where he was lying on the ground. On another occasion he was only 100 metres away from a temple that was bombed. It could so nearly have been his name on the casualty lists he spent his time compiling.

It wasn't just dangerous to travel around: speaking on the satellite phone was a risk. After a while Lokeesan began to suspect the Sri Lankan military were tracking his location from the calls. He would move quickly after every conversation, fearing an attack would come a few minutes after he'd hung up. He felt his was a voice the government side wanted to silence.

Lokeesan is convinced he first witnessed illegal white phosphorous being used against civilians in January, when he came across twenty-three dead bodies with none of the usual exit or entry wounds from shrapnel. White phosphorous is used to create a dense white smoke to mask military movements in battle; it sticks to the skin, causing third-degree burns, until it's either completely consumed or deprived of oxygen. 'Everything was burned – there was a yellowish-white fat all over the bodies. The skin had been torn off and it had melted the fat under the skin.' Some were killed while sleeping on the roadside, caught unawares in different postures. Some were hiding, taking cover. 'There were so many different ways of getting killed,' he says, now expert at surveying death.

But it's the stories he missed that most worry Lokeesan. There were many places where he never went, and that concerns him almost more than what he did see. 'There are still many things we don't know. There were no witnesses. A lot of people were killed that we don't know about.' In late January, he believes, tens of thousands of people were packed into the rebel graveyard in Vishwamadu, a small town on the main road down which almost the entire population fled. The Sri Lankan military encircled the area, trying to cut the civilian population off from the Tigers, raining shells down on the road to deter them from fleeing. 'We couldn't get in there because it was constantly being bombed…Those three days were unimaginable. So many died on that highway, but we have absolutely no idea how many.'

As the road became a death trap, Lokeesan and his family fled on foot through the jungle with tens of thousands of others. It was still raining heavily and everyone struggled to carry what they needed to survive. Lokeesan was pushing his motorbike through the mud, carrying just a bag of clothes, one of cooking utensils and one of rice. It took them seven days to travel just six kilometres. Shells were falling and there was a desperate rush of humanity heading for the sea, making it impossible to move fast. The sheer weight of the human beings and loaded vehicles meant the flooded road collapsed. The injured had no hope of reaching one of the makeshift hospitals; they died in agony.

'They were screaming to save their lives, suffering and asking for help right in front of your eyes. It was not unusual to sleep with dead bodies. This was the world in which we lived after January,' he says. 'I would wake to bombs and shells falling from the skies, like ripe mangoes from the tree.' Lokeesan photographed mothers searching for their children, calling out their names, desperate to find them alive. Many of the dead bodies would be so badly damaged they couldn't be recognised at all.

When they finally reached the sea, the sandy coast was so densely packed that there was no space or privacy; if a shell fell it would surely kill many at once.

At this stage all the Tigers could do was try and keep the Sri Lankan Army at bay, defending their tiny sliver of territory. They had lost all the major towns under their control, but human-rights groups documented how they still kept the civilian population captive, shooting at those who tried to escape to the army side. In total denial about their impending defeat, the rebels took yet more young Tamils to die for their dream of a separate state.

As the weeks went by, Tamils inside and outside the war zone hoped the international community would intervene in the conflict. Lokeesan saw it as the only solution, but it turned out to be a pipe dream.

On the beach, he pitched his tent in the ragged, disorderly settlement that had sprouted up near one of the two makeshift hospitals still functioning. The doctors worked in what had been a school building, on open ground clearly visible to the Sri Lankan Army. Army snipers were camouflaged in the jungle, just 250 metres away on the other side of a long lagoon that became the front line. The soldiers could see people coming and going with the naked eye, but the military also had drones flying overhead taking pictures.[1] Throughout the day there was gunfire coming into the hospital and on average Lokeesan says shells fell three times a week in or around the hospital compound. Rocket-propelled grenades (RPGs) were also fired and hit the hospital stores, wards and nearby tents, he says.

The area around the hospital smelled of dead flesh. 'It was like a butcher's shop. When you entered the hospital there was a tree, and under it were the injured and some of them would die.' The compound was packed with maimed, comatose human beings lying on blue plastic sheets and rags spread over the golden sand, cared for by what was left of their families.[2]

Of all the patients arriving, the medics were only able to save half; the others died before they could be treated. He remembers watching an elderly lady with a head injury expire right in front of him. 'She was suffering without even any bandages, shouting but unable to communicate because of the pain. I saw her waver in front of my eyes and then pass away,' he says, adding in a matter-of-fact tone, 'I watched so many die.'

There were no drugs, no gauze bandages and not even a surgical knife for amputations. It was here that the doctors started using butcher's knives for removing children's limbs without anaesthetic. People with head, stomach and chest injuries were often not even taken to hospital, because there was so little that could be done for them. Lokeesan estimates that only about a third of the people who were injured ever made it to a hospital to be recorded in the doctors' statistics. As the war intensified he observed the death rate increase dramatically: 'Before we fled to the beach, usually there were more people injured than killed. If ten people were killed, there would be twenty-five injured. But that was because people were still relatively healthy and fit and could respond to treatment. In the last weeks, I noticed the ratio of killed to injured was more or less equal.'

One day Lokeesan was in the hospital, counting the dead and injured, when he saw a mother, badly injured in the neck and chest but still conscious and screaming for her baby. An older lady – probably the grandmother – brought a child of about six months old, who was slightly injured. The mother took the baby, kissed it gently on the forehead, and offered her breast. She probably hadn't eaten herself for days, but knew her child must feed if it was to have any chance of survival in a world where milk powder was more valuable than gold. After a while, with the baby still drinking from her breast, Lokeesan noticed the woman was dead. That feed was the mother's parting gift to her child. She knew she was dying and that was why she'd been shouting so urgently for her baby.

On another occasion Lokeesan witnessed the area behind the hospital being shelled and the compound itself bombed. Just as the attack ended, a tractor drove in full of screeching, howling people, all of them injured. The medics lifted out seven pregnant women. Then Lokeesan noticed another woman, whose stomach was bleeding but was covered with a cloth. Nobody realised she was also pregnant because there were so many others to treat. 'Suddenly I looked at the stomach and saw something small and white sticking out. It was a child's hand poking out. The whole hospital went into shock.' Lokeesan thinks both mother and child died.

Lokeesan was sitting in his tent with his parents one evening when a missile – possibly from a tank – shot through the next-door tent. It passed horizontally, hitting an elderly man in the stomach, then through another tent, then through a vehicle and finally slammed into a house. It was too dangerous to bury the dead man anywhere away from the tent, so his family just put the body into the bunker they'd dug, filled it up with sand and left the place to search for somewhere else to stay. It was so hard to find even a couple of metres to pitch a tent that half an hour later another family came and took the spot, unaware a body had just been buried underneath. They slept on the previous occupant's grave.

In the third week of April the Sri Lankan Army managed to breach the Tiger defences and capture a portion of the sandy spit on which hundreds of thousands of Tamils were living. Lokeesan found himself confined for ten hours at a stretch to the bunker that he'd built using home-made sandbags. Multi-barrelled rocket launchers pummelled the densely populated area and shells went over their heads, causing horrendous deaths and felling trees. MBRLs were mobile trucks that could fire forty rounds of high-explosive fragmentation shells in one volley lasting just twenty seconds. The weapon sent hundreds of kilograms of explosives into a concentrated area of a few hectares, pummelling everything indiscriminately. The artillery barrages were incessant, coming from the east, the west and the north. By now the beach was in range of several different army positions. There was no sign of the Tigers, who'd started withdrawing south. Lokeesan is so tall that his head stuck out of the bunker if he sat up, so he had to keep his neck bowed down. Bullets were hitting the sandbags.

Lokeesan had all his reporting equipment with him – two laptops, a camera, a portable satellite internet dish known as a BGAN, and a hand-held satellite phone. He went to see the hospital, by now half burned down. 'People were screaming for help and they ran to the army area because it was the only place where there were no shells falling. They took off parts of their saris and used the cloth as a white flag. They were all dead by the time I went there. I have no idea of the number – there were so many bodies and the army was so close they could see they were civilians.'

In the middle of the road that passed the hospital were huge shell craters. By then the Sri Lankan soldiers were only 100 metres away. Lokeesan was cut off from the Tigers. 'I didn't know what to do,' he admits. 'I decided I would die if I stayed and die if I left. Whichever way, I was going to die.'

At four in the afternoon on 20 April, Lokeesan phoned in his last report to his boss, Jeya, in Oslo. 'I thought those might be my last words ever in my life,' he says. Jeya also remembers that last phone call; he told Lokeesan to save himself and his family at any cost and to destroy all the equipment.

First Lokeesan broke his laptops, then the BGAN dish – which proved almost indestructible – and then the phone. Removing the computer's hard disks, Lokeesan buried them under the wet sand inside the bunker, hoping the salty seawater would corrode them. 'Destroying all my equipment that I had protected for so many years, it felt as if I was killing a part of myself,' he says.

On that last day Lokeesan left a landscape littered with corpses, abandoned tents and bombed-out buildings and waded across the cool water of the lagoon which at times came up to his chin. Once he had passed the floating corpses, it took about an hour to cross the flat, grey-green expanse. Still carrying his father, Lokeesan helped his exhausted mother and girlfriend and carried a small bag of clothes and important documents.

As they approached the far shore, he spotted heavy weapons and soldiers holding mortars in the distance. It was petrifying to come so close to the enemy. The first soldier had a black cloth tied around his face to disguise his identity and was wearing a helmet and an ammunition belt slung over his shoulder.

'The immediate feeling I had was that it would have been better to have died in that place than come there. Just to see them was fearsome. All the time when I had been reporting on massacres, what went through my mind was: what sort of people are they that do these things? I tried to imagine the enemy. That first image matched what I expected. It was terrifying.'

Any Tamil would feel fear being at the mercy of victorious soldiers, who regarded all Tamil civilians as rebel sympathisers. But Lokeesan knew he was a wanted man. His reports of indescribable human suffering had exposed the Sri Lankan government's lies about 'zero civilian casualties'. What would the army do to him if they found out who he was? Had he survived the blitzkrieg of shells and dodged random bullets only to be tortured, stripped naked, blindfolded and executed and his body dumped in an unmarked grave?

Dripping, their wet clothes pasted to their bodies, Lokeesan and his family were completely silent, not daring to utter a word, paralysed by dread. By contrast the Sri Lankan soldiers were chatting happily and singing in their own language. They started to frisk the group to check for weapons, but there were no female soldiers to search the Tamil women so the male soldiers did it. Lokeesan was seized with fear for his girlfriend and mother. The soldiers' songs merged in his mind with another sound buried deep in the recesses of his memory. He'd been six years old when he'd heard a woman screaming in a paddy field. He'd been too young to know what it meant, but she was being raped by Indian soldiers, sent to Sri Lanka in the late 1980s to disarm the Tigers. 'To this day I remember the sound of that woman's scream,' he says, rigid with horror.

His terror didn't abate as they joined tens of thousands of people who'd fled earlier in the day. It was dusk and the soldiers told the dishevelled, damp Tamils to line up for more checking. Lokeesan thought it was better to get to the front of the queue and be searched before midnight; anything could happen in the middle of the night, he reasoned. He knew he had to keep his nerve if he was to evade detection; he'd also need a lot of luck.

Then without warning they came under attack: navy boats out at sea were firing cannon onto the land nearby and the barrage had come too close. 'Lie down, lie down!' the army officers shouted, quickly switching off all the lights they were using. Thousands and thousands of civilians were lying on the ground and the soldiers were sheltering in bunkers. It was the first time Lokeesan had seen the army take cover, just as Tamil civilians had been doing for months. He didn't know whether to laugh or cry.

At two in the morning they were sent to be searched once again, men and women in different places. All that ran through Lokeesan's mind was the sound of that woman screaming twenty years earlier. What would happen to his girlfriend and his mother? There was nothing he could do for them. It would take two days for the women to rejoin them.

Lokeesan and his father were out in the open, in a long queue, when they were ordered to take off all their clothing, including underwear. Destitute, starving and deadened by seeing so much killing, they were stripped of all remaining dignity. 'I don't know how to explain how that felt. To see my father naked, to see it happen in front of my eyes. Everyone was standing there naked, from my father whom I carried in my arms to small children.' Describing the humiliation years later, tears well up in Lokeesan's eyes.

After the shame of being strip-searched *en masse*, they were sent individually for questioning. Lokeesan knew his age would make them suspicious that he was a fighter.

'What did you do there?' they asked.

'I was a photographer,' replied Lokeesan, having decided it was best to tell a half-truth lest someone else reported seeing him with a camera.

'Were you a Tiger?' the intelligence officer asked in pretty good Tamil.

'No. My father cannot walk so I was exempted from service,' he said, making up the answers as he went along but knowing his father was there to back up the story.

'Are you married?' the man asked; married men were less likely to have been forcibly recruited.

'Yes,' he answered, though at this stage Lokeesan and his girlfriend hadn't yet married.

Under pressure to question thousands of people that night, the officer let Lokeesan go. He walked out into the glare of huge spotlights, watched by two Tamils in Sri Lankan military uniforms. Lokeesan remembered having seen them before, inside rebel territory. Either they'd infiltrated the Tamil Tiger ranks during the fighting or they'd swapped sides and turned informer at the end.[3] Luckily they didn't recognise Lokeesan with his beard and uncut hair.

The first time they were given food and water was when a group of reporters from state TV appeared to film the refugees. For the benefit of the cameras the Sri Lankan Army started distributing small, red packets of Maliban cream crackers. Starving, the people fought each other for a biscuit, losing any self-respect. Some men climbed the nearby mango trees, stripping them of even the unripe fruit in their hunger, but Lokeesan kept his head down, desperate not to draw attention to himself. By now the army were roaming around, randomly taking people away for questioning. Lokeesan pretended to lie asleep next to his father, not saying a word. He never saw those taken away coming back.

The refugees had to line up for two days in the scorching sun to be searched again before getting onto buses to take them to the refugee camp the government had prepared for them two hours' drive away. Lokeesan's father hadn't eaten for days and was so weak that he began to wonder if he would make it. Rainwater had gathered in small holes in the ground and some people started drinking from the dirty puddles in desperation.

There were no free seats in the crowded bus, and Lokeesan's father perched on their bag of clothes in the aisle. The rumour was they were all going for more questioning; Lokeesan was sure he would be discovered. 'It felt like we were a herd of starving cows being led to the slaughterhouse,' he says. Armed soldiers stood in the doorways of the bus to prevent the refugees escaping.

In a matter of minutes the bus drove back up the same coastal road on which Lokeesan had spent months documenting massacres. The yellow Sri Lankan flag now flew over this territory for the first time in two decades. Everyone knew the war was almost over – the Tigers controlled only a few square kilometres of beach, swamp and scrub jungle, their empire shrunk from nearly a quarter of the island in their heyday.

The bus joined the main north–south highway which runs along the spine of Sri Lanka, now in government hands for the first time in twenty-three years. It was strange for Lokeesan to see Sri Lankan soldiers in their khaki uniforms where once there had been Tiger traffic police stopping vehicles for speeding and issuing fines.

He heard a strange moaning sound. Nobody knew what it was at first – then in shock they realised that a woman was giving birth on the bus. An elderly lady started praying loudly, pleading with God to protect the mother. There was no way to give the woman in labour any privacy, and the passengers were too scared to ask the bus driver to stop.

As they drove through Kilinochchi, which had been the Tigers' headquarters, Lokeesan noticed that the district hospital now bore a banner announcing it was an army camp. They stopped at checkpoints along the way and then, at the last one, an ambulance was waiting to take the mother and newborn baby away. Lokeesan was astonished to find the soldiers had any pity for the woman giving birth; by now he believed the Sinhalese were a people without humanity.

Every Tamil who walked out of the war zone alive was sent to the newly constructed Manik Farm refugee camp, where soldiers armed with automatic rifles roamed freely among those they'd just defeated. Outside were armoured military patrol vehicles next to sandbagged bunkers. The entire site was surrounded by seven-foot-high wooden posts, strung with both barbed wire and coils of razor wire. A mechanical digger had carved out a trench around the perimeter to prevent the refugees escaping. From the air, the camp looked like a huge, ugly, bald patch of red earth in the green jungle, filled with white tents and corrugated-iron sheds laid out on a grid system. When there were strong winds, the sheds, which were held together only by a few nails, started to come apart and pieces of corrugated-iron sheeting would fly about, injuring people. Manik Farm was divided into zones of 20,000 people each, and as they filled up, construction workers chopped down more trees and extended the camp.

Civilians were detained for months – women and children battered by years of fighting, malnourishment, injuries and illness, people who could never have picked up a gun. Some in that camp were the only members of their families still alive; all were shell-shocked. The elderly just sat on the ground in the open, clasping their foreheads, unable to comprehend the extent of their suffering. Conditions were dreadful. The refugees bathed in dirty river water while chickenpox and measles started to spread. Most of the 282,000 refugees who ultimately wound up in Manik Farm had relatives nearby who would have happily looked after them. But the Sri Lankan government insisted on screening everyone, to ensure no fighters slipped through the net. It was a question of national security, they told the foreign donors who were expected to fund the camp.

At first Lokeesan hid; then he realised he had to go out and find food. His father was fading away, unable to eat what they were given because he had no teeth. Lokeesan begged a Tamil labourer working in the camp for some soft bread. 'Don't tell anyone,' the man said, 'or there will be problems for me; we are not allowed to do this,' but he took pity and brought them a loaf of white bread. The Sinhalese labourers extending the camp had a small canteen and sold cups of tea to refugees who could pay. Lokeesan only had Rs.1,000 (£5) on him, but he bought a cup. 'I felt sad to have been born as a human being. This was not a life; there was no point in clinging on to this sort of existence,' he says, recalling those forty-five days of detention.

Army and intelligence officers combed the endless rows of tents, picking up any young person without family, on suspicion of being a rebel. When Lokeesan registered at the camp he switched his first and second names around, to confuse those looking for him. The ruse worked for a while. Then, 'Lokeesan the reporter,' came the announcement on the camp loudspeaker system, 'we know you are here so come and surrender to Kushan the CID officer.'

Lokeesan immediately moved to a relative's tent, but he knew it would be only a matter of time before they found him. He managed to get a telephone call through to his brother in Europe, who paid a smuggler to take him and his family out of the camp and the country. It was expensive – Rs.1.6 million (£8,000) – but it was the only way to save their lives. This smuggler belonged to a pro-government Tamil political party, but it was often the police and army who took bribes to allow refugees to escape, turning a blind eye as they climbed under the barbed wire at the perimeter of the camp. If someone like Lokeesan could buy his way out, despite being actively hunted, there was little justification for locking everyone else up.

★

By the time Lokeesan and his family reached the capital, the victory celebrations were well under way. The city's broad avenues, with their white-stucco colonial mansions and shiny, glass shopping centres, were another world – nothing like rebel territory, even in the days of peace. The Colombo streets made it clear who wielded power: enormous banners praised the triumphant President as a 'divine gift to the country'. Tourists were already pouring back into Sri Lanka; arrivals up 8 per cent on the previous year with the news that the war was over. But for Lokeesan it was far from over. He paid an agent to procure passports and Indian visas for his family. He was on his way to meet the man when a white van drew up outside his hotel and the door slid open. Inside there were three strong men who ordered him to get in the vehicle. Lokeesan refused, but they pulled him in.

'Are you a Tiger?' was the first question.

'No, no, I am just a teacher. I am from Jaffna,' he lied, wondering if after all he'd been through he was now going to be abducted in one of the notorious 'white vans' that had become synonymous with disappearance and torture. Somehow Lokeesan kept his cool and they eventually let him go. It turned out the illegal-visa agent was also working for Sri Lankan intelligence. It had been a very close shave, and it was only the first.

The next morning his hotel was raided and everyone questioned, searched and photographed. The policemen suspected Lokeesan's family had escaped from Manik Farm, and they went off to check their records. By the time they came back, Lokeesan had disappeared; he quickly flew out of Sri Lanka with his family to southern India, where it was easy to blend with the local Tamil population.

Since the end of the war, thousands of Sri Lankan Tamils have transited through the Indian state of Tamil Nadu on their way to Western countries, by legal and illegal routes. They start off with three-month Indian visas and then pay bribes to extend them, aware of reports that Sri Lankan and Indian intelligence are conducting joint operations to hunt down former Tigers. Refugees say they are watched and questioned by the authorities, while some have been arrested and deported.

For many escapees, the time spent in India has involved months of nerve-racking waiting, hiding small children constantly indoors to avoid any attention and surviving off dwindling stocks of money.

Lokeesan was no different. He stayed in India for sixteen long months, during which time he married and had a baby boy. As the months went past, he became increasingly desperate, unsure how to get out as his passport had expired and he didn't dare go to his embassy to renew it. Help came from a very unexpected quarter: an exiled Sinhalese journalist who lobbied for him, preparing scholarship applications, arranging supporting documentation and translating the relevant papers. At first Lokeesan didn't trust the man at all; he'd never before spoken to a Sinhalese person who wasn't pointing a gun at him. Gradually they became friends.

Now they hope together they can tell people what happened in Sri Lanka. 'When I came out, I wanted to tell everyone what happened so that every single human being who died there would be worth something. There has to be an end to this thing. There has to be a point to it all. For me it's to tell the outside world,' he explains.

That's why Lokeesan agreed to tell me his story. The first time we met was in the town where he lives. We arranged to meet very early in the morning in his office. When he arrived and unlocked the doors, Lokeesan looked strangely familiar, which I wasn't expecting. 'Have we met before?' I asked. 'Yes,' he replied, equally surprised, 'at the time of the tsunami.' I had travelled to rebel territory in Sri Lanka to report for the BBC on the aftermath of the 2004 tsunami. As I stood by a destroyed church, the stench of death still hanging in the air, a young journalist had approached me on the first day to ask how I felt about what I'd seen. That time he'd interviewed me; now it was my turn. Neither of us could stop grinning. There was something so miraculous about meeting by chance again on the other side of the world.

A small twist of fate, but little consolation for a young man tortured by memories of bloodstained children. 'In my opinion everyone who was there is dead. There is no life inside us. We are just dead human beings walking around – empty skulls with legs,' he says.

Touched by the troubled young man in their midst, Lokeesan's colleagues clubbed together to buy him a new camera. His first instinct was to take photographs of his one-year-old son, but he couldn't. Looking at the world through a viewfinder again was too traumatic: 'All I could see when I looked through the lens were the bodies of dead children I had photographed during the war – like a two-year-old girl blown to pieces. She wasn't like a human being any more, but I could still make her out as a child who had once been pretty. She had long hair and the fragments of her dress were flowery. She was lying face-down, thrown by the force of the explosion, and the lower part of her body just wasn't there any more.' A photographer who can no longer look through a camera, Lokeesan can't watch the television news because the images of war elsewhere are too troubling.

Years on, he is still trying to work out who survived. He knew a lot of people in rebel territory, having grown up there. His school even became a makeshift hospital during the war, his A-level classroom next to the impromptu morgue. 'We're still counting the dead,' he explains, looking deep into my eyes and adding, 'I sometimes think it would have been better to have been killed too.'

Recorded Killings of Journalists and Media Workers, April 2004–March 2009

Source: Journalists for Democracy in Sri Lanka

1. Aiyathurai A. Nadesan, journalist, 31 May 2004
2. Kandaswamy Aiyer Balanadaraj, writer, 16 August 2004
3. Lanka Jayasundera, photo journalist, 11 December 2004
4. Dharmaratnam Sivaram, editor, 28 April 2005
5. Kannamuttu Arsakumar, media worker, 29 June 2005
6. Relangee Selvarajah, journalist, 12 August 2005
7. D. Selvaratnam, media worker, 29 August 2005
8. Yogakumar Krishnapillai, media worker, 30 September 2005
9. L. M. (Netpittimunai) Faleel, writer, 2 December 2005
10. K. Navaratnam, media worker, 22 December 2005
11. Subramaniam Suhirtharajan, journalist, 24 January 2006
12. S. T. Gananathan, owner, 1 February 2006
13. Bastian George Sagayathas, media worker, 3 May 2006
14. Rajaratnam Ranjith Kumar, media worker, 3 May 2006
15. Sampath Lakmal de Silva, journalist, 2 July 2006
16. Mariadasan Manojanraj, media worker, 1 August 2006
17. Pathmanathan Vismananthan, musician, 2 August 2006
18. Sathasivam Baskaran, media worker, 15 August 2006
19. Sinnathamby Sivamaharajah, media owner, 20 August 2006
20. S. Raveendran, media worker, 12 February 2007
21. Subramaniam Ramachandran, media personnel, 15 February 2007
22. Chandrabose Suthakar, journalist, 16 April 2007
23. Selvarasah Rajeevarman, journalist, 29 April 2007
24. Sahadevan Neelakshan, journalist, 1 August 2007
25. Anthonypillai Sherin Siththiranjan, media worker, 5 November 2007

26. Vadivel Nimalarajah, media worker, 17 November 2007
27. Isaivizhi Chempian (Subhajini), media worker,
     27 November 2007
28. Suresh Limbiyo, media worker, 27 November 2007
29. T. Tharmalingam, media worker, 27 November 2007
30. Paranirupesingham Devakumar, journalist, 28 May 2008
31. Rasmi Mohamad, journalist, 6 October 2008
32. Rasiya Jeynthiran, journalist, October 2008
33. Lasantha Wickrematunga, editor, 8 January 2009
34. Punniyamurthy Sathyamurthy, journalist, 12 February 2009
35. Sasi Mathan, media worker, 5 March 2009
36. Mahalingam Maheswaran, journalist, 13 March 2009
37. Anton, media worker, March 2009
38. Rajkumar Densey, media worker, 9 April 2009
39. Jeyaraja Susithara (Suganthan), media worker, 25 April 2009
40. Mariyappu Anthoneykumar, media worker, 14 May 2009
41. Thuraisingham Tharshan, media worker, 14 May 2009
42. Isai Priya alias Shoba, journalist, 18 May 2009
43. T. Thavapalan, journalist, 19 May 2009
44. Prageeth Ekneligoda, journalist and cartoonist, disappeared
     24 January 2010

In addition, more than fifty journalists exiled.

The Spokesman

He had a lot of time to think about his death, but in the end nothing went according to plan. For months he considered using the cyanide capsule hanging around his neck and the pistol he carried. For a senior Tamil Tiger, surrender wasn't really an option; martyrdom was the mantra of the group that pioneered the art of suicide bombing.

'You go and I will stay,' he told a friend. 'My body will be food for the dogs and crows.'

The final hours of the war were filled with frantic satellite-phone calls begging for help. He found he wanted to hold on to life at any cost. It was as if he'd suddenly woken from a deep slumber and realised nobody was coming to save him.

Crashing explosions shook the ground, bullets crackled and people screamed in terror. For months supersonic jets and artillery had pounded the tiny rebel enclave in northern Sri Lanka. By the end, more than 70,000 people were still cowering in bunkers on the beach, starving and shell-shocked, looking for a way to escape.

That final battleground was a place where to live or to die was as random as tossing a coin. There was no logic to it; some would survive and others wouldn't. This is the story of a man who knew the dice were loaded against him. His chances of survival were slim. Pulidevan, or Puli for short, was well known in Sri Lanka. He was the public face of the Tamil Tigers – the spokesman for one of the most successful and brutal ethnic insurgent groups in the world. If captured he was a huge prize for the Sri Lankan Army.

'They will kill you if they catch you,' I had warned months earlier, chatting with him on Skype. Even then defeat looked certain.

'Yes, I know,' he replied patiently.

'You're more of a threat than any fighter. Everyone knows what you look like, so you cannot sneak through some military checkpoint and vanish,' I said.

'I understand what you're saying,' he replied. Clearly the same thoughts had gone through his mind. He was a marked man.

For months I'd been asking Puli what the Tigers planned to do, as they lost one town after another to the advancing Sri Lankan Army. The rebels had retreated so fast that now they had nowhere to run except into the sea. I talked repeatedly of surrender but it was clear it was taboo. I wanted to put the idea in his head because there was no other option.

'We will prevail,' Puli would respond every time I asked him what was going to happen, quoting George Bush of all people. His evasion and flippancy were beginning to grate.

'You have to find a way to end the bloodshed,' I would press on.

'I see your logic,' he would reply politely, giving nothing away. It was infuriating that he didn't accept the idea of surrender until it was far too late. He was trapped as much by his own group's creed of sacrifice as by the enemy soldiers. Only when faced with annihilation did he try to save himself.

We chatted for months – him in Sri Lanka, me in London – but I never really understood what went through his head. How could I know what it was like to be bombed while hiding in the pitch dark with nothing to eat but watery rice soup? I took freedom for granted; how could I fathom the injustice that would propel an intelligent, educated man to join a proscribed terrorist group, instead of becoming an engineer or accountant?

I'd like to think that he had moments of doubt, that he wavered as his organisation became increasingly cruel, endangering civilians to protect its leaders, tearing children from their parents for a futile, painful death. But I am not really sure he was a dissenting voice. More likely he was obedient, unquestioning, obliging and loyal. These are the qualities of a good spokesman; ultimately they cost him his life.

The calls and chat messages increased with the fighting in 2009. The satellite line would be crackly and echoing and sometimes he'd ring off in a rush as fighter jets screeched overhead, dropping bombs. It was a hellish world where even the womb wasn't safe: babies were born with bullets already lodged in their tiny limbs. Little children clasped their hands over their ears to try and block out the sound of crashing explosions.

All those months, Puli never let on how bad it was. A strange blend of denial and bravado kept him joking right up to the end. Aware there was a rumour that the top rebel leaders had fled, he would pull my leg and pretend to be in Switzerland. The conversations were insistent, almost defiant: they said, we are still here, despite all the attempts to wipe us out. At other times there was sadness that the world didn't believe them. But mostly Puli wanted to escape the butchery – to talk about the heavy snow that lay on the ground that winter in England, the books he'd read and my mundane domestic life. He wished to imagine what it was like to live with a future; to pretend he was not marking time in death's waiting room.

One afternoon he telephoned when I was on my way out to hear a lecture by Daniel Goleman, the author of *Emotional Intelligence*. Puli astonished me by letting slip that he'd read the books, joking that women were better than men at emotional intelligence. What kind of rebels studied psychology, I wondered? I bought him a signed copy of the book, half believing that one day I could send it to him. I was just as susceptible to fantasy as he was.

At times it was surreal to be discussing everything except the carnage. I watched a man sleepwalk to his end and talked to him about the weather while he did it. Here was a man asking politely about my son's swine flu; a leader in the same organisation that was forcibly recruiting children just a little older than him to fight. I am ashamed to say that sometimes I pretended not to be there when Puli's messages beeped on my computer screen, ignoring the carnage as the rest of the world did.

I've often wondered why he reached out just as he was going under. I wasn't the only one he called. He was the kind of person who kept in touch, and as one of the few rebels who spoke fluent English, he had the phone number of every diplomat and journalist in the country.

At the beginning he hoped for help. Then when it became that clear the world wasn't going to intervene, I think he just wanted someone outside to remember he existed. There would be no funeral, no grave. He wanted to speak to someone he had known in much better days, when he had dreams for the future.

I had first met Puli during a period of extraordinary hope, when peace was blossoming. Posted to Sri Lanka as the BBC's correspondent in 2000, I lived in Colombo with my husband and newborn baby, juggling nappies and flak jackets. My employers sent a security expert to plaster all my windows in bomb film because a Tamil BBC reporter had just been murdered in the north of the island. But I was lucky: the four years I spent in Sri Lanka were arguably the best for a long time. The government and the Tigers began peace talks, and for the first time in years, journalists could actually meet the rebels.

Puli was not so important in those days. Six foot tall, with the rebel's mandatory moustache, he was a smiley, amiable and slightly scruffy man who still rode around on a bicycle. Later he had a huge four-wheel-drive jeep with tinted glass windows and a driver. That was when he headed the Tamil Tiger Peace Secretariat and shuttled back and forth to the capital negotiating, when he wasn't flying around the world on peace delegations. In early 2002 his political career hadn't started; nobody outside knew who he was and he didn't wear a suit and tie or carry a laptop in his briefcase to do PowerPoint presentations.

Back then, a visit by a BBC correspondent was quite a novelty in rebel headquarters. I sent complicated messages through front organisations in London and Paris to say I was coming; there was no direct communication. We were searched and registered by the Sri Lankan Army and set off into no man's land. On the other side of the front line, earnest-looking young rebels flagged down the car, demanding copies of our letter of permission to travel from the Ministry of Defence. The two groups might be bitter enemies, but they shared a love of bureaucracy and paperwork. My trip was so sensitive it had had to be personally approved by the Sri Lankan Prime Minister.

The roads were indescribably bad: potholed, bomb-cratered dirt tracks. Even in a jeep, it took five and a half hours to drive the seventy kilometres from Vavuniya, the nearest government-controlled town, to the rebels' headquarters. When we got there the media-savvy Tigers laid on a press conference to publicise the release of prisoners of war – captured soldiers from the majority-Sinhalese community who were delighted to be going home again. It was a goodwill gesture to the south, but the Tigers were still very unsure what would happen with the nascent peace process. Puli and his colleagues were always on hand to chat, picking up gossip, discussing the political situation, checking out the latest communications equipment we used. A young female fighter who spoke good English quizzed me on whether I was a feminist and explained that in 'the movement', as they called it, women were absolutely equal in every way. They escorted me to film a live-fire training exercise near the coast.

'Every time you mention us on BBC TV you use old footage from the 1980s; now you can be more up to date with these pictures,' said Puli shrewdly. Twenty years on, they were now a small army, with tanks and mortar guns and found it embarrassing to be depicted with just a few battered Kalashnikov rifles. The Tigers were nothing if not image conscious, and they put on quite a show. Teenage girls in stripy camouflage uniform nonchalantly slung grenade launchers from their hips up onto their shoulders and fired as they advanced on a derelict building. The noise was deafening. Elsewhere, all-female teams did target practice with 60mm mortar guns, dug into pits, computing the trajectory on tiny pocket calculators and shouting, 'Fire!' in their shrill voices. The Tigers were clearly not short of money or ammunition. After it was over, the female fighters stood in the shade under a tree, holding their guns but giggling like silly schoolgirls, wanting to pose for photos with me. Was this really equality, or just the right to die on the battlefield? I asked, noting that the decision-makers were all men. Yes, their husbands did do childcare and cook, the older ones reassured me.

It was very hard to reconcile these smiling feminist fighters with the civilian massacres and multiple suicide bomb blasts in the south.

They were on a charm offensive with the outside world. I was invited to dinner by the political wing's head, a fighter who'd lost a leg. White-gloved waiters served stuffed crab and prawns on white bone china; the event was so formal that nobody seemed to know what sort of conversation to make – they'd forgotten to train the guests. Who were these rebels, I wondered, who lived under strict economic embargo and yet managed to smuggle in bottles of mineral water and paper napkins for their guests just as easily as heavy weaponry?

Back outside, the poverty was extreme. There were no telephones and no electricity; at night only the odd kerosene lantern flickering in the pitch darkness. The government banned even torch batteries lest the Tigers use them to make bombs. There were very few cars: only bicycles pedalled by sinewy men who hitched up their blue and white sarongs so as not to get them tangled in the chains, and the odd tractor slowly chugging along the main road. It was a country in a time warp, nothing like the Sri Lanka we'd left in the south, with its factories, neon signs, traffic congestion and supermarkets with refriger-ated shelves full of packaged food. In rebel territory a few women sat on the earth with vegetables laid out on a tarpaulin cloth for sale; you could hardly call it an economy.

The outward scars of war were everywhere. Schoolchildren sat on discarded ammunition boxes to learn their lessons, the furniture having long gone. The buildings still had gaping holes in the cement walls where shells had blown through, as well as bullet marks. If you looked carefully many of the people had physical injuries too, including Puli, though he hid it well, always keeping one arm bent at his waist. This was a place with more landmines than people, and no proper equipment to de-mine; the rudimentary hospital was full of amputees.

Children in the war zone had never seen a train, or a computer – but they knew the difference between incoming and outgoing fire, or a Kfir and a Mig jet. Rebel areas were so isolated that when they first saw my car, with BBC written on the windscreen, people would stop in their tracks and stare, and then break out into smiles and wave as I went past. A foreign journalist was a sign that things were opening up.

The rebel territory might just as well have been a different planet. Two peoples lived just 300 kilometres apart, on a minuscule island. Young Tamils in the north, like Lokeesan, had never met a Sinhalese person who wasn't a soldier pointing a gun at them. They literally didn't speak the same language. Puli became pivotal in peace negotiations because he was one of the few who spoke fluent English, allowing him to communicate with the Sri Lankan elite.

After that first trip, I went back and forth to see the Tigers, getting to know them, filming their police stations, courts of law, banks, charities, computer training centre, graveyards and fighters, including the feared suicide cadres known as Black Tigers. It was the first glimpse for a decade into the strange world they'd created. I followed the Tigers to Thailand for peace talks with the Sri Lankan government, watching men who'd grown up in the jungle struggle to fasten the unfamiliar seat belts in the plane. Unused to luxury, in the mornings the room service trays outside their hotel rooms were filled with empty ice-cream bowls – evidence of harmless pleasures they couldn't get back home.

There were times when I fell out with these intensely committed men and women: they didn't like my stories about child soldiers and suicide bombers. For months they refused to cooperate, but slowly they realised they needed me because the Tamil diaspora, which funded them, watched the BBC. Puli was on hand to patch things up and crack jokes. When the Tigers tried to recruit my staff, it was Puli's office I stormed into late at night to vent my fury. He spoke to the intelligence wing and it stopped.

As the ceasefire took hold, Puli started travelling to the capital, wearing ridiculously flashy sunglasses in an attempt to go incognito. We met in hotel lobbies in Colombo, watched by security men hiding behind newspapers. I could speak my mind to Puli. Sitting in plush velour armchairs in the lobby of the Hilton, I told him it was wrong that the Tigers were taking advantage of peace to murder their Tamil opponents and forcibly recruit children. 'You've been very frank,' he said at the end of one conversation, taken aback but still managing his characteristic smile.

At one lunch my husband ordered a beer. Puli was utterly scandal-ised. Tamil Tigers were not allowed to drink alcohol, the sexes were strictly segregated and some commanders even checked their fighters had brushed their teeth at night.

Journalists invited Puli to the Foreign Correspondents' Association in Colombo – the first time a rebel had addressed a news conference in the capital. I later learned he'd been in a terrible state about what shirt to wear for the appearance. Puli even attended the BBC's fare-well cocktail party for me, held in the colonial seafront hotel, mixing with ambassadors, ministers, journalists and the wheelchair-bound science-fiction writer Arthur C. Clarke. The Tigers looked as if they had adapted to the demands of modern diplomacy, but it was super-ficial; mindsets formed in jungle warfare were not easy to change. They were sent to Northern Ireland and South Africa to study peace processes. They thought they understood the outside world, but in the end miscalculated by counting on the international community to save them, with tragic results.

By the time Puli was desperately telephoning me in 2009, he was no longer a budding Sri Lankan Tamil politician, a future leader in a federal system; he was a terrorist banned in thirty-two countries. The peace process had broken down; the Tigers had lost 6,000 square kilometres of territory in the east of the island. The world had tired of their intransigence. They'd been given their chance to compromise during the peace process and failed to seize it. Many countries believed the only hope for Sri Lanka was to start again to solve the economic and cultural problems of the Tamil minority – decades of injustice had led many Tamils to feel they belonged to a separate nation – but without the troublesome Tigers. Some diplomats were willing to turn a blind eye to the killing, hoping the government would get it over with quickly.

Instead the rebels prolonged the end by keeping hundreds of thousands of women and children trapped with them. They hoped for a humanitarian intervention. Puli had been quite open about this approach. He told European friends that, just as in Kosovo, if enough civilians died in Sri Lanka the world would be forced to step in. It was callous brinkmanship, played with innocent lives.

For its part, the Sri Lankan government did its best to hide the human cost, precisely to *prevent* international involvement. International aid workers and journalists were barred from the battle, to prevent independent reports seeping out. Gruesome pictures and videos emerged but were quickly dismissed as rebel propaganda.

The Tigers didn't exactly win friends in the international community either. In January 2009 they took local employees of the United Nations and their families hostage in a desperate and counterproductive bid to draw attention to their plight. At that point I was among the very few people who still had contact with Puli or anyone senior in the Tamil Tigers. I was asked to facilitate a conversation on Skype, which failed because Puli deliberately dropped offline and only returned once he was sure the UN man had gone. I told him the Tigers couldn't expect the world to help if they behaved like this. I could never tell from his non-committal responses whether or not he agreed.

Then reports came in from the Catholic Church that the Tigers were preventing civilians from fleeing the war zone by beating and shooting at them. 'How can you claim to be the "legitimate representatives of the Tamil people" if you are shooting them yourselves?' I asked Puli in horror. Again he didn't contradict me.

I lobbied the Church of England to take a moral position on the war, thinking the Archbishop of Canterbury could raise awareness about more than 300,000 Tamil civilians trapped in the battlefield. After our meeting, his advisers went away saying they didn't see how they could play a role; Puli was supposed to talk to them but again he vanished offline.

What I didn't know at the time was that the Tamil Tigers had been offered a civilised way out by the Norwegian government, with the backing of the US and senior figures in the UN in New York. There were months of top-secret discussions over an internationally mediated laying-down of arms, which could have involved an American naval ship docking off the east coast to pick up civilians. The surrender would have saved thousands of lives and prevented all the rape, disappearance and summary execution after the war. The only snag was that the Tigers didn't accept it, preferring to hold out for political or military intervention and talks on power sharing. In the process they inflicted unspeakable tragedy on their own people. Though many more civilians were killed by the Sri Lankan Army in 2009, the moral responsibility must also lie with the Tigers for deliberately putting their own people in harm's way and refusing to surrender even when they'd clearly lost.

Much later, after the end of the war, I met the two Norwegian diplomats who had flown to Malaysia to discuss the surrender plan with a senior Tamil Tiger representative. They told me how they took the high-speed train from the airport to the central station and walked to a nearby hotel, where a couple of Tamil men were waiting to lead them up to a room. The two diplomats had no idea what to expect of their interlocutor. He was the Tigers' legendary arms dealer, a man best known by his initials, KP, who lived undercover in South Asia. The Norwegians had been shocked when the Tigers suggested they negotiate with a man who was on Interpol's Most Wanted list and reportedly had scores of aliases and false passports. They were surprised to find themselves with someone soft-spoken and polite, who looked like a typical businessman in a suit. The Norwegians discussed the surrender plan and left believing they were making progress and that KP at least understood the mess the Tigers were in.

The next step was for KP to visit Oslo in April – no mean feat to organise, considering he was an international criminal. The Norwegian security team was already on its way to Oslo Airport to receive the visitor when a telephone call came in saying the trip had been called off. The rebel leader Velupillai Prabhakaran had suddenly decided KP shouldn't leave Kuala Lumpur after all. Talks stalled because Prabhakaran now insisted that any cessation of hostilities must come as a step towards political negotiations on power-sharing.[1]

'They had no sense of reality,' commented one of the Norwegians involved in the talks; 'they were not engaging. We watched in horror.' Perhaps surrender just wasn't in Prabhakaran's vocabulary. Some believe his martyrdom best ensured his legacy and mystique, keeping the Tamil separatist cause alive for future generations. Others say he received bad advice and even misinformation as he became increasingly politically isolated.

If the Tigers weren't keen on surrender, nor was the Sri Lankan government, which feared a nationalist backlash from extreme Sinhalese chauvinists. Colombo initially agreed, reluctantly, to an amnesty for all rebel fighters, except the leader and his intelligence chief, who would be put in internationally supervised custody.[2] In diplomatic cables the American Ambassador in Colombo warned the Sri Lankan government that it needed 'a more public effort to communicate the offer of an amnesty' or it wouldn't work.

In late April 2009, the international community asked for a pause in fighting to allow a UN team into the war zone to try to arrange a surrender.[3] The Sri Lankan government was loath to be involved in anything that looked like negotiation with the Tigers, just as it was winning. It deliberately excluded the Norwegian Ambassador from the meeting to discuss the surrender proposal, to the horror of his colleagues.

By the second week of May, victory was so close that the Sri Lankan military wouldn't countenance a Tiger surrender. Advancing soldiers were just a kilometre from the rebels, relentlessly pummelling them with heavy weaponry. Caught in the middle were tens of thousands of civilians, being indiscriminately shelled on a daily basis.

It was chaos; Puli and his boss, Nadesan, were the only ones still in regular contact with the outside world, and they sent out conflicting signals. One day Puli spoke to a friend abroad and seemed deeply disturbed, aware for the first time that he was in real trouble. But two days later Nadesan sounded bizarrely upbeat, telling an overseas Tamil journalist: 'Don't worry about us – we will astonish the world with a new way forward.'

That last week Puli sent me a photograph of himself in a bunker, smiling as ever but shockingly thin. He had a pen in the pocket of his short-sleeved shirt. The background was a tent lined with bloodstained white sarongs. At one level it was a bit like a holiday snap, but we both knew why he sent the photo. It was for his obituary. The next day Puli was full of bravado on the phone to a Tamil friend in London. 'No, no, we are still fighting, we will do something,' he said. When asked exactly what he planned to do, he just answered, 'We have cyanide.' The following day he told a priest, 'Father, we believed India and others but they have all betrayed us.'

In the last days of their lives, Puli and Nadesan started reaching out to everyone they knew for help, among them the *Sunday Times* journalist Marie Colvin, later killed in Syria while bravely reporting on civilian suffering. In 2001 she had lost an eye in Sri Lanka and won the adoration of Tamils for telling a similar story of hidden humanitarian disaster in rebel areas. By the end of the Sri Lankan conflict she found herself acting as an interlocutor for the Tigers, relaying desperate messages to them through South Africa. 'I remember wondering if Nadesan was really completely in touch with how desperate the situation was because he was still giving conditions, although the conditions had softened by the end.[4] The man was desperate, so I didn't think I could argue and say it was already too late,' she recalled.

On the last weekend of the war, Puli and Nadesan telephoned Colvin and asked her to persuade the United Nations to oversee their unconditional surrender, along with a group of forty fighters and family members.[5] Puli made his wife leave the war zone with the exodus of civilians, promising they would meet up again but warning it might take several years.

'There were no more jokes, no pleasantries; they were really waiting for an answer,' Colvin said. She called the UN Secretary-General's special envoy, Vijay Nambiar, who was travelling. The first time they spoke, Nambiar told Colvin he thought it would be an uphill struggle to persuade the Sri Lankan government to accept a surrender: 'They seem to want to go all the way.' The second time they spoke, Colvin had woken Nambiar up at five in the morning. He said he'd been invited to witness the surrender of the group of Tigers but didn't think it was necessary to go in person.

'Shouldn't you go? This is a very, very fraught situation,' Colvin asked, horrified that he didn't seem to want to seize the opportunity. Nambiar told her he'd received assurances from President Rajapaksa that the Tigers who surrendered would be safe, and he thought that was sufficient.[6]

I too received a call that weekend, from a Tamil doctor in London who wanted to tell the media that rebel medics wished to cross into army territory, bringing with them hundreds of civilians and injured people. He'd already tried the UN and the Red Cross, who were unable to help. The doctor was flustered and distraught, unsure when he'd be able to speak to his colleagues on the ground again, aware their lives hung in the balance. I told him it seemed odd to negotiate surrender through the media – direct negotiations with the government might be better given that time was running out so fast. He consulted colleagues in a Tiger front organisation in London, who insisted the medics should take their cyanide capsules because surrender was not an option. I was left wondering if they just wanted to score a propaganda point in the media, rather than actually save lives.

What happened in the final hours of the war is still unclear. It appears the top Tiger commanders tried to sneak across the lagoon and into the surrounding jungle in three separate groups, disguised in army uniforms and wearing suicide belts packed with explosives. None survived. Today there are many rumours and contradictory versions of how Velupillai Prabhakaran and his close associates met their end. Puli and Nadesan, however, chose a different route. They sent messages to the then Sri Lankan Foreign Secretary, Palitha Kahona, through an intermediary in Europe, saying they wanted to give themselves up. He knew Puli well from the days of the peace process. Today he denies organising the surrender, but just after the war showed a British journalist this text message on his mobile phone: '0856 Sunday 17 May 2009. Just walk across to the troops, slowly! With a white flag and comply with instructions carefully. The soldiers are nervous about suicide bombers.'[7]

Nadesan also called a Tamil MP in the Sri Lankan Parliament, Rohan Chandra Nehru, asking for help and suggesting he come to the battleground to witness the surrender personally.[8] 'The army are very close to us but we are three thousand cadres here and about twenty-two thousand civilians,' Nadesan told the MP, who noted down the numbers in his parliamentary desk diary. During the call Nehru heard a woman's voice in the background screaming, 'Brother, I want to die, give me cyanide,' as well as the rhythmic thud of falling shells and the sound of gunfire.

The MP passed on the message to the President's brother, Basil Rajapaksa, as well as diplomats from Norway, Britain and the United States. Just after six in the morning Nehru received a call from a man saying he was the President of Sri Lanka.

'No, no, don't fool around with me,' he answered, assuming someone was playing a practical joke on him.

'No, I really am the President,' the man replied, and went on to confirm that he'd consulted with his other brother Gotabhaya Rajapaksa, the Defence Secretary, and all the plans were in place for the Tiger leaders' surrender. Nehru asked to go as a witness but the President said, 'No, our army is very generous and very disciplined. There is no need for you to go to a war zone. You don't need to put your own life at risk.'[9]

According to Nehru, Basil Rajapaksa spoke directly to Nadesan and told him which route to take for the surrender. The army wanted to know how to identify the Tiger leaders from the civilians as they left the war zone, so Nehru thought back to all the movies he'd seen and suggested the Tigers carry a large white flag, held higher than usual.

At the last minute, Nehru managed to get through to Nadesan on his satellite phone; the noise of gunfire was even louder. 'We are ready,' Nadesan told him. 'I'm going to walk out and hoist the white flag.'

'Hoist it high, brother – they need to see it. I will see you in the evening,' replied the MP, confident it would all go well. Little did he know this was to go down in history as 'the white flag incident'.

Before he set out to surrender, Nadesan telephoned his brother Ravi in London to warn him what was happening.

'Are you sure? Is there not any way you can escape?' Ravi asked, stunned that the end had come so fast.

'Don't you know what's happened? We are surrounded on all four sides,' Nadesan replied.

'Won't they humiliate you if you surrender?' his brother asked.

'We have only two options – surrender or suicide,' Nadesan replied, adding that there were more than 1,000 injured rebels with them who urgently needed medical treatment.

'You know the ground situation best. You decide,' his brother advised, unaware that would be their last conversation and that Nadesan's daughter would disappear without trace.

Sunday 17 May happened to be Norwegian National Day. In Oslo, Tomas Stangeland, former political secretary in the Norwegian Embassy in Colombo, had gone to bed early. It was midnight when he received the first call. He was surprised to hear from his old friend Puli; they hadn't spoken in months, so it came out of the blue. Tomas asked what the noise was in the background and was told it was shooting. Puli said he was going to surrender and needed help. Tomas agreed to ask the Norwegian Ambassador in Colombo to inform the Sri Lankan government and the Red Cross.

At about 3 a.m. Norwegian time, Puli rang back, and now sounded desperate. It was clear something was really wrong. His voice was serious and there were none of the usual jokes and bonhomie. Not long after, Puli called his sister-in-law in Canada and a European friend abroad to inform them he was setting out.

What happened next is disputed. One account says the Tigers started surrendering in batches, with Puli or Nadesan crossing first and being received by soldiers who were aware that other Tigers wouldn't come unless the surrender looked successful. A large group, including Nadesan's Sinhalese wife and young son, and more than thirty rebels were to follow.

One version of the story says that as the group was halfway towards the army, the shooting started. Nadesan's wife reportedly cried out in Sinhala, so the soldiers would understand, 'He is trying to surrender and you are shooting him,' but was killed in the hail of machine-gun fire. Even her own father had refused to speak to her once she married a Tamil Tiger. For many in her own community she was a traitor.

The Sri Lankan government said the political leaders were all shot in the back by their own side for daring to surrender. However, it never let anyone inspect the corpses and burned them two days later. There was no funeral for any of the dead Tigers – only rumours that the army has been incinerating the bones in the former war zone to leave no trace. The area of sandy coast where the rebels made their last stand is still off-limits to all: a patch of paradise that needs to be hidden.

Within hours I received a call telling me that Puli had been killed. The news of his death quickly hit the headlines but it was a month before his wife, detained in the refugee camp and then on the run, discovered she was a widow. Two years later, when I finally found her, she pulled out a tiny crumpled cutting from an Indian newspaper with a black-and-white photo of Puli from her wallet. It was the only picture she had for all those months of clandestine mourning.

There was another picture, which eventually appeared online – of Puli's corpse. His white teeth can be seen poking out from under the moustache that extends almost the width of his dark face. The gradually balding forehead seems smaller than in real life, when he towered over most Sri Lankans. His body is laid out on the earth, arms stretched out flat by his side – not a natural pose for a man who always kept his left arm bent because of a war injury. There's nothing peaceful about his passing: there are laceration and burn marks around the waist. It was definitely not the death he'd planned.

Tamil Tigers

Trained Fighters

2006	15,000 + 10,000 auxiliaries, according to the Sri Lankan military
2008	20,000 + 10,000 auxiliaries according to the Sri Lankan military
JULY 2006– MAY 2009	22,247 Tigers were killed, according to the Sri Lankan military
	11,700 Tigers said to have been detained at the end of the war
BY 2007	81 suicide bombers (63 men and 18 women) had died on land, 241 (169 men and 72 women) at sea

Child Soldiers

JANUARY 2002– SEPTEMBER 2007	More than 6,000 children known to have been recruited by the Tigers. Approximately one-third were girls.
SEPTEMBER 2007	Reports of 400 children recruited by a pro-government Tamil militia. Almost all were boys.[1]

Political Figures Assassinated by Tigers, according to Sri Lankan Ministry of Defence

Prime Minister of India
President of Sri Lanka

Opposition presidential candidate
10 leaders of political parties
7 cabinet ministers
37 MPs
6 members of provincial councils
22 members of local councils
17 political party organisers
4 mayors

Government–Tiger Peace Talks (After 2002 Ceasefire)

SEPTEMBER 2002	Thailand: Sattahip Naval Base, Chonburi
OCTOBER 2002	Thailand: Rose Garden Hotel, Nakhorn Pathom
DECEMBER 2002	Norway: Radisson SAS Plaza Hotel, Oslo
JANUARY 2003	Thailand: Rose Garden Hotel, Nakhorn Pathom
FEBRUARY 2003	Germany: Norwegian Embassy, Berlin
MARCH 2003	Japan: Hakorn Prince Hotel, Kanagawa
FEBRUARY 2006	Switzerland: Chateau de Bossey, Celigny
JUNE 2006	Norway: Thorbjornrud Hotel, Jevnaker
OCTOBER 2006	Switzerland, International Conference Centre, Geneva

The Doctor

It was in the lobby of an empty hotel on a windswept, rainy Atlantic coast that I had arranged to meet the Tamil doctor. A political refugee from the tropical jungles of northern Sri Lanka, he now lives in a tranquil landscape of pine trees and glaciers. Wrapped in a thick fleece against the damp chill outside, the doctor was extremely nervous about delving back into the past. He had just been through a month of intensive trauma counselling. There were times when he'd contemplated suicide.

On several occasions during our interview he had to break off to visit the bathroom and wash his face, to control the emotions he was reliving. Two years on, the doctor still recounted the war through traumatised flashbacks – the anecdotes exploding in random order in his memory, zigzagging back and forth across the months. He rushed to describe each one quickly before it faded again. Often he seemed to be actually back in the war zone, seeing the scenes of horror flash in front of him, constantly pulling himself back into the present. These snapshots were punctuated by apologetic, high-pitched laughter.

Short, dark and balding, with big eyes peering watchfully from behind a prominent nose, you wouldn't know he was a hero. He looked like an ordinary forty-seven-year-old man, even a little plump – a far cry from the emaciated figure who escaped at the end of the war. Though he had many opportunities to flee, he chose to stay till the end in order to save lives, believing he himself would not survive.

Pieces of shrapnel narrowly missed him as he operated in makeshift field hospitals. He's convinced they were deliberately attacked, even though he repeatedly gave the Sri Lankan government details of their positions so they'd be spared. He calculates that his team of doctors, nurses and medics saved at least 20,000 people, but he is tormented by 150 patients he abandoned under a tree on the very last day of the war.

He wants to forget the hands clawing at his sarong, the voices asking to be rescued, as he tore himself away and ran through a hail of bullets to surrender to the Sri Lankan Army.

Now in exile, living in safety with his wife and three daughters on icy, unfamiliar shores, he is still fearful for his extended family back in Sri Lanka.

'Call me Niron: I have to be careful. Any problem caused by me and they will take revenge,' he says, referring to the Sri Lankan authorities. 'Recently one friend told me that the police came with my photograph and showed it to him, asking if he'd seen me. That was after I'd left. They were looking for me, but it was too late. At first they were searching for the Tiger leaders; we were the second priority. Now they realise our importance as witnesses.'

He was one of just a few government doctors who stayed on throughout the war to serve their people. Even though the northern jungles had been under rebel administration for years, such was the power of the government bureaucracy that it still deployed doctors and civil servants in these areas. Increasingly desperate, on rare occasions the doctors spoke out about the carnage in telephone interviews with the international media. At the end of the war, the other doctors were captured and forced by the Sri Lankan government to retract everything they'd said. Niron was the one who slipped through the net.

At first Dr Niron worked in proper hospitals, the patients lying on clean sheets in beds, tended by nurses in starched white uniforms. Soon he was setting up makeshift operating theatres in public buildings, homes, tents and then finally in the open, under a tree. By the end, many of the nurses were dead and the doctors were amputating limbs with minimum anaesthetic, using butcher's knives, as witnessed by Lokeesan.

Niron spent six months working around the clock, taking short naps sitting upright in a chair between operations. The last time he had had a good night's sleep in a bed was in December 2008.

In early January 2009, he was busy at work when he received a message that his own wife had been injured. In the middle of the night he rushed to a nearby clinic, to discover she'd been unconscious for nine hours, with a head injury and fractured arm. Their youngest daughter was by her side, but unhurt. His wife, a teacher, had been speeding on her motorbike, in a panic to reach her children during a shell attack, and crashed into an auto-rickshaw at a junction. Their older girls, aged eight and ten, were left alone at home, wondering what had happened. They only stopped crying when their father eventually appeared, but even that night he didn't sleep at home, quickly returning to his hospital to be on duty.

Mrs Niron regained consciousness but developed epilepsy. Without the right drugs it was impossible to control. The terrified children wanted their father. Dr Niron felt torn in two directions: his patients needed him, so did his family. With one arm in a sling, it was difficult for Mrs Niron to climb in and out of the bunkers. A few weeks later, she fell on her fracture again.

Dr Niron decided to evacuate his family on a Red Cross ship taking the injured out of the war zone. There was no question in his mind but that he must remain. For the next four months he had no news of his wife and children, and no way of contacting them. After a while, he tried not to think of them. He simply assumed he was going to die.

Now, sitting in an armchair opposite me, Dr Niron abruptly recalls the horrific image of a charred body left on the road outside his hospital. A blackened corpse sat in the driver's seat of a wrecked tractor, his hands stuck to the steering wheel. For a week all the traffic just went round the tractor as if it were a perfectly normal obstruction. Passers-by were impervious to the sight of death. 'I can't describe that situation because it was an entirely different world, a place of inhumanity,' he says. 'I lived there but now I am afraid to go to such a place as that.'

Towards the end of January 2009 the attacks intensified, the puddles running red with blood. Inside the improvised hospital, desperate mothers fanned their wounded babies with their bare hands in a pathetic attempt to ease their suffering. People would arrive with all the flesh blown off their limbs, the white bones visible like chewed joints of raw human meat.

On the afternoon of 26 January, Dr Niron emerged from hours of surgery, exhausted and spattered with blood. He had a quick chat with a nurse, whose job it was to inspect the incoming patients; the twenty-three-year-old woman had just discovered her own brother among the injured in the admissions tent that morning. After thirty-six hours on duty, she asked Dr Niron for a rest. A few minutes later she walked out into the yard to take a break, just as a shell landed. She was killed right in front of the doctor, who'd been the last person to speak to her.

It was one of 2,000 shells Dr Niron says landed on or around Uddayarkattu hospital in the last ten days of January 2009.[1] During one of the attacks, the Red Cross witnessed the destruction of the admissions room, dispensary, injection room and dressing room as well as damage to wards.[2] This was when the fighting intensified, just as Sri Lankan aircraft dropped leaflets instructing civilians to move to a newly declared 'safe zone' inside rebel territory. Dr Niron's hospital, which was already in the 'safe zone', suddenly faced an influx of patients, as well as people seeking shelter. The problem was that the government had unilaterally decided the location of the 'safe zone' and chose to place it very close to the Tigers' front line, which was not at all safe. The result, says Dr Niron, was more casualties, not fewer.

Later a United Nations official with first-hand experience of the war put it this way: 'The intention was not so much to protect civilians as to cause pandemonium behind the Tiger lines. If the government had been really serious about saving lives, it wouldn't have located the "safe zone" on the front line. It would have been as far away from the fighting as possible.'

Inside the new safe zone, Dr Niron struggled to perform surgery as the shells fell around his hospital. 'It is luck that I am still here,' he says, perplexed by his survival. As the vans pulled up outside the hospital, nurses, hardly much older than schoolgirls, ran to unload the injured on to bloodstained trolleys. All the medical staff moved at double speed in the rush to save lives. When the hospital was attacked, the shells would kill the injured – people who had escaped death once and erroneously believed they'd been rescued by being brought to hospital.

At first the doctors assumed the direct strikes on the hospital buildings were a terrible accident. They made desperate telephone calls. Every time they moved the makeshift hospitals to a new site to escape the bombardment, Dr Niron would paint a large red cross on the roof. They knew the government had drones flying overhead throughout the daylight hours, providing a live stream of detailed pictures to military headquarters. To be on the safe side, the health service administrators would also send the GPS coordinates to the Red Cross to share with the Sri Lankan Army. They trusted this would protect them.

The doctors shared the details of the location of their hospitals on seven occasions. Every single time, the buildings were attacked within a matter of days, if not hours. Eventually they learned their lesson. There were five smaller hospitals, with no red crosses on the roof, whose locations they never passed on to the army or the Red Cross.[3] Not a single one of those five buildings was ever hit. Eventually Dr Niron concluded that the military were deliberately targeting hospitals. 'They were attacking purposefully; they wanted to kill as many as possible,' he says gently, his eyes watering at the horror of what he's saying.

His conclusion is borne out by a United Nations report that also found that civilian hospitals were systematically attacked by the Sri Lankan government during those months. The report said that in early February one of the two remaining hospitals in rebel territory was attacked with multi-barrelled rocket launchers and artillery for five days in a row. According to the UN there were several direct hits within hours, while up to 800 patients were inside. One incoming rocket was captured on video, as a man cowered near an ambulance, the high-pitched, deafening whistling clearly audible as it approached, and then the clattering thud of impact.[4] Inside, men picked up rubble and smashed roof tiles from the hospital verandah. During one of the attacks, international staff from the Red Cross were present, collecting the injured, and they called the army six times to warn them their shells were falling dangerously close the the hospital building, whose coordinates they'd already communicated.[5] The Red Cross had very limited access and this was the last time they went into the war zone by land.

It was rare to have independent witnesses; the Red Cross publicly confirmed that it came under fire from positions held by the Sri Lankan military. The organisation even broke its strict code of silence, predicting in a statement from Geneva that there could be 'countless victims and a terrible humanitarian situation'. Nobody heeded their warning. When the fighting ended, the Red Cross said it had seen a lot of wars, but rarely one where civilians had been so badly affected. They called it an 'unimaginable humanitarian catastrophe',[6] but by then it was too late.

Today it's the constant sound of crying that Dr Niron can't get out of his head. It wasn't just his patients. Relatives came to search through the corpses piling up at the hospitals. Peering under the cloths covering rows of bodies laid out on the ground, they would explode with grief when they found what they'd been looking for. Prostrate mothers howled, beating the earth with their hands and pulling their hair in the dust. Unshaven men sobbed, their hands clasping their heads in utter incomprehension.

It wasn't long before Dr Niron and his colleagues received orders from their employer, the Health Ministry, to quit the war zone. The doctors bravely defied the instruction, continuing to work, now without pay, while bombs crashed around them.

Dr Niron trained his medics to prepare the patients for surgery, cleaning and opening up the wounds. It was like a conveyor belt. He would perform the complex part of the operation, leaving the patient to be stitched up by an assistant while he went on to the next operating table. With only a handful of doctors, it was impossible to treat everyone and many injured were left to die.

Post-operative 'care' meant being laid out on an old sarong on the dusty, cement floor in a half-built, windowless breezeblock shed. Everyone suffered from chronic exhaustion, unable to sleep at night because of the explosions that made the earth vibrate and the children scream in fear. They were always hungry. There was no way to harvest crops and the government controlled the flow of food, sending in only a fraction of what was needed, effectively blockading rebel-held territory. It's a war crime to cause starvation; after it was all over, the United Nations found there were credible allegations that the government deliberately underestimated population numbers to justify sending less food. American diplomats also commented that the Sri Lankan government wanted to keep civilians hungry enough that they'd have an incentive to abandon the rebels.

One morning in February, a man brought three children to be examined by the doctors. 'We checked and they had no heartbeat at all; they were dead. One child had been frothing at the mouth. The man told me the children were starving and in desperation had been eating the root of a fruit bush that is poisonous. All of them were between seven and ten years old; the same age as my own children.' The doctors reported many cases of children who starved to death.[7] A photograph from early May shows children scavenging in piles of rice husks, hoping to find individual grains to cook.

Now, surrounded by supermarkets and cafés, Dr Niron finds it hard to believe he once lived in a place where children died of hunger. He apologises for the fact that he has 'very terrible stories' to tell.

It wasn't just food that was in short supply. In just a few days at the end of January, hundreds of Tamil civilians were killed and more than 1,000 injured. The doctors typed an urgent appeal on official Ministry of Health notepaper – a reminder that they still belonged to the government that was attacking them. The letter, headed 'Human Catastrophe & Medical Emergency', was addressed to the Sri Lankan government, the United Nations, the Red Cross and the international community. It warned that if medical supplies such as anaesthetics, antibiotics, suturing needles and blood bags didn't arrive within twenty-four hours, many more would die of their wounds. The supplies never came.

As more and more government soldiers perished in the fighting, the military became less keen on sending life-saving drugs into enemy territory. Dr Niron says the supply of medicine was already inadequate in 2008, but when the war was at its height, in 2009, he received no useful drugs whatsoever. All the government sent him was paracet-amol, allergy tablets, vitamins and a local anaesthetic used for dental extraction. He received nothing to treat war wounds. As the United Nations later commented, the denial of medicine by the Sri Lankan government 'imposed enormous suffering and unnecessarily cost many lives'. At the time the Americans privately told the Sri Lankan government it was unconscionable to deny medicine to injured civilians, but their words had no effect.[8]

The government argued that it couldn't send anaesthetics because there was no trained anaesthesiologist in the hospitals in rebel areas. This overlooked the fact that they had sent anaesthetics in the past, and that there were many medics who knew how to administer the injections. When the doctors openly complained that they hadn't received a single bottle of intravenous fluid, antibiotic or anaesthetic to do life-saving surgery, they were threatened with disciplinary action for 'embarrassing the government'. Increasingly they had to rely on the rebels, who ran a parallel medical service for their front-line fighters. The Tiger medics gave them some of their precious stocks of essential drugs, blood bags and fuel to operate generators.

In the run-up to the war, Dr Niron had run a programme to train 10,000 students in first aid. His foresight paid off. The first-aid training meant members of the public knew how to identify the most critical injuries. They had to choose who would survive the journey – who would live or die. Volunteers then ferried the injured to hospital on the back of motorbikes. On arriving at the hospital patients had their wounds cleaned and splints or tourniquets applied.

Blood transfusions were a problem. Before the war, Dr Niron had run a blood-donation campaign, issuing people with cards identifying their blood group and educating villagers who were wary of needles. Despite malnutrition, people came to the hospitals to give blood they could ill spare, knowing it was a matter of life and death for others. But shortages meant a patient's own blood was often collected from his bleeding wound into a plastic bag, filtered through a cloth and then retransfused back into his body.

In the final weeks Dr Niron, desperate to save a sixteen-year-old-girl who needed bowel surgery, donated his own blood before operating, despite the fact that he'd lost fifteen kilos in weight and was constantly hungry. 'I gave blood twenty-six times over my career,' he says proudly. 'Without blood I couldn't save that girl. She was all alone.'

Over those last few months of the war, the divisional hospitals of Kilinochchi and Mullaitivu kept on relocating to new buildings, until finally they ended up on the beach in Mullivaikkal. Dr Niron was now reduced to working in a bunker, reinforced with layers of sturdy palm-tree trunks and sandbags. One day a bomblet flew into the room and lodged itself in the roof. He believes it belonged to a cluster bomb – a weapon he and others saw several times, though the Sri Lankan government denies having used them. They heard the crack of the initial explosion, followed by a whizzing sound as the bomblets exploded.

Sometimes all the injured were women and children, like the day hundreds of mothers were queuing for rations of milk powder when a drone flew overhead and then not long after a shell exploded on top of them. Many remember that incident as one of unparalleled horror. In the hospital, the doctors struggled to insert needles for the intravenous drips into the tiny veins of injured toddlers: 'That day we faced a lot of problems with these young children. We couldn't find a vein because they were so small the veins would collapse. So we made small incisions and took the vein and put the drip in that way. We had to save them, no? They were tired and hungry and always crying. We couldn't look after them and it was very difficult to manage them.'

Throughout the war, indeed, a disproportionate number of the serious casualties were children. They didn't survive because their smaller bodies were less able to withstand the gashes from pieces of burning, jagged shrapnel. The same piece of metal might have caused less havoc with an adult's larger body.

Soon even bandages started to run out. Volunteers went around collecting old saris to be cut up into strips and boiled. Loudspeakers warned people not to drink the water without boiling it first. 'Nobody can imagine; they simply wouldn't believe our story,' says Dr Niron, 'with all those shells and rounds of fire coming in, we still had a public-announcement system and I have to tell you we didn't get a single case of a communicable disease right up until the end.' He's proud that they managed to prevent an epidemic, despite so many weakened, starving people all living in close proximity, with woefully inadequate numbers of toilets.

As the area controlled by the Tigers shrank, it was hard to cure people so exhausted by continuous attacks, bereavement, hunger and displacement. Hundreds of patients were admitted daily, lying dazed with pain on the golden sand next to dirty drains. Many were sent home immediately after operations, with oral antibiotics to self-administer. By now anyone with a relatively minor wound simply wouldn't risk coming to a hospital, knowing it was a target.

Early one morning Dr Niron had been expecting his best friend, a psychiatrist called Dr Siva, when someone rushed into the operating room to tell him a person with a stethoscope had been killed outside.[9] 'I went as fast as I could and saw that he'd been killed. It was just ten metres away from where I had been. He was very close to me and always he would come and talk to me if he had any problem…I wondered what a world this was.'

Dr Siva wasn't the last of his dwindling band of medical colleagues to die. A few weeks later another nurse was killed, and then the hospital's administrative officer.

By the final week of the war, tens of thousands of shattered people were crammed into three square kilometres of beach. Rebels and civilians, the living and the dying were all side by side. The doctors told the UN that many of the injured hadn't received treatment for days, there were no antibiotics left and half their staff hadn't reported for work because of heavy shelling.[10] Dr Niron was lying in his tent one night when something exploded above him. As the tent caught fire, he crawled out on all fours. In the dark he put his elbow down on something scorching and then from above a flame dropped on his back, burning the flesh.

'It was different from a normal fire. It burned as if in a circle. There was no flammable material in our place, but suddenly there was a blast and then it ignited. It was as if a petrol can was on fire but there wasn't any petrol there. The area on fire was like a big tree. It was huge. One of my colleagues died – a young assistant called Selvan. He did preventative medicine normally. All the rest of us – all six people – were injured that night.'

The doctor believes the Sri Lankan government was using white phosphorous – and other survivors also report seeing it being used, although international law prohibits its use against civilians in populated areas. Dr Niron still has the black scars on his arm and back, though he says the colour of the burn wound has changed. 'I worked in the surgical department for so many years, but these phosphorous wounds are different from normal burns,' he says.

Dr Niron lost all his possessions in that attack, except the sarong in which he'd been sleeping. He had to borrow a shirt from a friend to protect the wound on his back from the buzzing flies. His doctor's card, his clothes, spectacles, pen – all were destroyed.

Two days later all the doctors held a meeting. The others wanted to leave because there was no medicine, no food and nothing more they could do for their patients. They shared a last supper with the area's top civil servant, who had remained behind to try to administer the civilian population. Someone found a bit of white flour and they made a kind of pancake with no oil, milk or eggs.

In the morning Dr Niron's colleagues left. Later he found out that they had been arrested by the army, interrogated for months and then forced to retract everything they'd said during the war. They appeared at a press conference to declare that they'd lied about the civilian casualties and in reality very few people had died. After the war, a United Nations report confirmed what most knew: that the doctors had been put under pressure by the government. Secret US Embassy cables made public by WikiLeaks revealed that the doctors had been 'heavily coached for the press conference, given specific lines to say, and even practiced with several members of the local media beforehand'. The US Embassy worried that the doctors were at risk of abduction or extrajudicial killing. Later the government accused all the doctors of being Tigers.[11]

The last makeshift hospital on the beach ceased to function on 15 May.[12] Dr Niron tried to set up his remaining equipment in a tiny building nearby, hoping he could do some emergency surgery. He was forced to move the next day, burying three bodies under the soft, blisteringly hot sand before he left. The patients who were still alive were laid out under a big, overarching mango tree – scores of emaciated people, bandaged in rags.

Peering out from his bunker, Dr Niron thought he'd spotted a fallen fruit from the palmyrah trees that dominate this part of Sri Lanka. Starving, he told his assistant to run and fetch it quickly so they could share it. The young man came back, having found not a dark, round coconut but a small baby's head, severed from its body. 'I have terrible memories of that whole coast,' he says, 'bodies without heads and babies missing both legs.'

On the last morning of the war, 17 May, rebel territory had been reduced to a tiny dot of land about 150 metres in radius. Tiger fighters were nowhere to be seen; they'd either been killed or had switched to civilian clothes to try and escape. All around there was gunfire.

Dr Niron and his assistant knew there was nothing more they could do. They had to cross to the army side if they wanted to stay alive, but even that wasn't guaranteed. Would they be safe if they made a run for it? How would the army treat them if they surrendered?

'I left around one hundred and fifty patients there under a big tree,' he repeats. 'It was the worst thing I did in my career.' Fleeing on that final morning, Dr Niron felt the injured and dying tug at his clothes, calling out his name, pleading for help.

They ran, bent double to avoid the shooting. Most people had already left. The only protection against the bullets was other human beings – a small group of about a dozen people also taking their chances. They tried to take cover behind anyone else moving. Every time they halted for a few seconds, the doctor would ask his assistant if he was injured and check his body for bullet wounds. It was like playing Russian roulette. 'We had a fifty:fifty chance of coming out alive,' he said.

Around them corpses were strewn – people like themselves, who'd been hit that morning. Some of the elderly wouldn't leave the dead behind. 'I told them to go,' said Dr Niron. 'The firing was so intense that they stood no chance if they stayed.' The shots seemed to come from all directions.

Dr Niron remembers the first soldier he saw very clearly. He wore a helmet and ammunition belt and was peering down his rifle at them from inside the forked branches of a tree. That meant they were already in government-controlled territory. The doctor and his companions had their hands up in the air. 'Go!' barked the soldier in broken Tamil, 'but don't look back.' Shocked to see the army at such close quarters after so many months, Dr Niron couldn't help wondering what was happening to all those left behind.

They moved through a scorched landscape of beheaded, blackened palm trees towards a long earthen bridge across the lagoon. Dr Niron noticed the corpse of a soldier lying near a tree stump. He was a big man, covered in ants. It looked as if he'd been dead for a couple of days, but nobody had been able to move him. Bullets whizzed over their heads as they hurried across the bridge.

Once across the water, in seeming safety, civilians had to line up in a queue for checking. Dr Niron was separated from his colleague, the medical assistant, who has disappeared without trace after treating more than 100,000 patients in the last three years of the war. It torments the exiled Dr Niron that he couldn't save even one of his loyal helpers. 'They were with me in my tragedy days,' he says, trying to explain the emotional bond.

What happened next is a blur. Dr Niron remembers how painful it was to be body-searched because the soldiers touched his burn injuries, where the shirt had stuck to the raw wound on his back. It's the thirst he remembers next; his mouth was parched with anxiety. Sweating in the sweltering midday heat, he thought he would faint. Spotting a Tamil man with a gallon container of water, he asked him for a sip.

'He didn't know me and he wouldn't give it. At that moment I reflected how I had given blood twenty-six times for my patients and now I couldn't get one drop of water. I didn't tell him who I was, but I begged him to give me water and he refused.'

The only consolation was that his companions didn't turn him in to the authorities. 'Other Tamils in that place knew me very well – I had always helped them – but they kept silent and didn't tell the authorities who I was, which was lucky…Later on I found out they were looking for me. I was a wanted man there.'

The army did register his name, but it was a common one and they didn't realise who he was. Transported to the Zone 4 refugee camp well inside government territory, Dr Niron was assigned to a tent with sixteen other people. There was so little space that he spread a few pieces of paper on the ground and slept in the open. It was only here that he finally got a drink of water.

All Tamils leaving the war zone were detained in the camp, irrespective of their age, profession or political persuasion. Priests, doctors, United Nations employees, foreign-passport holders – it made no difference. Paying bribes was the only way out at that stage. Dr Niron didn't have a penny, but he had a network of medical colleagues. One by one they came to his rescue.

When he stepped into the clinic in the refugee camp, Dr Niron was immediately recognised by the doctor on duty. 'He saved my life,' he says of his colleague. The doctor quickly wrote out a slip of paper ordering urgent treatment for chest pain. Dr Niron was put into an ambulance with other patients being transferred under armed guard to the district hospital.

The hospital was watched by the police and army to prevent Tamil refugees escaping. The doctor on duty there also recognised Dr Niron.

He quickly hid him in a side room, being careful not to register him as a patient and leave a paper trail. Then he dressed Dr Niron in his own jeans and T-shirt so he'd look like a member of staff. They waited till night and then got into the official staff van that dropped doctors home at the end of their shift. Together they drove out of the hospital compound, past the police sentry post at the entrance, without being questioned. 'Most of the doctors were Tamils and they wanted to save us. Not only me – a lot of other people too. They took risks,' says Niron.

That night Dr Niron remembers stopping at a soft-drink stall, before even looking for his wife and children. 'I was very excited to drink Coca-Cola because I hadn't had it for months.' His friend bought him a huge bottle and he knocked it all back in twenty minutes.

After several phone calls, Dr Niron tracked down his family. For four months Mrs Niron had been praying her husband would emerge alive, but he had lost so much weight, she didn't recognise him on the doorstep. He laughs about it, saying if she didn't know him, how could the authorities spot him? They probably missed him because he'd grown a beard and moustache and looked so bedraggled. He arrived at one o'clock in the morning, but all the children woke up and were running up and down, laughing in excitement.

He was so hungry that his wife cooked him a meal in the middle of the night; he still remembers exactly what she cooked him and how it felt to have a proper food again after months of near-starvation.

For the next fifty-five days, Dr Niron hid with his family in one tiny room. Money was tight because the government had stopped his salary. They sold his wife's gold jewellery to get him a passport and friends smuggled him through the military checkpoints to the capital and helped him survive. He flew to Singapore, went overland to Malaysia, then spent four desperate months in Thailand and finally arrived in Europe. It took ten more months and the generosity of many other doctors to get his wife and children out of Sri Lanka.

Today the only possession Dr Niron has left from his old life is his wedding ring, which he sent out of the war zone with his wife. It's taken him two years just to be able to snatch some sleep at night. Not a man to remain idle, he spends the dark hours writing poetry in Tamil. In his first year of exile, he published a collection of his poems under a pseudonym in Sri Lanka.

Dr Niron doesn't want to draw attention to himself for the sake of his relatives still in Sri Lanka. For years his father worked as a doctor in rebel areas and even now some of the people whom Dr Niron saved have discreetly been to thank his parents. 'People will do anything for me,' he says. 'I have a lot of goodwill there.'

Soft-spoken and self-effacing, Dr Niron is a witness to the crimes of the Tigers as well as those of the army. Living in rebel territory, he saw the Tamil Tigers forcibly recruit one person from every family to fight from 2007 onwards. In the final months he says younger and younger children went to the front line, including the teenage children of top rebel leaders.

The death toll is still uncertain, but Dr Niron is in a good position to make an estimate. It was his job to pass the names of the injured to the rebel radio station so they could broadcast the information to the families. At every makeshift hospital the medics kept records of how many people they had treated, but the documents were captured by the Sri Lankan Army. From March 2009 onwards Dr Niron says they treated 300 injured people a day, but in January and February the numbers were also high. This does not include the dead. 'On some roads there were lots of bodies and nobody counted them. Some gravely wounded people who later died never made it to hospital,' he says. There were no funerals and no marking of the graves; many were hastily buried in bunkers and under the sand. By the last few weeks, when the casualties were at their highest, movement was so restricted that it was impossible to collect any information at all. Dr Niron believes one person in every two was injured in the final weeks, himself included. He first calculated the 2009 death toll as at least 27,000 in five months. Today, as he hears that more and more people he once knew are dead, he's revising that estimate upwards.

★

Looking at the cruise ships in the icy harbour, I ask Dr Niron if he thinks he will ever see Sri Lanka again. 'If it was secure I would go back,' he says, 'but not to the places where the fighting took place.' He tells me about a headless torso he saw: 'The head was on the junction,' he says, and then adds with a nervous giggle, 'It was a place where our landmarks were bits of exploded bodies. It was a horrible place to live. I can never, ever go back to those areas.'

Home is now a Hanseatic trading port, with shops full of toy trolls and chunky knitwear for the tourists *en route* to the glaciers. Dr Niron spends his days learning the language of his adopted country, twisting his tongue around the unfamiliar, guttural sounds. He is a faceless refugee, conspicuous only for his dark skin. None of his new friends know who he really is. He finds it easier that way.

'I can't concentrate on anything. I am not normal. I can't plan ahead. It's very difficult. If someone says, " You can work next year," my mind goes all blank. If I tell the truth, in my heart of hearts, I don't want to work as a doctor any more. I can do any job, but not that one.' He is now a surgeon who cannot stand the sight of blood.

Astonishingly, Dr Niron feels he failed as a doctor. There was one woman he met on the last morning whom he cannot forget. She was kneeling by the side of her husband, whose legs had been blown off. Dr Niron asked his assistant if they could carry the man out, but there was gunfire everywhere and they couldn't. 'Please rescue him, please rescue him!' the woman begged several times, refusing to give up on her husband.

This doctor who did so much still feels he should have done more. We argue for some time over what else he could have done. 'I did my job, I agree with you,' he says eventually, 'but if I meet that lady again, what will she think of me?'

Some of the Attacks on Hospitals

Source: Human Rights Watch

15 DECEMBER 2008	Mullaitivu General Hospital: shelling
19 DECEMBER 2008	Mullaitivu General Hospital: five shells hit hospital
20 DECEMBER 2008	Mullaitivu General Hospital: shells hit hospital grounds
22 DECEMBER 2008	Kilinochchi General Hospital: aerial bombing near hosptial
25 DECEMBER 2008	Kilinochchi General Hospital: shells hit hospital grounds
30 DECEMBER 2008	Kilinochchi General Hospital: shells hit hospital
8 JANUARY 2009	Tharmapuram Hospital: shells hit seventy-five metres away
19 JANUARY 2009	Valipunam Hospital: shells land in hospital yard
21 JANUARY 2009	Valipunam Hospital: shell hits hospital
22 JANUARY 2009	Valipunam Hospital: shells hit hospital compound
26 JANUARY 2009	Uddayarkattu Hospital: shells hit hospital
31 JANUARY 2009	PTK Hospital: shrapnel from shells hits hospital
1 FEBRUARY 2009	PTK Hospital: three attacks – shrapnel and shells
2 FEBRUARY 2009	PTK Hospital: shell hits hospital
3 FEBRUARY 2009	PTK Hospital: two attacks on hospital
5 FEBRUARY 2009	Ponnampalam Memorial Hospital: shelling
9 FEBRUARY 2009	Puttumatalan Hospital: shell hits near by, causing damage to wall
10 FEBRUARY 2009	Puttumatalan Hospital: shelling

16 MARCH 2009	Puttumatalan Hospital: RPG hits inside the compound
23 MARCH 2009	Puttumatalan Hospital: RPG in front of building and two shells nearby
9 APRIL 2009	Puttumatalan Hospital: several shell attacks
20 APRIL 2009	Puttumatalan Hospital: heavy shelling and gunfire, hundreds injured
21 APRIL 2009	Valayanmadam Hospital: aerial attack
23 APRIL 2009	Mullivaikkal Hospital: three shells hit hospital
28 APRIL 2009	Mullivaikkal Primary Health: heavy shelling and aerial attacks
29 APRIL 2009	Mullivaikkal Hospital: shelling
30 APRIL 2009	Mullivaikkal Hospital: shelling
2 MAY 2009	Mullivaikkal Hospital: two shell attacks

Source: International Committee of the Red Cross

24 JANUARY 2009	Uddayarkattu Hospital: hit by two shells, five dead, twenty-seven injured
7 FEBRUARY 2009	PTK Hospital: video shows attack, date not confirmed
12 MAY 2009	Mullivaikkal Hospital: shell attack killed admin officer and others
13 MAY 2009	Mullivaikkal Hospital: video shows attack, date not confirmed

The Nun

Sixty-four years old, with greying curly hair that doesn't match her young face, Sister Ignatius is a quiet and modest Tamil woman who's devoted her life to practising her Christian principles.

When I went to meet her she was living in a convent, a suburban red-brick house in Europe. She had an air of informality, wearing trousers and a sensible navy-blue cardigan, with a cross around her neck.

In the traditions of Sri Lankan hospitality, she fed me a huge tea – home-made bread, cream cake and biscuits spread out on the tablecloth in the kitchen – all the while gearing herself up for the ordeal of remembering. She waited till the house was empty and then took me into the front parlour, firmly shutting the door behind her, as if symbolically separating the past from the present. Even after a year spent recovering from her ordeal, she was still extremely nervous talking about the war.

I've called her Sister Ignatius because she told me not to use her real name – she's not even sure it's a good idea to mention that she's a nun. Speaking out could land her in grave trouble when she goes home to rejoin her congregation, nuns who serve Sri Lanka's one-million-strong Catholic population, which includes both Sinhalese and Tamil.

Faced with the escalating war, Sr Ignatius made a conscious choice to bear witness, knowing it would test her courage, but she had no idea to what extent. An intensely moral and upstanding woman, she absorbed the psychological pain of strangers, comforting them at a time when nobody else had the capacity to worry about others. The doctors tended to physical wounds while Sr Ignatius and her colleagues eased people's souls, giving them human tenderness and generosity just when the world seemed most cruel. She says she will be haunted for the rest of her life by the appalling suffering she saw.

For hours she recounted the horrors to me, speaking in a half-whisper, as if the experiences were too dreadful to tell out loud. They were experiences that made her question her faith in a loving God. For the first time in her life Sr Ignatius came face to face with pure evil. She was still reeling from the shock.

After the first time we talked, Sr Ignatius was up all night, tormented by memories she can't put to rest, memories of mothers howling and cursing because the rebels had seized their precious children to fight, of a priest whose leg was amputated without anaesthetic, of young children blown to pieces, of dead bodies abandoned on the roadside.

It was a struggle to accept that her God had allowed so many innocent people to be killed. 'Where does this evil come from?' she asked herself repeatedly, eventually reasoning that the jealousy, power and hatred she witnessed came from Man, who had been given the freedom to choose his actions by God. 'Sometimes I fought with the Lord. "Why all these killings? What are you doing? Don't you see these things? How many killings and wounded?" Literally I fought with him like this,' she says.

Sr Ignatius' story begins on 29 January 2008, a full year before the climax of the war. She was in rebel territory, visiting Sri Lanka's holiest Catholic shrine in a village called Madhu. In this part of western Sri Lanka the war was already in full swing, the front line just ten kilometres from the shrine. The army was advancing from west to east, capturing rebel territory and in the process driving Tamil civilians out of their homes.

The sprawling compound of the Madhu church had become a magnet for thousands of fleeing refugees. They assumed that one of Sri Lanka's most important shrines would protect them. Camping in flimsy tents, they cooked on small fires around the white-stucco buildings. The Madhu shrine is very special to all Sri Lankans, even Buddhists and Hindus. Tamil and Sinhalese alike believe the 400-year-old shrine's tiny statue of the Virgin Mary, known as Our Lady of Madhu, has miraculous powers to protect people against wild animals. The shrine's soil is considered so precious that every year in peacetime, tens of thousands of pilgrims scoop it up into little bags to take home, believing it will protect them from snake bites and scorpion stings.

Sr Ignatius was about to leave for the capital when an explosion on a school bus close to the church killed thirteen children and seven adults. Years later, she finds it hard to forget the sight of so many dead children in one place. 'That was terrible. My God,' she whispers, pulling her cardigan a little tighter around her.

She was one of the first to see the green and white bus tipped on its side in the bushes. Passers-by had already started pulling the children, in their blue and white uniforms, out of the wreckage. Many of the small corpses laid out on the grass still had school backpacks attached to their shoulders. Everywhere there was wailing and sobbing, injured children calling out for their mothers. The windows of the bus were blown out and many of the dead passengers still sat in their seats. At the entrance to the bus, a boy's dead body was sprawled head-down across the bottom step. The steps themselves were awash with blood. Inside, a dead teacher sat slumped against the grey-upholstered front seat, as if still alive, a book perched on her lap.

The blast had been caused by a large mine attached to a tree trunk and activated by a booby trap. It was probably meant for rebel vehicles transporting ammunition which used the road. At the time the Sri Lankan Army denied responsibility, but it was clear to all that both sides used guerrilla tactics, infiltrating each other's territory and planting explosives. A fortnight earlier the Tigers had blown up a bus in the south of the island, killing twenty-eight people. The two main communities generally experienced the horror of the war in isolation from each other, leading to very different narratives of the conflict.

In Madhu, Sr Ignatius changed her mind and stayed on for another month, attending the funeral for the victims. It was arranged by the bishop of the nearby town of Mannar, a fragile white-haired man with a slight stoop, who personally collected the corpses from the hospital and arranged coffins for families too poor to buy them. While at the funeral, they could still hear the thud of shells falling in the distance.

Weeks later, back in Colombo, Sister Ignatius heard the news that Madhu itself had come under attack. The Tigers had ordered the refugees deeper into rebel territory and moved mortar launchers into the jungle around the church, firing at government forces.[1] Clerics say it wasn't the first time the rebels had violated the sanctity of a holy place – neither side showed respect for churches or temples, with the result, they say, that most of the Catholic churches in the western part of the rebel territory were damaged or destroyed.

In early April shells started falling on the Madhu church compound. After hours of artillery attack, the four priests and three nuns who were guarding the precious statue feared for their lives. At dusk they unceremoniously packed Our Lady of Madhu into a suitcase and put her in a car. Several times they had to get out of the vehicles and lie flat on the road to take cover from incoming shells, one of which fell right in front of the convoy of fleeing cars. The statue eventually escaped undamaged but the shrine itself suffered. A shell fell on the church roof and a side chapel was destroyed.

As the fighting worsened throughout 2008, Sr Ignatius visited rebel territory twice more, trying to help the elderly and sick. By December she was in the capital, watching as hundreds of thousands of Sri Lankan Tamils were trapped between the rebels and the army, seemingly abandoned by the United Nations and the outside world. She grappled with the idea of whether or not to return to the war zone, knowing she might get trapped there.

'Nobody could tell me to go, I had to decide for myself. Some thing was telling me to go and another thing was saying, How will you manage?' After a sleepless night worrying about whether she could cope, her mind was made up when she went to church the next morning. 'As I walked in, the entrance hymn was *Whom Shall I Send*, which goes, "I will go, Lord…I will hold thy people in my hand." Those words touched me. I went and knelt there and said, "Lord, I am going!"'

Three days before Christmas 2008, Sr Ignatius travelled into rebel territory, along with a young novice whose sister had just been killed fighting for the Tigers. It was the last chance for the girl to see her parents before she embarked on two years of religious training, but she couldn't travel alone.

They boarded a public bus to the war zone. It was extraordinary that, just as the main rebel town was about to fall, a middle-aged nun and a young girl were able to travel with such ease into a battle area. They drove along potholed dirt roads, the only way in because the main highway was being bitterly fought over. The bus passed abandoned homesteads set back from the road, surrounded by fragile stick fences. There were tiny thatched huts perched tentatively on top of the yellow sand, shaded by towering palms. Normally there'd be people walking around and chickens scuttling about pecking in the dirt, and bony, cream-coloured cattle grazing absent-mindedly; but everyone had gone.

They walked across the front line, carrying bags full of vegetables, which they knew were scarce on the other side. After a while they found a Tamil Tiger rebel sitting in the open at a table under a tree, filling in immigration forms. Sr Ignatius went straight up to one of the Tigers and discreetly confided in him that the girl's sister had died, though she didn't know it yet: all she had told the girl was that her sister was injured, fearing if she knew the truth she'd become hysterical, making the already difficult journey impossible.

The rebels operated very strict controls on all movement in and out of their territory, to prevent civilians from leaving the war zone, so as to use them as human shields. Sr Ignatius was worried that, for the girl to return to her training on the government side, she needed a special travel pass that might prove difficult to get. She was terrified the Tigers might try to recruit the novice by force, as they probably had her dead sister. It was nerve-racking, but when she saw the Tiger official had given them both the same-coloured travel papers, meant for religious officials, she breathed a sigh of relief. It meant the girl could go back to her education and would not be imprisoned in the war zone.

Sr Ignatius found the nuns from Madhu living in a makeshift shelter in a large field. She broke the news to the novice that her sister was already dead, the funeral having been held the day before. Then she escorted the distressed girl to her parents, who were about to spend Christmas in a tent, mourning the death of their daughter.

That Christmas, 300 kilometres to the south in Colombo, the military commander, Lieutenant-General Sarath Fonseka led the army carol concert. An ardent Sinhalese nationalist and architect of the war against the Tigers, the general had boasted of wiping out 15,000 terrorists in the previous three years. Soldiers sang 'Ding Dong Merrily on High' and 'Silent Night' while schoolchildren donated their pocket money to the families of war heroes.

On Christmas Eve the Catholic Archbishop of Sri Lanka and other Sinhalese priests sat on chairs covered in freshly laundered white cotton in the tropical garden of the President's colonial mansion, known as Temple Trees. Dressed in their long, spotless white robes, the priests watched nativity plays surrounded by colourful fairy lights, ignoring the fact that most of the people in rebel territory, a few hours' drive north, were held against their will in a war zone that was becoming increasingly brutal.

The Church was divided. Most Sinhalese priests supported the government, while Tamil priests pleaded for a ceasefire. Some Sinhalese Catholics ridiculed the Tamil priests as supporters of terrorists, calling them 'terrorist bishops', 'neo-colonialists' and 'Judas priests', while many Tamil Catholics regarded the archbishop as a poodle of the Sinhalese hardliners.

Christmas Mass in the capital that year took longer than usual because of all the prayers for the country's rulers and a speedy victory over the terrorists. There were no prayers for the sixty Tamil priests and nuns quietly working inside the war zone. In fact the government soon decided it wanted all clerics out of rebel areas, for their own 'safety'.[2]

Sr Ignatius didn't celebrate on Christmas Day that year: heavy fighting made it impossible to meet up with the rest of her order, who were spread out along the east coast, living with different groups of refugees. It was on Boxing Day that they managed to come together, in their last remaining convent building in Tiger territory, for a prayer service, sharing a special meal made out of the carrots Sr Ignatius had brought with her.

After Christmas, Sr Ignatius persuaded two elderly nuns to evacuate to government territory, taking the novice with them. Leaving was not easy: only the elderly and those needing urgent medical treatment were allowed out by the rebels. Everyone else had to defend the Tamil homeland, whether they liked it or not. Astonishingly, an erratic bus service still operated along a back route, travelling in and out of rebel territory until mid-January. Sometimes the women would travel to a certain point and hear shelling, or learn that the army was not allowing people to cross the front line that day, and turn back. Many times they set off, only to return a few hours later. One day they made it out.

In the convent, Sr Ignatius could hear the artillery fire coming nearer while she visited the sick and comforted the bereaved. One day she found herself at the graveside of a girl she knew – an orphan adopted by an elderly couple with the help of the Church. 'A lovely girl,' she says. 'I can still see the picture. A beautiful girl lying in the coffin with her mother and father, also dead, on either side.' The girl's brother was the sole member of that family left alive, but Sr Ignatius doesn't know if he survived.

'That was the worst thing: you are in one area together and then you move and they move and you have no idea if they are living or dead,' she explains, getting up to turn on the gas heater, chilled perhaps as much by the memories as by the unfamiliar harsh European winter.

On the evening of 16 January a priest showed up unexpectedly on the doorstep of the convent, urging them to leave immediately. Sr Ignatius was stunned. How could she move? The only other nun in the convent that day was in her seventies, and they had four teenage girls in their care: orphans who could be snatched at any moment by the rebels to fight. When forced recruitment intensified, distraught parents turned to the nuns and priests to hide their children.

'We were really scared about travelling about with those children because the Tigers could easily stop us and say, "Where are you taking these girls?"' Deciding it was too risky to move in the dark, Sr Ignatius turned to her companions and declared: 'Sisters, we will trust in the Lord and stay tonight.' The women lay awake throughout the night, listening to the thud of shells falling.

In the morning Sr Ignatius stopped a passing stranger, who agreed to give them a lift. After they'd squeezed in all their precious food stocks, there was no room left in the car for Sr Ignatius. She locked the door of the convent and walked through the eerie empty town to the bus stop, hoping some transport would come. In the streets were armed rebels, all with short hair, the girls in dark baggy trousers and long white men's shirts belted at the waist, the boys with baby moustaches wearing green ammunition jackets, their radio communication sets crackling in Tamil, rifles at the ready. Sr Ignatius' prayers were answered: a bus arrived, probably the last to leave town.

She fled to a village — ironically called 'Freedom City' in Tamil — which four days later was declared by the Sri Lankan military to be part of a thirty-five-square-kilometre 'safe zone' for civilians. 'You can't imagine: from all over people had come and there was no place anywhere, just tents everywhere. What a sight! Seeing the misery of the people there,' Sr Ignatius says, 'I don't think anyone can bear that.' Then, almost in disbelief, she asks out loud: 'Oh Lord, where was I?'

The nuns hired labourers to dig bunkers, but before they could even finish the job the men leapt into the unfinished holes, as shells started landing in what was supposed to be a safe zone. Sr Ignatius hid under a camp bed in her tent, listening to the shrapnel flying about. 'For four hours I was under that bed, thinking what had happened to the other sisters and the girls…Four hours of continuous shelling, and that was supposed to be a safe area!'

By now Sr Ignatius and other nuns in the area didn't just have the orphans to look after. Several families had left their teenage daughters in their care, terrified they'd be forced to fight for the Tigers. The hope was that the bands of roving rebel recruiters wouldn't dare snatch the children right in front of the nuns. Not only did families have to struggle against hunger, degradation and shells but also the terror of the rebel child snatchers who like ogres could strike at any moment.

Parents would go to any length to protect their sons and daughters from conscription, hiding them for hours in sacks or buried underground in wells or metal drums. Teenagers were hastily married off in the hope that their married status would prevent them from being taken to the front. The nuns and priests quietly did what they could to help.

One day when Sr Ignatius had stayed behind to guard the young girls while her colleagues were visiting the war-injured and bereaved in the makeshift hospital, the younger brother of one of the nuns turned up unexpectedly. A science student, he'd just managed to escape from the Tigers after being forcibly recruited a few months earlier and sent to the front line.

'Please, sister, I can't go back there,' the boy begged. 'Please, please keep me here. I want to be free.' Heartbroken, all Sr Ignatius said was 'When did you last eat?' She never asked any other questions, maintaining that his story was written in his face. 'For three days we have had no food. We were moving here and there,' he answered.

Hiding an escaped fighter was extremely risky, especially as the nuns were already sheltering twenty girls of fighting age. As she cooked up a packet of instant noodles for the boy on a small wood fire, Sister Ignatius wondered what it must be like on the front line if the fighters didn't have enough to eat. Then she heard a jet roar overhead and ran to take shelter. After it had gone she couldn't find the boy. He had lain down to shelter under a pile of wood and broken furniture and instantly fallen into a deep sleep, oblivious to the deafening screech of the supersonic jet. Sr Ignatius hid him long enough to find his parents, but she has no idea what became of him afterwards.

Living in a tent in the 'safe zone', Sr Ignatius and the other nuns used a steel cupboard to partition the space into a sleeping area and a chapel. During one assault, Sr Ignatius sheltered behind the metal cupboard while another nun hid under the altar table. Later she found a hole in the cupboard, just where she'd been sitting. 'This shell piece had missed me by a few inches,' she said, adding, 'There was no time to get frightened. One after another, things were happening.'

On 29 January two priests came to tell them to leave immediately because it was too unsafe. In the pitch dark the nuns and the twenty girls in their care set out on foot on a long journey that would have taken fifteen minutes in a car. Sr Ignatius calls it 'the great exodus'. A mass of humanity was on the march, on a wide dirt road leading south-east towards the coast, fleeing the 'safe zone' that had proved anything but safe. Ancient tractors laden with belongings inched slowly forward, amongst people on foot, motorcycles carrying whole families and bicycles staggering under the weight of sacks slung over the handlebars. People spilled over into adjacent fields to find a way of bypassing the enormous human traffic jam. It was a time when many still hoped to salvage their possessions.

When they arrived at the next village, Sr Ignatius could hear shelling. 'It was chock-a-block. Can you imagine all those people living in that area – washing, cooking and eating and finding somewhere to go to the toilet. Just forget it. Jesus Christ! We were packed, just like sardine fish,' she says.

Here the sisters heard that shelling had destroyed vehicles and stores belonging to the Catholic charity Caritas. All the certificates of baptism, marriage and death for Catholics had gone up in flames in the attack, completely erasing family records.

After only three days they came under intense artillery fire again. Many people rushed to the church for sanctuary. Badly shaken, the priests and nuns felt they had to show leadership, but they couldn't agree on what to do. Some of the clergy had the idea of hoisting a white flag and leading the people out of the war zone to surrender to the army. Others, like Sr Ignatius, worried that either side might attack, resulting in carnage.

The Tigers were shooting at groups of civilians trying to flee the war zone. Militarily, the rebels kept the civilian population with them to slow down the army's advance, using women and children as a human buffer. Politically, they claimed they were fighting for the Tamil people and that would be difficult if all of them had run away. Strategically, they also gambled that heavy civilian casualties would stir the outside world into intervening. They put the survival of their own organisation before that of innocent civilians.

In the church, the clerics were in a terrible dilemma – whether to risk leaving or take their chances and stay. One group of civilians left with an Anglican priest, walking towards the army. Sr Ignatius heard shooting but couldn't tell who was firing, although some claimed it was the army. Later on, she also heard a report that an elderly nun had been shot in the leg by the Tigers while leading 2,000 civilians out.[3]

In early February, desperate to stop the outflow of refugees, the Tigers even sent a woman suicide bomber to mingle with a group of escaping civilians. There is a video showing the aftermath of the attack in which she blew herself up, killing twenty soldiers and eight civilians, many of them small children, and injuring sixty others.[4] The Tigers were sending a clear message that everyone had to remain.

Moving deeper into what was left of rebel territory, Sr Ignatius and a small group of nuns packed all their tents and food stores onto a tractor and walked. During most of February they would move from one place to another, staying in a succession of tiny villages until they reached the coast. Along the way they lost everything they had loaded onto the tractor: the driver abandoned the vehicle because he was unable to start the engine in the panic and it was too risky to stay.

Sheltering in a stranger's garden with many other families, Sr Ignatius was so close to a shell that she actually saw it fly past. The temperature had been steadily rising and she was sitting on the ground in the shade of a mango tree in the crowded compound, waiting to wash at the well in the garden. Every time she was about to go, someone else would beat her to the well and she would hold back politely. Suddenly the area came under attack.

'I saw a cylindrical shape. It came between the coconut trees and fell near the well and exploded. Jesus Christ! It hit one of the big mango trees and the pieces flew everywhere. We were all covered with sand and dust. We were there, a few yards from the well. If it had landed on the other side, we'd have all been dead. We heard the noise: zzz. My God, even now I feel scared,' Sr Ignatius says.

After a near-miss like that, the only thing to do was to flee. As they drove out on another tractor, Sr Ignatius saw Tigers moving around, not in uniform, but wearing sarongs over their trousers in order to look like civilians. The rebels disguised themselves because of the drones, which now flew overhead constantly. The Sri Lankan Air Force were using drones purchased from Israel to send live video to headquarters, with pictures so detailed that it could make out individuals moving about on the ground below. With the Tigers dressed like civilians, it was harder for the military to pick them out.

By March the nuns had moved right up to the seashore, into the narrow spit of land fourteen kilometres square that the government had demarcated as a second safe zone. Hundreds of thousands of people were already packed into the tiny space. The parish priest directed Sister Ignatius to an abandoned house where there was still one empty room. Just as she started cleaning it, some rebels arrived to ask what she was up to.

'As a rule when someone abandons their house, it is taken over by the movement,' a Tiger explained. This house had belonged to someone who'd escaped on a fishing boat, dodging fire between the navy and the rebels.

'Maybe, I don't know,' replied Sr Ignatius, 'but we want to stay here. You know we are here for the people. If we wanted to we could have left this place, but we stayed on for them.'

That gave the Tigers pause for thought, and they went away.

Soon the nuns were sharing the tiny house with a man from the Red Cross, three families and a group of small children from the rebels' orphanage. There was only one bunker for everyone, so during attacks the nuns just sat on the cement floor of their room, leaning against the walls for protection. One day a nun moved a metre and then, just where she'd been sitting, a sharp fragment of metal hit the floor like a bullet. When they picked it up a few minutes later, it was still hot. There were so many near-misses, Sr Ignatius can't understand how they survived.

'Sometimes I wondered why He saved us and not other people.

That was a mystery for us. A miracle of miracles it was...I used to reflect, maybe the Lord saved us to be with the people right through. I had one beautiful picture of Jesus. I carried it with me, right through all that. A child seated on His lap, looking at Him, and He's smiling. That was always with me wherever I slept. Before I went to bed I prayed that He would take care of us and the people.'

Every day the nuns witnessed countless individual tragedies. 'It is hard to listen, and people appreciated that,' Sister Ignatius said modestly. 'People didn't have much to eat – everyone had been reduced to begging – so we were able to help certain people very discreetly and quietly, otherwise they'd be ashamed.'

Just as they were running out of money, one of the sisters met a man who had Rs.500,000 (about £2,500) in cash that he'd withdrawn from the rebel bank while it was still operating. He feared he might not live to spend it, so offered it to the nuns, if they would arrange for the Church to repay the money to his relatives in a government-controlled town.

'It was a blessing. How the Lord had been leading us,' said Sr Ignatius, astonished by their good fortune. She sent a handwritten note out by the Red Cross ship to the bursar of her congregation, who repaid the money to the man's family; but she doesn't know if he survived.

Two nuns always stayed at the house, to guard the twenty girls, who hid out of sight of the armed rebel groups that were press-ganging young people into the fighting force. As more and more of the population gathered in the tiny enclave on the coast, the nuns managed to find some of the girls' relatives and persuade them to take their children back. The families were planning to escape to the government side and waited for their moment.

Hundreds of people had taken shelter in the nearby church building, turning it into a refugee centre. Mixed with the civilians were rebel deserters and Tiger spies who'd infiltrated to catch them. A priest described how one day 200 armed Tigers encircled the church and took away somewhere between 100 and 150 boys and girls, some as young as sixteen years old.[5] Parents wept and pleaded with the rebels, trying in vain to offer themselves up for military service instead of their precious young sons and daughters.

At night Sr Ignatius would hear mothers shouting and cursing in the bunkers because their children had been stolen by the Tigers. 'Whatever came into their mouth they would say, abusing the Tigers, abusing both sides.' She remembers one lady lying on the ground, crying and throwing sand about, cursing and swearing. Her son had just been caught and taken to fight and she was hysterical. 'People were angry because they'd gone through so much difficulty to bring their children up, educate them, save their lives, moving from place to place,' she says. 'They were very angry with the Tigers and it was not just one or two cases of recruitment.' Bombed by the government, their children stolen by the rebels, ignored by the outside world, many had lost hope. All Sr Ignatius could do was to listen to the stories and show she cared.

Many of the nuns were elderly and falling sick. Sr Ignatius had no choice but to send them out of the war zone one by one on the Red Cross ships that periodically evacuated some of the most gravely injured. Even in the chaos of full-scale war, the Tamil Tigers exercised such strict controls on movement that any nun leaving needed a doctor's letter and an exit pass signed by three separate rebel officials.

On 23 April Sr Ignatius was sitting in her room, gently weeping after saying goodbye to a sister who'd just left by ship accompanying an injured priest,[6] when suddenly a blast jolted her out of her gloom: 'There was this huge vibration and then sand came and covered me from head to toe. It was such a huge one. I just sat there like that. I didn't know what to do. I was frozen. Then I heard people crying. After a few minutes I heard them saying a father, a priest, was among the injured. I was hearing the crying and talking, but wasn't able to move. I was in shock.'

A huge piece of shrapnel had hit the priest's left leg before he passed out. He was carried to the doctors, who had to amputate his leg – without anaesthesia – to save his life. Thirty-five-year-old Father Vasanthaseelan, who ran the local Caritas office, was put on the next ship out of the war zone.

The Sinhalese archbishop never publicly protested that his clergyman had been injured inside a church compound in the 'safe zone'.

That shell explosion marked the start of a relentless onslaught by the army, which was now within walking distance of the Tigers – less than a kilometre away and closing in fast. Sr Ignatius spent her days and nights scrunched up, hardly able to straighten her knees, in one of the eight underground bunkers around the church, as the ground constantly shook and sand rained on to her head. A priest who was also there remembers reciting thirty rosaries in one night alone while the area was pounded by shells from multi-barrelled rocket launchers, artillery and mortars. He still had a wireless telephone that was working and used it to call his bishop to urge the Sri Lankan Army to stop the shelling as there were more than 10,000 civilians still living around the church.[7]

In a brief lull in the fighting, some families decided to risk rushing along the coast, hoping to escape into government territory. Sr Ignatius sent the orphan girls out in two groups with them, worried that it was dangerous for young girls to go alone, but worse for them to stay. It wasn't long before one group leapt back into the bunker in tears, saying they'd been fired on from the government side.

The next day the Tigers ordered the nuns to move southwards to the tiny enclave still under their control. They were hoping the people would follow the clergy. It transpired that they needed to clear some open space between their forward positions and the army approaching from the north. The area was covered with tents and bunkers, which the advancing army used as cover to creep forwards. The Tigers eventually forced the unhappy civilians out by burning their tents, which also meant they could have clear sight of the enemy advancing.

The fighting was heavy. The rebels fired rounds out of the safe zone but Sr Ignatius says the army's incoming fire was even more ferocious. An ambulance and a van parked near the church caught fire and even the fresh green foliage on the trees was in flames. She also believes white phosphorous may have been used; a priest there said he suffered skin irritation from the chemicals present in the air. By now the rebel enclave was so densely populated that it was impossible to target only combatants.

During a pause in the firing, Sr Ignatius sent the teenage girls off again with some families who were desperate enough to try to escape northwards to the government side. Frantically waving white flags, they risked being shot by the Tigers from behind and by the army from in front.

Meanwhile Sr Ignatius followed the crowd walking in the opposite direction, as ordered by the Tigers, to Mullivaikkal in the southern-most part of the spit of land. She'd eaten nothing for days except a few biscuits. Shells smashed into the earth behind them as they passed dead bodies on the road: she counted nine. When fighter jets roared overhead they could only stand under trees for cover.

By now the enclave under rebel control was only about four kilo-metres long and two kilometres wide, and home to more than 100,000 people, living in the open in squalid conditions. They were surrounded by the sea on one side and a lagoon on the other, a shallow river to the south which was the front line, and of course the advancing Sri Lankan military to the north.

Sr Ignatius remembers arriving and then sitting in the open air on a towel on the beach, listening to the roar of the fighter jets swooping low in the sky and dropping what she thought were cluster bombs: 'The noise was terrific. Then there was the sparkling of the bombs. I think those were cluster bombs. *Tuk, tuk, tuk* was the noise; they were exploding all over, I thought. My God!'

The orphan girls they'd sent north never made it and returned south. Miraculously they met up again with Sr Ignatius, who by now had found shelter in a house occupied by another group of nuns. Sr Ignatius had developed diarrhoea and was in acute pain when walking since stepping on a rusty nail some weeks earlier. A piece of rubber from her flip-flop had become lodged inside her foot and turned septic. She went to the makeshift clinic in Mullivaikkal, the tiny village whose name has become synonymous with the final bloodbath, arriving just as the clinic came under attack and the doctor ordered everyone to lie down on the floor. When the attack was over, a nurse used forceps to remove the piece of rubber from Sr Ignatius' foot.

Still unable to walk properly, Sr Ignatius realised she had to leave before she become a burden to the others. 'That was the worst decision I had to make in my life,' she says, loath to abandon the last nun from her order and the girls in their care.

It was the end of April 2009 when she boarded a Red Cross ship – an enormous three-storey vessel, like a liner, which docked a mile out to sea. A huge Red Cross flag was spread out on the beach to mark the assembly point. Little speedboats ferried the injured passengers to the ship, transporting three stretchers at a time. It would take a whole morning to load 400 or 500 patients. Inside the ship the floors were covered with bandaged, bleeding passengers, some missing limbs, who considered themselves very fortunate to be escaping. Red Cross staff served the starving passengers biscuits and water.

Looking back at the teeming shore, Sr Ignatius saw tents pitched everywhere and grey smoke rising among the trees. Keen to hide the extent of human suffering, the Sri Lankan government consistently downplayed the number of people in rebel areas; Sister Ignatius herself had heard the radio news bulletins from the capital claiming there were only 10,000 people left in the war zone. At a glance, however, she could see there were many more along the long flat coast. Just before she left, the senior Tamil civil servant working for the central government as an administrator in rebel territory had told her there were still 165,000 people camped on the beach. His figures turned out to be more accurate than those of the government, which had a hard time explaining why 72,000 people whom they said didn't exist emerged from the war zone in the last two days of the war alone.[8]

Sr Ignatius boarded the ship in the morning; by the time they docked, just a few kilometres further down the coast, it was night. She held her breath as she watched the injured, wrapped in sheets, being perilously lowered off the huge ship into tiny boats for the journey to shore. She feared they would tumble into the water. Then her turn came: 'Practically I had to jump into the sea from the big ship. Two people helped to drop us down. They lowered me while in the little boat two men caught hold of me. It was terrifying. I thought I might fall in and drown,' she says.

Getting off the ship in the dark, on a sandy beach, surrounded by police and military, the first inkling Sr Ignatius had that something was wrong was when a tag was tied around her arm with a number on it. It made her feel like a prisoner. 'What an inhumane thing to do – just a number issued in sequence,' she said.

The army sent the refugees to be searched. After the Tiger suicide bomber disguised as a refugee, the authorities were understandably nervous of anyone coming out of rebel territory.

Sr Ignatius went into a booth where a policewoman said in Sinhala, 'Remove your sari!' Shocked, she stared in disbelief at the person ordering her, a nun, to strip naked.

'That was the first time I ever got really angry in my life. I was so furious. Sick and tired, I looked at her and she just repeated, "Remove your sari!" I said, "Yes, I am a nun." So she looked at me a little, turned and spoke to someone who said, "Go!" I thought to myself, This must be happening to everyone. Can you just imagine? This is the way they had been treating people coming from there who were so mentally and physically worn out. That made me sick. The thought of it: a woman asking a woman to do that. Why not use a metal detector, or frisk people by hand?'

After strip-searches that included removing all underwear, the refugees were sent to a huge shed, where a charity handed out hot rice parcels and gave everyone a bag with a mat, bedsheets, towels, a sarong, a mug, toothpaste and soap. Still convinced she'd be sent home in the morning, Sr Ignatius initially refused the emergency bag, but then took one just in case. She tried to eat some rice but her mouth was so dry after the many days of starvation that she found it hard to swallow.

At midnight they were all put on a bus and driven north to a temporary detention camp in a school building near the war zone. One of the officers in charge recognised Sr Ignatius as a nun and said very respectfully, 'Sister, we didn't know you were coming. Stop for a while and I will find somewhere for you to stay. I have a building with two rooms and I will find some beds and you can come and occupy this.' He turned out to be extremely kind to Sr Ignatius, giving her permission to go to a small shop opposite the camp gate to buy things for the refugees.

Sr Ignatius waited patiently for a day, then asked the soldiers what was happening. They didn't know either. Later a senior officer came to talk to her.

'How are you?' he asked in English.

'Very tired' was all she could manage. The man drew up a chair for her and started to chat.

'How many people are there; what is it like there?' he asked.

'Yesterday there were one hundred and sixty-five thousand people there,' she told him.

'That's impossible. No! There can only be ten to fifteen thousand left now.' [9]

'I have seen it with my own eyes and heard it. I can't say more than that,' she replied, too worn out to argue.

The officer apologised that he couldn't release her without an order from headquarters. He instructed his junior officer to let her use the camp telephone to contact her bishop.

'Among all the hundreds and thousands of people, I was the only one who had that privilege to use the telephone,' she says, pleased with the small token of respect. She called the bishop and found he'd already been pushing for her release. It was to take the Catholic Church, with all its considerable clout, ten faxes and a month to obtain her freedom.

Sr Ignatius relayed short messages for people to their relatives through Church officials, who would call her on the camp commander's telephone. After a while, she heard that all her orphan girls and her colleague had managed to escape and were being detained elsewhere. It was a huge relief, but they were close enough to the fighting to be able to hear the explosions in the distance.

Still suffering from the wound in her foot, Sr Ignatius went under guard to the local hospital. There she noticed a couple with two children close in age but clearly not related, and asked about them. The mother explained that her husband had gone to search for water and found a dead woman sprawled on the ground with a baby lying next to her, still alive. He'd picked up the baby and a briefcase lying on the ground, hoping it would offer clues to the child's identity. Sr Ignatius was full of admiration for their kindness, but she couldn't talk any more because the bus started hooting to take her back to the detention camp.

A few days later the couple arrived at the camp and sought out Sr Ignatius to tell her the rest of the story. They'd opened the briefcase and found it contained baby clothes, a woman's dance-training certificates from India and a photo album. These were the last treasured possessions of the mother, the things she didn't want to leave behind when fleeing for her life. The couple had started searching the pictures in the album for someone they might know. When the ten-month-old baby saw one of the photos, she stamped her little hand over the picture, covering it. It was clear she recognised her dead mother. Then the couple spotted someone they recognised in one of the pictures. The woman told Sr Ignatius: 'At least now we have a clue to go on. When we get the chance to go home, if ever, we will put an advertisement in the newspaper and try to find out if anyone from her family is still alive. If nobody comes to claim the child, we will bring her up ourselves.'

Sr Ignatius was touched by the goodness of the couple, but chilled by the baby's demeanour: 'I saw the child; it had no smile. You will never see a smile on the child's face. The face was frozen. I haven't seen a baby like that. Even if you tickled her, there was no reaction.'

Everyone came to share their stories with Sister Ignatius, including a mother separated from her baby, unsure if he was alive or dead and crying hysterically all the time. 'The Lord had a purpose keeping me there for a month,' she reasoned.

After a couple of weeks, an army commander asked her: 'Did you get the news?'

'What news?' she asked, hoping it was her release. Instead he told her that Velupillai Prabhakaran had been killed, after three decades of outsmarting the Sri Lankan Army.

'Did they find the body?' she asked immediately. Nobody quite believed Prabhakaran, an almost mythical figure, could be dead. Even after his corpse was paraded on television, some Tamils still maintained he was alive.

'As far as I know they were travelling in a van and were caught in a blast,' the commander replied. Later other versions of his death were to emerge.

When the refugees heard the news of the rebel leader's demise, the mood in the camp was subdued and unusually quiet. 'They were sad, but we never spoke about it,' says Sr Ignatius. Nobody wanted to be singled out as a rebel supporter while in army detention; but their feelings about the Tigers were anyway very mixed. Tamil civilians in the war-torn areas of Sri Lanka always had a love–hate relationship with the Tigers. They loathed them when they stole their children. They also disliked paying the so-called 'rebel taxes', in effect extortion of hard-earned money. But when the Tigers hit back against an oppressive army they revelled in their strength, feeling they could stand a little taller because someone was fighting back in their name. At their best, the Tigers made them proud to be Tamil; at their worst, they made them feel doubly cursed.

In late May Sr Ignatius received word that she was being released, while the rest of the refugees were being transferred to Manik Farm, where five Tamil priests who'd been in the war zone were also being detained.

Sr Ignatius spent the next few months living in Vavuniya town and visiting Manik Farm, taking food and clothes to people there, trying to ease their suffering. After a while the strain of the war started to take its toll on her health and the Church sent her out of the country to recover.

Once abroad, Sr Ignatius shared a house with a Sinhalese nun, determined to show that, even after all she'd been through, Sinhalese and Tamils can live together. Reluctantly she admits there is an ethnic divide in the Sri Lankan Church. Many Sinhalese and Tamil Catholics disagree over the issue of war crimes. Like the government, Sri Lanka's current Sinhalese archbishop does not support an international investigation into the conduct of the war, while the Tamil bishops insist the truth must be investigated, because 'forgiveness comes from confession'.[10]

Sr Ignatius believes that, to move forward, both communities in Sri Lanka need to accept their wrongdoings. She acknowledges that the whole country has suffered and is aware there are many Sinhalese war widows and bereaved parents in the south of the island. Her own family history illustrates the layer upon layer of suffering the Tamils have undergone. In 1958 her father had to shut up his shop in Colombo and flee for his life, tipped off by his Sinhalese neighbours that race riots were coming. She was fourteen years old at the time. 'Can you imagine our family life, a father without a job?' she asks. In 1978 more riots forced her sister and her brother-in-law to flee the capital by ship. In the 1980s her family had to flee again, this time on foot.

'Displacement runs in our blood,' she says. 'The wounds go very deep. It's not only the war and the present, it goes back decades. So all those memories are buried in the people. National reconciliation is wishful thinking. Justice has to be done. It's not enough simply to talk of peace. You cannot have injustice and speak of peace.'

The Catholic Church in Sri Lanka

Number of Catholics in Sri Lanka: 1.4 million (7 per cent of the population)
Number of priests and nuns inside the war zone in February 2009: approx. 60

Casualties Among Catholic Clergy in 2007–9 War

Father Francis Joseph, disappeared after surrendering in May 2009, presumed dead
Father Mariampillai Sarathjeevan, died 18 May 2009
Father James Pathinathan, injured April 2009
Father Vasanthaseelan, leg amputated April 2009
Father Karunaratnam (Killi), died due to claymore attack 2008
Father Pakkiyaranchith, died due to claymore attack 2007
Sister Louise, shot in leg February 2009

Churches Damaged or Destroyed in Fighting 2008–9

Paranthan Church, damaged
Dharmapuram Church, damaged
Vishwamadu Church, damaged
Puttumatalan Church, destroyed
PTK Church, destroyed
Iranapalai Church, destroyed
Mullaitivu Church (just rebuilt after being badly damaged in tsunami), damaged
Alambil Church, damaged
Mohamalai Church, destroyed

Valayanmadam Church, damaged
Mullivaikkal Church, destroyed

Convents damaged
Kilinochchi
PTK
Paranthan Holy Cross
Rosarian Community convent
Mullangavil

The Teacher

Uma was late for our appointment at a friend's house in a suburb of south London. She'd gone for a routine check-up at the local hospital, but as soon as the doctors saw her legs they went into a spin, ordering immediate X-rays. Two years after the end of the war, Uma's legs were still peppered with tiny pieces of shrapnel. 'The doctors were panicking and I was laughing,' she said, brushing off their concern. She peeled off her socks and showed me a piece of metal still sticking out of the sole of her foot. It must have been agony to walk but she didn't complain. It wasn't her first war wound either. Opening her blouse, Uma revealed scar tissue across one side of her chest – an injury caused by a Sri Lankan air strike decades earlier in which she'd lost a breast. At the age of fourteen it had been devastating, but over the years she learned to compensate by cracking jokes and being the life and soul of the party. 'I don't want to upset others,' she explained. 'I try to be jolly and strong.'

It's this resilience and vivaciousness that allow Uma to make friends easily. She won the heart of the immigration officer who heard her case in London, and astonished a charity for refugees by striding into their offices and demanding trauma counselling. It helped that she spoke fluent English, having been a language teacher back home.

She launches into her life story by telling me how happy she was building a home with her husband, Bhavan, before the last phase of the war shattered her dreams. 'Ours was a love marriage,' Uma proclaims, proud that she rebelled against the norm of an arranged marriage. Initially her family objected to her choice. Her husband, who only had one leg, was from a working-class family in the poorer east of Sri Lanka, while her family was educated, wealthy and from the north. 'In a way Tamils from the north of Sri Lanka think they are superior, but I think they are fools,' she explains, exploding in laughter at the thought of their prejudice. Uma's parents didn't stand much chance. 'I fell in love with my husband and I said, "Whether you accept it or not, I am going to marry him."'

There was no question but that the couple, both former Tigers, would live in rebel territory. They bought a plot of land on which to build a house, using their bare hands to clear away all the thorny bushes and plant lemon, mango, jackfruit, coconut and papaya trees. 'I wanted to have at least three children and I wanted them to enjoy all the fruits I could give them without paying money. I planted everything and watered them, counting the days for my not-yet-born children to come and enjoy the fruits of my labour,' she exclaims colourfully.

After several miscarriages Uma realised she was unable to have a baby. Now she says it was better that she didn't have to bring a child through the final stage of the war. 'I can't even answer myself; how could I answer a child's questions?' she says.

Instead Uma's twenty-year-old nephew came to live with them. 'He filled the gap of my barren womb. I considered him the child I never had. After four miscarriages I thought it was OK to have a child with a moustache. He treated me like a mother. He loves me.'

Uma's day started at four-thirty in the morning. She would clean the house and cook before going to work on her motorcycle. Her nephew grew vegetables on their land to sell in the market for extra money. In their spare time Uma and Bhavan helped him, working in the garden. 'My husband is more comfortable with his hands and me with my head, so I learned so much from him. I came from such a cosy, rich family. I didn't have any real life experiences,' she says nostalgically.

'We had a lovely life until everything was broken. We were never rich, always struggling. We laughed a lot, making fun of ourselves and everyone else. That was our great wealth.'

Uma remembers the war starting in the distance, slowly deflating her dreams as refugees start to arrive from the areas closer to the front line: 'You could identify them because they would have an I-don't-know where-to-go look on their faces and an I-don't-know-where-the-next-meal-is-going-to-come-from look. The ones with money would hire tractors or lorries and load everything on them. They would even remove doors and beams, hoping they could go back and build their homes again. It was so pathetic to see. Chicken coops and some of the children's toys would be sticking out because the children were very, very particular about taking their toys with them. I used to watch it because my college was near the main road. The fighter jets were almost constant visitors in our lives then: they would come, they would go, they would bomb.'

As the battle inched towards them, Uma had time to prepare mentally for what was coming. 'In a way, a little bit of normalcy was still there. I worked. I had a miscarriage…we had almost one year to get used to it.' One day Bhavan told her it was time to start preparing to move. In mid-January the couple opened their gates to anyone fleeing; they knew it wouldn't be long before they too would depend on the hospitality of strangers. Seven families were already staying inside the modest house, but they cleared the chilli plants and paddy fields to make room for others to pitch tents. 'I don't know who lived there because there was no time to get to know them,' she says, explaining that they would come with all their belongings and beg for shelter. My husband said, "Dear, open your door to anyone who comes, never mind who they are." He thought we were all going to die.'

They weren't the only ones to be generous; it became the norm in those strange times. Everyone shared what little they had, realising how precarious life was. 'Tamil people are not like that usually,' Uma says, laughing cynically.

Uma and the other families built a big bunker in their garden, lined with logs and earth-filled barrels. As soon as they heard the whistle of a shell they'd all get inside, putting the children to bed there every night. Outside, people had dug trenches everywhere: on the road, near schools and at the food-distribution points where the rebels gave out rations.

'There was shelling every day, around the clock. At night-time you can't imagine. You had to catch sleep whenever you could. The nights were worst; if the shelling starts all the children will holler, "Amma, Amma!" They were scared and it was hard to control them,' she remembers.

Bhavan started working as an ambulance driver, rushing the injured to hospital. One day in the last week of January, while he was out at work, she heard the doctors on the radio appealing for blood and decided to donate. 'It was my seventh time,' she says, explaining for my benefit, 'You see, if you live in a war-torn country, you do it often.' Uma's nephew wanted to come with her, but he'd never given blood before and was nervous.

They rode their bicycles the one and a half kilometres to the local school, which had been turned into a hospital. It was shocking to see the classrooms and even the verandahs filled with wounded, while in the hospital grounds the dead were laid out next to the injured. 'You couldn't make sense of anything because everybody was wailing and the relatives of the patients were trying to get attention for their loved ones, and the staff, who were so few, were desperate,' Uma recalls. 'When you go to hospital you think, now everything will be all right, but that wasn't the case there.'

As his blood group was being identified, Uma's nephew said, 'Thank God we decided to come.' But after they'd finished the boy began to feel a little queasy at the sight of the blood. Under all that stress, the hospital staff somehow managed to bring him a cup of hot tea, though without milk, which was already scarce. Suddenly the hospital building came under attack.

'*Bam, bam, bam* – the shelling started. So many shells fell into the school grounds. My nephew just threw the cup of tea away. But where to go and what to do? The wounded were being wounded again. Their relatives were being wounded. We rushed out of the building, leaving our bikes there. We didn't even remember we'd brought them. We ran all the way home. There was human flesh torn and hanging from everywhere and blood. It was horrible.'

They arrived home with their clothes splattered in blood, alarming their friends and neighbours. They'd lost the little piece of cotton wool they'd been given to press down on the vein where blood had been taken, and all the exercise had pumped the blood out of their veins. Today Uma can't stop thinking about all those people milling about in the hospital. 'They were calling on all the deities, begging the gods to save them, but all they got was shells,' she says, adding that she can no longer believe in God after what she's seen.

By the first week of February 2009, the time had come for them to flee. Bhavan told her to pack three sets of clothes each, some bedsheets, a few cooking utensils, a first-aid kit and all the dry food they could carry, as well as documents and identity cards. They also took a hoe, a big knife and screwdrivers to repair their motorbikes. Each of them prepared a backpack of essentials. 'Do you know what I put in my backpack?' she asks: 'Panties and sanitary napkins! Since I had so many miscarriages, I had very heavy periods and I needed them.'

Uma had no jewellery to pack because she'd sold everything to build the house. 'I never cared about gold jewellery. Most Tamil women won't agree, but it was not a big issue for me,' she says, relishing her lack of convention. Instead Uma had kept the dried flower garlands from her wedding day in a drawer. Whenever her husband tidied up, he would make fun of her, saying, 'There's something here to go in the bin.' 'Throw it away only if you want a divorce,' she would joke back.

All she has left today of her former life is one small gold bracelet her father gave her, which was too tight to take off her wrist. She lost even her earrings, which were removed before surgery in a government hospital. 'It's shocking to have nothing of your past. It's like being erased or obliterated. It's like losing one of your limbs, or losing your memory.' She struggles to explain. I am struck by the comparison to losing a limb. It's not a simile she'd use carelessly, given that her husband had been through exactly that. When they moved, Bhavan took his crutches as well as his artificial leg, mindful that somebody might need them. In the end they both needed the crutches.

Leaving home, Uma says she half expected they would never return. Like many in that area, they had photographs on the walls of dead friends and relatives who'd fought for the Tigers. Many families took the pictures down and buried them underground, thinking this would save their homes from destruction when the army occupied them. Uma's husband instructed her to leave the photographs where they were, but she decided to go one step further and honour the dead before she abandoned the house.

'We grew about forty rose bushes in the front yard, all of them nodding their colourful heads. I cut some and put them on the pictures, most of which were our heroes. We knew if the army decided to destroy the place they would do it one way or another, whether the photographs were there or not. We knew we were nearing the last stage of the war. It was sort of like gambling. The dice can fall this way and you're dead, that way and you're alive. There was no use doing small things.'

Hope did get the better of Uma and her nephew: they couldn't help running around burying farm tools in the trenches, in case they came back one day. Bhavan was more realistic. He urged them to leave immediately, saying, 'We can buy them again, if we're still alive.'

Dead cattle, their feet sticking up from swollen bodies, dotted the landscape; the stink lingered in the air. The road was empty, abandoned vehicles left untouched. Everyone else preferred the muddy interior lanes, even though they'd become swamps after the continuous downpour. 'If you're game, let's go on the main road,' said Bhavan. 'If we drive at seventy kilometres an hour, we can get there in eight minutes.' They loaded the two bikes with their belongings. Uma drove alone, following Bhavan with their nephew perched on the back of the larger bike. Shells were falling in front and behind and Uma struggled to keep up. 'Aunt, hurry, come!' her nephew called back to her desperately. 'My husband said, "If you're not wounded, just pull on the accelerator and go!" You couldn't see where the next shell would fall. But if something blows up in front of you, your instinct is to stop. I did that and he would shout, "Come on!"'

They made it through and stayed with a cousin, in a place so small, Uma says, you can't even describe it as a village. The army was only two

kilometres away and there was gunfire from all directions. Nowhere
was safe in those days, but it was better than their own home. Then, on
15 February, Bhavan was hit by a stray bullet. It pierced the upper thigh
of his amputated leg, passing right through the stump. Uma quickly
tore a clean sarong into strips and used it to tie two sanitary towels on
the wound as a dressing. With the help of her nephew she lifted her
wounded husband on to the back of his more powerful motorbike.
She doesn't know how she did it, but somehow she drove him to
the overflowing hospital, through those roads clogged with desperate
people moving in all directions. All the time she feared the worst.

'I didn't know if the bone was affected or not. They couldn't
remove any more. I would lose him; they couldn't amputate any more.
So you can understand what I felt. I can't tell you how much time
it took to get him to hospital. I had to rush, but I couldn't. He was
feeling faint and I would put one hand behind and say, "We are nearly
there." You see, I used to lean on him a lot, but now it was my turn to
stand firm.'

Luckily it was just a flesh wound. Uma refused to allow the doctors
to admit Bhavan: she knew hospitals were being targeted so she insisted
on taking him home, with dressings, medicines and instructions about
what to expect. The staff knew him from his work as an ambulance
driver, and Uma was very lucky to get the precious antibiotics. 'I
begged them. There was a shortage but somehow I managed to get
them. I don't think at that stage many people would have been able
to persuade them to give the drugs, but I literally begged them. He
had already lost a leg. It was a matter of life and death for him. They
couldn't amputate again.'

After less than two hours in the makeshift hospital, Uma drove
Bhavan back on the motorbike. Fearful of handling the big bike, Uma
made him sit astride the saddle lest he fall off as she swerved to avoid
people on the crowded road. It was bumpy and excruciatingly painful,
but they had no choice. It felt dreadful to return to the same place
where he'd been wounded. They found that their cousin had fled in
fear, leaving other families camping there. In those days, Uma explains,

everyone escaped when they thought the time was right; there was no sense that the homeowner packed up and left last. 'My dear,' said Bhavan, 'this place is as dangerous as anywhere else. Let's wait a day or two until I can sit on a motorbike again and then we will go.'

Two days later they moved nearer the hospital, thinking it would be easier to get the dressings changed if the wound became infected. They dug an open trench on someone's land and erected a tent on top. If you went inside the tent, half of it was ground level and the other half dug out. They had no money to buy logs to reinforce the structure. It was an illusion of protection: 'An open trench is only a tiny, tiny bit better than being completely in the open, but somehow it felt safe when you were under the tent,' explains Uma. Her husband refused to go into the trench, because it was too narrow to enter with only one leg and he couldn't use his artificial limb yet, his stump being too swollen. When he moved about, the pain shot up his leg because there was still a slight infection in the entry wound. The couple forced their nephew to lie in the trench, saying they needed him to stay alive to look after them. 'Whenever a shell came near, he used to cry out, "Aunty, come in!" Poor boy, he was so frightened for us,' she remembers.

Being so close, the three of them panicked every time they were separated. If one person had to get out of the bunker to fetch drinking water and got delayed, the others would assume the worst. They would argue over who should take the risk of running everyday errands. 'If the shell attacks were heavy and I wanted to go to the toilet, I had to get permission from both of them,' she remembers in amusement. 'Aunt, are you serious? Can't you wait?' Uma's nephew would ask. 'We loved each other and we wanted each other to be safe, if you could call our tent safe,' she says.

Again they moved, this time right up to the coast, near where the Red Cross ships came and took away some of the injured. During March they lived near the sea, being bombed and shelled continuously. 'Everything flew around your head – shrapnel and rounds of bullets,' she says casually, as if describing bad weather.

Gradually Uma nursed Bhavan back onto his feet. After a month he was able to use his artificial leg again, but still had to move slowly.

They rationed the little rice they had left. Before midday Uma would make gruel with three scoops of rice and some salt and they would all drink it. Suppertime was delayed as long as possible to make the food stocks last longer. Five scoops of rice as porridge again and, once or twice a week, Uma would throw in a handful of lentils or soya beans. It was too dangerous to go out and look for vegetables. They didn't have much cash and had no idea how long the fighting would go on. A distant relative who was a fisherman would try to smuggle a tiny fish to Uma to give her husband some protein. It wasn't easy to fish in the sea as the Sri Lankan Navy was positioned off the coast, but they managed to catch some in the nearby lagoon.

Worried that Bhavan was lacking protein, the normally frugal Uma astonished her family by purchasing some milk for nearly thirty times the normal price. 'One packet of four hundred grams of skimmed milk was normally a hundred and thirty-five rupees, and I used to buy just four a month from my housekeeping budget and ration them. If they asked for tea with milk too often, then for the last week of the month they had to drink plain tea. When my husband was wounded, I bought one packet for three thousand five hundred rupees [£17]! His hands were shaking and he couldn't hold anything. My husband and my nephew made such fun of me. "Aunty used to scold us and ration it," they teased.'

To pass the time, Uma and her boys would read romantic novels and play cards in the bunker. 'It kept us sane,' she says; 'we played non-stop.' Amazingly the three of them kept on telling jokes. 'Before the war we used to laugh a lot and share everything, every titbit,' she remembers fondly. 'Those days were so happy. The only shortage we had was money, but in every other sense we were so rich.' Even under bombardment they found something to laugh about: an old woman making a racket calling upon all the gods, or someone they knew who used to be very stuffy now sleeping on the ground like everyone else. 'My guys would make fun of it all and say, "See what she's doing!"

I would say, "Put a lid on it, they might hear you." Whenever we had the chance to capture some normalcy, we grabbed it with both hands,' she explains.

As they moved towards the sea, it became impossible to dig trenches because the sand was too soft. People built up walls of sandbags instead, chopping up the best silk saris into five strips and then sewing them into bags that could be filled and emptied as they moved location. An ornate sari that would normally cost thousands of rupees now sold for just twenty. It was a world where milk cost more than a fridge, where a car could be traded for a bag of rice. People broke into shops in the town and stole the saris, and a few enterprising tailors started a business stitching them into sandbags. Uma was the tallest in her family so they would measure the height of the wall of sandbags by making her sit down and then adding a couple of inches. If they made it too tall, the structure would fall over, but it needed to be high enough to shield the top of her head.

One day in March Uma was at the coast trying to buy some fish to feed Bhavan when she saw a foreign woman, small, with blond hair tied back into a ponytail, wearing a Red Cross vest. She'd come ashore for a few brief hours with a ship collecting the wounded, and was trying to talk to the crowd of people on the shore, with the help of a translator.

'They were surrounding her as if she was a god or a prophet, everyone trying to tell her about their suffering. They were begging her to go and tell the outside world about what was happening there.'

Uma noticed the translator was giving himself airs and graces. In her own frayed, crumpled dress, she pushed herself forward, telling the others she could speak English.

'Will you allow me to talk to her?' she asked the crowd.

'Yes, go!' they replied.

'Hello, I would like to speak to you,' Uma addressed the astonished aid worker, whose expression showed that she didn't expect a dishevelled refugee on that beach to speak impeccable English. 'What are you doing?'

'We are trying to take the injured away,' replied the Red Cross worker.

'How many injured?' pressed Uma. When she heard the figures, she said: 'Do you think these are the only people who are wounded?'

'No, we are only taking a small proportion of the injured. We have limitations, you know,' and the woman began to explain why the Red Cross couldn't do more.

'You are recording the dead and you are taking away the people who are going to die. So are you not like the Nazis, who while killing people recorded everything? What is the meaning of this? You are not trying to stop all of this. You are not even planning to stop it. Aren't you justifying it, by taking away the most wounded people? You are not helping us. You are just pretending to help us. I have lost my faith in the rest of the world. If you call these people terrorists, what are you going to call me, if I escape this and am given the chance to live again? What will these people do, the future generations? Do you have a more appropriate name for them than terrorist?'

'I am just an aid worker employed to do a job,' replied the stunned woman, but Uma wasn't ready to let her off the hook yet. She was like a madwoman, possessed.

'I know you are doing a job, but I would like to know your opinion. You are here, witnessing this. I can't talk to the rest of the world, but I am here on this beach, speaking to you. I am a person and you are a person. I can't ask anyone else. See these people: they are grovelling to you for a Panadol or a packet of milk – grovelling for a chance for their children to live. If the world can't give it to them, what will they be in future? They are crushing Tamils and claiming they are liberating them. Do they look liberated? Are the shells liberating us from life? Is death a liberation?'

Then Uma gave up trying to get the Red Cross woman to respond to her as a human being. She walked away, exhausted. As she put it, the gas of her rage had exploded and spent itself. Without saying a word, Uma returned home. When her family heard the gossip about a woman who had scolded a Red Cross official to the point that she was nearly in tears, Uma owned up that she was the culprit. Her husband hugged her and told her she'd done well.

Today Uma feels guilty about being so rude to the lady on the beach. She'd love to meet her again and apologise, but her views haven't changed: 'What is the meaning of them coming and going? What is the point of them having access to the war zone? It was not helping us. For outsiders it is better that the Red Cross was there, but for us, inside the war zone, it was the same whether they were there or not. They were just assuaging their consciences. What about the rest? Who carries the cross of being alive, like me? Of being alive, when thousands were denied that chance. It is a great burden to survive.'

Uma hides her grief with humour. 'What have we done to deserve all this? Who dished out all these things to us: God? Then He's like the United Nations and Red Cross people who abandoned us,' she jokes, adding, 'I don't know what will happen in future but I am so angry with God that I will punch Him in the eye. That's probably why He's not around, because He's scared of people like me!'

Suddenly she starts talking about books, her passion. There were few up-to-date novels in rebel territory, but Uma read whatever she could find. She had devoured all the Second World War stories of Leon Uris, never thinking her own life would one day resemble the plots she adored. She tells me about a character in his book *Exodus*, a Polish Jew whose sole ambition is to fight back after escaping the Holocaust. 'Fighting back is called terrorism,' she says indignantly, 'but he is the sole survivor – his whole family is wiped out. In a way he is like me.'

Then, almost in passing, she mentions casually that she had a miscarriage on the beach at the climax of the war. In fact, being briefly pregnant had its upside. Because she'd missed two periods, she had more sanitary towels left over to use as wound-dressings.

As the fighting intensified, everyone congregated on the final strip of beach where the war culminated. It took two days to move there because they had to wait for a lull in the shelling, gradually emptying the sandbags and transporting them to the new location, where Uma's nephew would start digging the new shelter. Ferrying their meagre belongings even a few kilometres along the coast was nerve-racking, each person worrying about the other and constantly forced to take cover from incoming shells. By the second day, 6 May 2009, Bhavan had a fever and she implored him to rest while she went back to fetch their last belongings. Reluctantly he agreed, conceding he was too tired to cope.

Uma returned to the junction where they'd lived in a tent under a fruit tree. On one corner of the crossroads was a small tailoring shop, where a lady stitched sari bags for customers. On the opposite corner were a well and a toilet, where they would queue at night to wash. 'Having a toilet was like having five million pounds in your hand, like being a billionaire there, just having a bit of privacy and being able to shut the door,' she remembers. Uma's motorbike was parked opposite the well. In front of her were three tractors and another behind, the engines revving, making a din. All around people were getting ready to flee to the open beach, leaving behind the jungles, bushes and marshes of the previous months. Uma put the key in the ignition of her motorbike and turned it. To this day she doesn't understand how the key fell on the ground. Normally it wouldn't come out of the keyhole unless she first turned it back to the starting position, but that day was different.

'I had a feeling as if someone was walking over my grave, as if a shadow was passing over me. It was chilling. I had goosebumps all over my hands and felt queasy. I never felt like that before. I was wondering how the key could have fallen out. I stood there for a minute just thinking and then I bent over to pick it up.' It was a matter of seconds, but the decision to bend over at that exact moment saved her life.

A shell fell diagonally behind Uma, just six metres away. She was thrown to the ground. Glancing at her rubber flip-flops, she spotted a tiny piece of shrapnel in her toe. Her first thought was that it would be a good joke to share with her husband. On the opposite corner there had been a grandmother standing at the well, holding her grandchild in her arms and trying to make her eat by pointing out all the tractors. 'I saw her last moments of life. I stooped as the shell fell and I turned and saw her blasted into pieces,' says Uma. Only after she'd tried to stand up three times and failed did Uma realise that she was badly injured herself. When the dust and smoke abated, she became aware of all the shouting and the tractors. Then she turned and saw the other corner of the junction where the tailor and a mother and daughter had been blown to bits. 'I don't know how I escaped,' she says, adding: 'It can't have been an act of God, because if there were a God, what about all those other people who died?'

Uma didn't know it yet, but her leg had multiple fractures and damage from scores of shrapnel fragments. Someone told her cousin, who was a rebel, and he came on his motorbike to take her to the last functioning hospital in rebel territory. They abandoned her bike and didn't even stop to bandage the wounds in the hurry to get out of there as quickly as possible. Bleeding and stunned, Uma was deposited on the ground at the hospital, where she was considered a mild case because all her injuries were below the knee. The nurses didn't even clean the wound, just applying a gauze dressing to stop the bleeding. There were no painkillers and no antibiotics to give. 'They did what they could for me. They had their hands full with more seriously injured people. Even I could see that. I considered myself lucky and I didn't expect anything from them,' she says.

Bhavan came and collected her, cleaned the wounds and boiled strips of cloth in a cooking pot, using them to tie the sanitary towels as sterile dressings to her legs. He realised her leg was fractured because he'd suffered multiple fractures himself in 1990 when he'd been a fighter. Always in pain, Uma never cried or fussed, but couldn't stand even her husband's sarong brushing against her injury. He said: 'Until a doctor says otherwise, you are not putting your foot on the ground. I will carry you. I will not let you lose your leg, because I know what it will mean for you.' Both Uma's legs were swollen from her waist to her toes with secondary infection and she was already weak from the miscarriage and lack of food.

In mid-May they threw away everything except their national

identity cards. Bhavan emptied their last remaining bag to reduce the weight, so he could carry her out of the war zone. She watched him discard her laptop, keeping only three plastic water bottles between them. 'We were well and truly destitute then,' she says. Bhavan carried her in a fireman's lift while walking on his artificial leg.

In those last terrible days she watched sons and daughters abandoning elderly parents in the rush to save their own lives. 'They left the wounded and the dead without even checking if they were still alive, but my husband and nephew somehow dragged me, pulled me, carried me and helped me to hobble. They saved my life,' she says. They'd begged some heavy-duty painkillers from the doctors and Uma took 1,000 mg every four hours, rendering much of that awful journey a hazy blur. Concerned that the men she loved were making themselves a target by carrying her, she remembers repeatedly imploring them to leave her and to run to safety. They refused. She saw the Sri Lankan Army shooting to herd people across the bridge and she started crying hysterically, sure that she wouldn't be able to make it out. For the first time, Bhavan slapped her, saying, 'Would you leave me if I was injured? I am not going to leave you. Who do you think I am? Now shut up and cooperate.'

'Go, go, go!' she implored him in terror. 'If you leave me I will live on because you will remember me.'

Today Uma says her husband may not have remembered her birthday but he more than proved his love in that terrible situation. 'He was a funny man,' she says fondly, and then tells me about her first birthday after getting married and how excited she was, wondering what he would buy her as a present. Unfortunately he'd completely forgotten and Uma was furious for days. Now she says those memories of their life together fuel her through her darkest days.

Crossing over into government territory, it took the three of them fifty-six hours to reach the refugee camp. 'They put us in a barbed-wire enclosure like sheep. They made us remove all our clothing. Each and every one, regardless of age and sex, even infants, had to strip,' she says, still outraged at the indignity. In agony for hours on the bus, Uma went numb below the hips and started crying, fearing she was going to lose both her legs because she couldn't stand up or raise her feet. In the camp it was two weeks before she was sent to hospital. It took four days just to see a doctor because so many people were wounded. The doctor thought her outer wounds were healed and assumed it was just an infection. After six days of her staggering back and forth to the camp clinic to pick up medicines, the doctors realised there was something wrong. 'Thank God for that, I was lucky,' she says, grateful that they transferred her to a nearby hospital run by Médecins Sans Frontières.

'There I was treated like a human being, after such a long time. Being treated like a human was the best thing I recall; being treated for a fracture was secondary. We used to be a very proud people. Being reduced to a sub-human being is worse than death. You could die but at least you would still have your dignity.'

With a plaster cast on her leg, Uma was returned to the camp, because the hospital had no space. When the fracture didn't heal as expected and she developed bronchitis, she was hospitalised again. While she was away her nephew was taken away and jailed. He had nothing to do with the rebels but the Sri Lankan authorities were suspicious of all young Tamil men of fighting age. Uma was in and out of hospital, terrified every time she left the camp that they might also arrest her husband. In September 2009 they started taking him away for questioning. Bhavan was tied to a tree and tortured but she can't bring herself to tell me how. In January 2010, eight months after the war had ended, they came for him for the last time. 'I know I am the luckiest woman in the world to have had a husband like him,' she says, 'and the unluckiest woman to lose him in such a way and not know where he is.'

Today Uma is racked with guilt about leaving Sri Lanka. Mostly she tells herself that it will be easier for her husband to escape now that she is safely out. 'It's so hard to keep the faith going, sometimes I despair. I haven't come here to earn money or be rich. All I want is a life with my husband.' In her dreams Uma imagines finding a small place in the green English countryside and settling down to farm with him one day. 'I want to try normal life,' she says. 'We would be happy anywhere, even in the Sahara or Mount Everest, so long as we are free.'

Alone in exile, Uma talks to Bhavan in her head, sharing the new experiences with him. When she ate her first strawberry – a fruit she'd read so much about in books but never tasted – she told him all about it. 'Subconsciously I am speaking to him. I carry him with me. I imagine what he would have said to this or that and how he would have laughed at me.' Nobody around her knows she's doing this, but it's her way of holding on to him. 'I know if I stop laughing, I will start to cry. I have done a lot of crying, you know, and I am fed up with it. Nowadays I cry behind closed doors or under quilts, but before I didn't even have that luxury, to cry in private.'

Uma's nephew was released after four months in jail and returned to his parents in the east of Sri Lanka. They talk almost daily. For more than a year she has heard no news of Bhavan, but refuses to give up hope. 'They took away our individuality, our intellect, our confidence, our hope, physical wealth comes last. I used to be a teacher, a fighter, a wife, and then I was reduced to being a fugitive, a person in hiding. Now they have taken everything from me.'

As they dragged her husband away, that last time in the refugee camp, Uma will never forget the one word he mouthed to her: 'Escape!'

Bhavan fell into that vast category of the Sri Lankan 'disappeared' – people the government talks about as if they've been carelessly misplaced somewhere, rather than brutally wiped out. I wondered at Uma's tenacity, her conviction that he was still alive. She told me on her birthday she'd woken up in the middle of the night absolutely certain that he was thinking about her. But after a year with absolutely no news of him, I personally assumed he was dead.

Almost a year later I contacted Uma again, and was astonished to learn she was waiting for Bhavan to join her. She'd found a job working at a cash till in a supermarket, to support him. In an email bursting with expectation she wrote: 'My only extravagance is spent on phone cards. Both of us are counting the days to the reunion. I hope with all my heart that it will be soon. When he comes, you can have the raw material for a thriller-romance!!!!!!!!!!!!!!'

Disappearance

Sri Lanka has the second highest number of unresolved disappearances in the world, after Iraq. As of 6 February 2012, the number of disappeared in Sri Lanka is 12,460.[1]

Disappearance of Tamils after the Surrender in May 2009

20 cases (Human Rights Watch)
32 cases, including groups of people (UN, *Report of the Secretary-General's Panel of Experts on Accountability in Sri Lanka*)
1,379 written complaints of disappearance (Sri Lankan government's Lessons Learnt and Reconciliation Commission). The commission said 21 of the disappeared were abducted by Tigers and 1,028 arrested by the army.

Number of Ongoing Disappearances According to Media Reports Collected by the Groundviews Website

OCTOBER 2011	4
NOVEMBER 2011	7
DECEMBER 2011	10
JANUARY 2012	6
FEBRUARY 2012	14
MARCH 2012	15[2]

Missing in 2011

17 JANUARY	Two schoolboys abducted by men in a white van in Mannar

4 MARCH	Thushara Jayaratne, a final-year Law College student, was abducted
1 MAY	Jaffna teenager Thiruchelvan Kajeedan reported missing in Colombo
20 MAY	Diluxon Anandarajaha reported missing in Batticaloa
2 JUNE	Malathi, a fifteen-year-old girl, abducted
26 JUNE	Balachandran Satkurunadan abducted and killed in Jaffna
28 JULY	Human-rights activist Pattani Razeek found dead after being reported missing in February 2010.[3]
13 NOVEMBER	Businessman Kapila Chaminda Bandara abducted in Nugegoda
21 NOVEMBER	Fish trader abducted in Dematagoda
29 NOVEMBER	Jaffna University student Vetharaniyam Latheesh reported missing
3 DECEMBER	Ruwan Chandimal 'Navy Ruwan' reported missing
5 DECEMBER	Businessman Christopher Fernando abducted in Kotahena
6 DECEMBER	A Tamil youth reported abducted in Jaffna[4]

The Rebel Mother

Uma's friend Usha is an unemployed single mum living in a council
house in south London. The first time I met her was on an icy winter
morning when the whole country was blanketed in snow. She stood out
a mile as a former Tamil Tiger rebel, even in London's crowded Waterloo
Station, her butch self-assurance totally out of character for an Asian
woman. She wore unfeminine clothes: jeans and a black Adidas tracksuit
top with white edging along the zip. A large woman in her forties, with
curly hair around her temples, she had an intensely serious demeanour.
There were no rings on her stubby fingers and her dark hands bore the
pale pink scars of tiny shrapnel wounds. The only feminine decoration
was small flower-shaped diamond earrings and a modest gold medallion
hanging on a long chain around her neck. I didn't know it then, but
this was a substitute for the gold necklace that Sri Lankan Tamils give
in place of a wedding ring. Usha's original wedding necklace had been
in the shape of a tiger's tooth and identified her as part of a rebel cadre.
Before she surrendered with her two young daughters at the end of the
war, she buried the necklace underground.

Usha's story begins on a hot July night in 1983, at the boarding
house of Jaffna Ladies' College, one of the top schools for girls in Sri
Lanka. All was quiet outside; even the stray dogs were asleep. In the
vast industrial-size dormitory, fifty Tamil girls lay in beds, neatly laid
out in rows. Among them was Usha, the youngest daughter of a bus
driver for the Ceylon Transport Board. At fifteen she still wore her hair
in two long pigtails and was the baby of the family. Every weekend
she would feign illness, hoping to be sent home for some pampering
by her parents.

Usha loved nothing more than to borrow storybooks and comics
and secrete them inside her exercise books to read during study time
in the boarding house. When she was supposed to be preparing for her

O levels, Usha was reading adventure stories, unaware that one day she would live through escapades far more dramatic than anything in her books.

The lights had been out for three hours in the junior dormitory when suddenly there was a thunderous explosion, followed by gunfire, distinctly audible a kilometre away in the calm of the night. In those days bombs and bullets were unheard-of in the tranquil tropical island.

All the girls in the dormitory woke up, screaming in panic. The matron rushed in to calm the commotion. That attack would change Usha's life, and those of all Sri Lankan Tamils, for ever. Thirteen Sinhalese soldiers had just been killed in an ambush by a handful of young Tamil rebels.

Sri Lankans know very well what happened next. Tamils call it 'Black July'. In the capital, Sinhalese mobs used the killing of the thirteen soldiers as the trigger for a pre-planned pogrom. They attacked Tamil shops and homes, burning them and hacking people to death in the streets. The rioters came, armed with electoral lists as well as machetes, so they could distinguish who was Tamil. In such a divided nation, it seems strange that it's so tricky to spot the enemy. There are tell-tale signs – how a woman ties her sari, religious markings, places of birth – but none of them is foolproof. Electoral records with full names made the most reliable death lists.

Usha wasn't aware that her brother, who was studying engineering at university in Colombo, had a narrow escape on a bus. With quick thinking, he leapt off the vehicle, picked up a club and followed the mob, pretending to be one of them, until he reached his hostel. It was a month before his family knew he'd survived, a month in which many Tamils began to feel they were never going to live securely in Sri Lanka. It wasn't just a question of being gradually squeezed out of universities and plum civil-service jobs, a process that had started in the 1950s with legislation that marginalised Tamils. Now they could be dragged out of their homes and set on fire while the government did nothing. Incredibly the rioting went on for five days before the President addressed the nation. Even then he failed to condemn the killing, instead suggesting it was a natural reaction to provocation. Fifty thousand Tamils were left homeless; nobody knows how many thousands were killed. Sri Lanka has never been very good at counting the dead.

The 1983 riots were the turning point, when many young Tamils lost faith in democratic politics and took up arms. It took some years for Usha, but eventually she walked into a rebel base to sign up. She was instructed to come back once they'd run background checks on her. Not telling a soul, she went about her life as normal until one day she simply disappeared. Her widowed mother was frantic, visiting all the offices of the Tamil Tigers to ask about her daughter. Eventually she saw Usha's name on a list, but it was too late. The day before, she'd been sent off to the jungle for a month's military training – mostly physical exercise and political indoctrination, but she did get to handle a rifle briefly.

Usha was soon put to work in the Tigers' media unit, trained as a photographer and then a camerawoman. Her mother begged her to return home. 'She was crying and said, "It's because your father isn't here that you did this. Society will blame me for bringing you up wrong. What will the relatives say that I let my daughter run away?"'

Over the years Usha rose up the rebel ranks, setting up the all-female video units that produced propaganda films. She was never part of a fighting unit, but on many occasions dodged army patrols and came close to being captured or killed.

'On one trip in 1999 we were taken by boat near a Sinhalese area and marched for five days in the jungle. There were three hundred male and female cadres and nine of us from the video unit. The Sri Lankan Army came to know we were moving – maybe they were tipped off – and we had a lot of trouble with them in those five days. We had just got to a place where we thought we were safe. I was dead tired. I couldn't take a single step more. Then all of a sudden the army came at us. We all ran for three or four kilometres. I tried to hide behind a signboard. The others had gone ahead and I was lost in that unfamiliar place. Then luckily a girl from my unit came back to find me. We lost five of our people there.'

On that trip Usha's team spent months documenting the extreme poverty of the Tamil villagers, who collected honey, hunted wild animals or went to the nearest town to beg food for their children. These were the people the Tigers were fighting to liberate. The video unit wanted to show how deprived Tamils were, in order to raise money from the diaspora to buy arms.

The Tigers certainly knew the power of information: rebel bases had sophisticated video-editing suites and kept an extraordinary archive of battle footage. Commanders also knew their fighters would be more inspired to acts of bravery if they were being filmed. They would scrutinise the footage from the front line to devise better tactics. In one major battle six cameramen died filming. Each carried a gun as well as a camera, and had orders to defend the tape with their lives.

Usha's trip to the east was not front-line combat, but army patrols were a constant threat. In these remote jungles, the boundaries were fluid and the soldiers generally patrolled only at night. 'In the daytime we were with the people. At night we would go to the jungle to sleep. In the morning we would wait for a temple bell to ring the all-clear to say it was safe to come out.' They had to trust the local people not to turn them in.

Specialist rebel guides led Usha and her team through the unfamiliar jungles, showing them the hidden food stores that were a lifeline. They found stocks of dry rice and lentils, sealed in polythene bags, secreted inside wooden treehouses, out of reach of the wild animals. When the mission was finished, Usha had to wait three months to be picked up by boat. 'I was going mad without any books to read or anything to do. When people went to the village for food I would look forward to reading the old scraps of newspaper in which they wrapped the food parcels.'

It was not the life Usha had expected, lugging around camera gear instead of babies. By the time she reached her early thirties, even the Tigers thought she should marry. They had a rule that female recruits had to serve for five years and men for eight in order to be eligible to marry. Usha had more than done her time.

In September 1999, a thin, gaunt-faced Usha put on a heavy silk sari, gold with an ornate pink border, and decorated her curly hair, which was drawn back into a bun, with white flowers. Like many nervous Tamil brides, Usha didn't know her future husband that well. Nirmal looked more sure of himself in the photographs. He wore a long white shirt with an extravagant white and gold turban perched on his head, making it hard to see his moustachioed face very clearly at first. The couple had been introduced by an older lady who played the role of matchmaker. Friends, colleagues and a few relatives gathered to watch the couple take their vows.

It sounds like a typical Sri Lankan wedding. It was anything but. There was no Hindu priest, no exchange of gold jewellery and definitely no dowry because the Tigers disapproved of the custom. The bride was thirty-three and Usha was actually her *nom de guerre*. The groom had done time in jail and some of the more important guests were on Interpol's Most Wanted list. Usha was marrying well, though. Her husband was a rising star in the Tigers. He had worked for their special intelligence wing, which spied on army camps, and then for their fledgling air force. He'd joined the Tigers early on – in 1982 – and was sent to set up their political office in London, and then to India. There's a lot that even Usha probably doesn't know about his past. Secrecy was key to survival for a man like Nirmal.

A rebel leader conducted the austere ceremony and witnessed the signing of the marriage certificate. The happy couple solemnly pledged to live together for the rest of their lives according to the principles of the Tamil Tigers. The special rebel wedding vows were identical for bride and groom: the Tigers preached feminism to lure women on to the battlefield. Officials presented Usha and Nirmal with a wristwatch each to commemorate their union. A more romantic touch was the exchange of white flower garlands dotted with pink, green and yellow blossoms. Afterwards everyone celebrated with cups of tea and savoury snacks. The Tigers even footed the bill.

As Usha prepared for the birth of her first child, the Tigers were launching a big offensive to expand the territory under their control.

Her house was taken over by rebel medics to treat the wounded. Just when most expectant mothers are painting the newborn's room in a pastel shade, Usha had blood splattered over her walls as the surgeons worked frantically on the injured.

The day after her baby was born, Usha got up and walked out of the hospital, ignoring the custom that women spent several days in bed recovering. She recalls a man on the maternity ward commenting admiringly to his own wife, 'Look at that lady, walking so smartly out of here.' The little girl with the pigtails had developed into a tough woman, highly motivated and politicised. Nowadays Usha might be a refugee with faltering English, but back home she was the boss, respected and obeyed. She still has a burly confidence that comes from having once issued orders.

Usha's two daughters had scores of aunties and uncles who loved them – Usha and Nirmal's comrades, bound together by a shared conviction that armed struggle was the only path. The rebel family was also her support when Usha suddenly found herself widowed after just four years of marriage. One day she received a telephone call saying her husband was gravely ill, in government territory. It was during the ceasefire in 2004. Nirmal had been travelling in the south of the island. Usha does not say what he was doing there, only that he made regular visits. Nirmal was rushed to hospital with chest pains and vomiting, and died aged just forty. By the time Usha managed to get to the hospital it was too late. There was no time for a post-mortem so she never found out the cause of death. They had to get the body across the border to rebel territory before the army asked too many questions and stopped them. By six o'clock that evening, Usha was back home with her husband's corpse and two toddlers.

Today all she has to remember Nirmal is the photograph that she sent her sister in England after their wedding. It's the sole decoration on the pale pink walls of her spotlessly clean, two-bedroomed terrace house in south London, and every day she lights a candle to honour his memory, a small token of her steadfast devotion.

*

The last time Usha saw her home in Sri Lanka was on New Year's Day 2009. She was standing on the porch of the bungalow before the three large front windows, each with elaborate metalwork and dainty lace curtains. Usha had already moved her children away from the artillery range of the advancing Sri Lankan Army, but nipped back home to pick up some belongings, knowing this could be her last chance. The day before, the house had been shelled. Soon Sri Lankan soldiers would be standing on her verandah, or what was left of it, establishing an army checkpoint on her neighbour's land.

The ceasefire had fallen apart and the army had been steadily advancing into rebel territory, pushing the Tigers and the people towards the coast. A true believer, Usha was convinced the Tigers were doing the right thing by preventing anyone leaving the war zone, and would soon regain their lost territory.

As she stood on the polished maroon cement next to one of the red-brick pillars, a Sri Lankan fighter jet flew overhead. There was a small crack as it released the bombs and then an ear splitting thud as they impacted, the earth vibrating with huge force. Usha was literally thrown off her feet on to the ground a few metres away in the garden, her head bleeding and her body burned so that the fabric of her clothes stuck to her flesh. She had injuries to her head, back and arms.

There was chaos and screaming. Some of the trees were burning. Expecting another attack, Usha sprinted over the rubble, intent on getting into the narrow bunker dug into the earth behind the house. Roof tiles had been blown off the bungalow, leaving the wooden beams underneath exposed.

Five people had been killed in the garden next door. Men arrived to check the smouldering ruins for survivors, only to find twisted bicycles, house beams and tree branches all mixed up in the wreckage. Dry palm thatch from the fencing lay around and some of the palm trees had no tops, their leafy fronds blown off by the explosion.

Usha was only in the bunker for a few minutes before she decided to walk down the road to find a vehicle to take her to hospital. Luckily, after only half a kilometre a passing rebel truck picked her up. On the bumpy ride, sitting on the dirty floor of the truck, they heard more bombs falling and saw more people injured.

The BBC news report for 1 January 2009 quoted the rebels as saying that eighteen civilians had been injured in government air raids that day. Usha was one of the faces behind the statistics. The government had banned all journalists from the war zone, with the result that the reporting of the war had degenerated into a series of rival claims and numbers, with no sense of the individual human tragedy.

The hospital at Tharmapuram was tiny, just a branch clinic with a morgue built to accommodate just one body at a time. It was one of only two medical facilities trying to serve hundreds of thousands of people in the midst of war.

The injured were loaded on to metal trolleys with no sheets or mattresses. Video from the time shows two children sharing one trolley. One boy, no more than ten years old, had his stomach bandaged and an intravenous drip attached. The other, younger, boy had a bandaged hand and is sitting at the end of the bed, his eyes brimming with silent tears.

The verandah and the corridors of the tiny clinic were packed with the war-injured. In the wards, the beds were so close together that it was hard for the nurses to walk round them, but Usha thought herself lucky to have one at all because so many were lying on the floor.

While Usha spent days forced to lie face-down in the hospital bed because of the burns to her back, the Sri Lankan Army captured her childhood home town of Kilinochchi, the rebels' *de facto* capital. Government troops hadn't set foot in the town for eleven years. It was a huge blow to Usha and the Tigers.

For the army it was a psychological boost, even though every building in the town was damaged by the fierce fighting. Share prices in Colombo surged 5 per cent on the wave of optimism that the news sparked in the south. Newspapers there asked if this was the end for Sri Lanka's three-decade-long ethnic conflict. President Rajapaksa called the capture of the Tigers' main town 'an unparalleled victory', and there were celebratory parties. Spirits were only slightly dampened by a Tiger suicide bomber attacking air force headquarters.

In the crowded hospital, Usha was having the minuscule shrapnel splinters painstakingly picked out of her leg with a pin. Reassuringly, amid the chaos the nurses still wore starched white aprons over their blue short-sleeved shirts and had neat white caps pinned to their heads. Visitors squeezed in, bringing more bad news. The army had captured the whole of the strategic A9 highway – the only road linking the north and south of the island. Yet Usha still assumed the Tigers' losses were a temporary setback. Over her twenty years in the rebel movement, she'd seen various defeats and watched the Tigers bounce back. Why should it be any different this time?

It wasn't long before the doctors sent Usha home because they needed the space for more critical injuries. Today she still walks around London with two small pieces of shrapnel in her foot that they never had a chance to remove, but she's not complaining. The day after she was discharged, a shell fell just seventy-five metres from the hospital building. She was grateful to have been sent away in time. By mid-January the army had captured the little hospital.

The Tigers were steadily retreating, unable to do more than slow the government forces down. Occasionally they released videos of their fighters, wearing camouflage helmets with jungle foliage hanging off them like green dreadlocks, fiendishly spraying the enemy with machine-gun fire from behind earth bunds. The footage showed off the bloated corpses of scores of dead soldiers, young men with innocent faces, frozen by a bullet as they ran. Their captured rifles were neatly lined up as trophies to demoralise the next wave of young village boys sent out to fight. Soon there were no victories to film, and the Tiger videos concentrated on the humanitarian crisis instead, hoping the gruesome pictures would prompt international intervention.

Released from hospital, Usha, her mother and her two girls, aged six and eight, began to flee. They often slept by the roadside, spending one night near a school building, the next in a tent, the next in the grounds of an abandoned government office. Sometimes they would pass a tiny red Tamil Tiger flag fluttering in the wind and a uniformed rebel policeman, in his dark blue trousers, light blue shirt and military-style cap, gun slung over his shoulder, directing the traffic. Every few hundred metres vehicles broke down or ran out of scarce fuel. People were stuck for hours and the ambulances couldn't get through the traffic. At some points the flat road simply disappeared under lakes of dirty floodwater from the heavy monsoon rains, and people crossed in small boats. One night Usha saw a vehicle with its headlights on as it moved among the displaced people. In the pitch dark, in an area without electricity, a plane quickly spotted the light and bombed.

When the army announced it was establishing a safe zone for civilians, it didn't take Usha long to realise it was anything but safe. She decided to make for the coast, further away from the range of the deadly artillery.

Tens of thousands of civilians fled into the dense jungle on foot under heavy shelling. The journey took Usha ten days. Every time they heard the screaming of a fighter jet, flying overhead like a giant black bird of death, they would take cover in ditches, lying flat in the mud and shielding their heads with their arms. Her daughters would cover their ears with their hands to block out the terrifying roar of the planes. There was a thudding *boom* as the bomb fell and then a cloud of black smoke mixed with red dust from the earth. Usha told her children not to look, but decapitated bodies would lie by the roadside like butchered cattle. 'People would die and their families would just leave them where they fell and move on,' she recalled: there was no time for burials. She saw a hundred dead people in one place where ten shells had come whistling in with a flash, their point of impact marked by the dark grey smoke rising above the treetops. Passing the spot, they smelled the high explosive mixed with blasted wet earth.

'We had to wade through the water while there was shelling. The motorbike wouldn't move. I gave one child to a friend to carry and put the other on the bike and had to push it through the water. Death was so close it sent shivers down the back of my neck,' she says, remembering the sound of bullets whistling past.

All this time they were lucky if they were able to cook one meal a day, a tasteless, watered-down rice porridge to feed the children. By February there were no vegetables on sale, by March not even a sliver of fish, despite being quite near the coast. At the start of 2009 Usha's eldest child weighed twenty-eight kilos, by May she was less than half that weight, an eight-year-old weighing only twelve kilos. The children were always hungry, always asking for more rice porridge. 'Mummy, when we go back home will you buy potatoes and cook nice food for us?' they would ask. None of them realised they would never go home again. 'We still had hope. We thought the United Nations wouldn't let people die like this, so many of them in those months. We believed they would definitely come and save us. They had the power to save us,' she says.

At first Usha moved with food stocks, spare clothes, a photo album, a picture of her late husband and her laptop all loaded on the motor-bike. Gradually their belongings shrank to what they could carry in their hands, in February the photo album was left behind, in May the computer.

She travelled with some friends from the Tamil Tiger newspaper, which carried on printing till mid-April. Usha used the discarded aluminium foil from the printing rolls to fashion home-made toilet bowls, which she connected with a pipe to a pit. Living on the sandy strip of beach, it was easy to collect water that looked clean, by digging a hole in the sand and waiting for it to fill with water.

When they reached a new spot, the first thing was to dig a bunker or erect a shelter with sandbags. A tarpaulin cloth would cover the trench. It was hot inside and the children would beg their mothers to fan them all the time with the leaves of young palm trees. Restless and bored, they would make up any excuse to get out of the bunker, saying they needed to go to the toilet more often than was plausible. Every time an attack started, the children would start screaming in terror. By April, families had to spend the whole day in the shelter because of the shells from multi-barrelled rocket launchers.

One day in April Usha was inside the safe zone, sheltering in a bunker with a friend called Priya, who had her baby girl on her lap.

'The shelling was heavy and we all had our heads down because sand was flying everywhere. I looked up and saw Priya put her hand over her neck to stop the blood coming out. There was so much blood because she'd been hit in a vein. 'Check my baby!' she cried. The baby was dying: a shell fragment had entered the child's head and exited at the neck. There was no blood on the baby's head – it was just coming out of the mouth. I watched the baby close its eyes as its life went slowly out.' Then on the floor of the bunker Usha noticed a girl's pigtail, neatly severed by a piece of flying shrapnel. It belonged to eight-year-old Surenyah, a child whose mother was outside cooking rice. They were taken to hospital but the baby was already dead and Surenyah survived only one more day.

By now Usha's children were petrified of the noises. They still are: any loud bang and they will come running. Young as they were, they understood how tenuous their grip on life was. One day Usha over-heard the older girl tell the younger one, 'Our life is teetering on the very edge, like this,' showing her the edge of her fingernail, 'and any small thing can finish us off and push us over the edge.'

Three times Usha asked her mother if they shouldn't kill themselves by walking into the sea and drowning together. She just couldn't bear the idea of dying one by one. Every time the subject of suicide came up, Usha's eight-year-old would put them off, begging them to 'wait one more day and see what happens'.

By the final weeks of the war, in May 2009, tens of thousands of starving civilians were camped on a tiny patch of beach. There was no order to the settlement: ragged, dirty, makeshift tents were pitched at chest height, packed incredibly close. Motorbikes and vans parked amid the tents were unable to drive out because there was no longer any path free.

More and more families arrived, rushing barefoot along the hot golden sand. On one side was the beautiful sea, the waves lapping the coast, and a few beached fishing boats reminiscent of better days. It was just the kind of place a child would love to stop and paddle or build a sandcastle, but if you looked out at the horizon there was black smoke and gunboats. On the land side there were palm trees, their dark green branches swaying in the breeze, the picture of an otherwise idyllic beach. But the crackle of gunfire and children crying could be heard in the background. Everyone had their heads down in fear as they rushed through the tropical paradise that had become a living hell.

Three hundred metres back from the sea, where Usha lived, there was no breeze or shade. As they moved into May the temperature rose steadily. Farmers who'd transported their possessions on bullock carts had long ago killed their animals to eat them. Usha dug up a leafy plant that was just about edible when boiled. Firewood was running out. They resorted to pulling up roots to burn.

Still Usha thought the United Nations wouldn't let them die. She believed the rumours that a ship would come to rescue them. On 15 May it became apparent even to a fervent devotee like Usha that the end of the Tamil Tigers had come. 'We were in an area full of young dry palmyrah trees that had been set on fire by the shelling. I knew the Tigers had their ammunition nearby and feared it might explode,' she remembers. They had to move but it was dark and they couldn't find anywhere to take shelter. Every bunker they approached was already full and the people inside shouted, 'Go away; don't stay here.'

'Where can we go?' Usha shouted back in the pitch dark, until some women Tigers recognised her voice and called her over to share their bunker.

By now civilians and fighters were all mixed up in the same tiny area. Around them was the stench of death and the smell of burning vehicles. It was impossible to let the children out of the bunker; they had to let them go to the toilet in the corner of the trench. 'I am unable to understand how they tolerated it all,' Usha says now.

On 17 May, at dawn, they started to walk to the bridge that separated the rebels from the Sri Lankan Army, along with tens of thousands of people. Usha left a scene of utter devastation. Billowing grey smoke made everything look a hazy, dirty-green colour. Smouldering buses were reduced to crumpled metal skeletons. Bloodstained clothes and belongings were strewn among hastily abandoned tents and the twisted wreckage of makeshift huts. It was a beach where the only bodies lying on the sand were dead. And the bodies were many: sprawled in the open, burned, maimed, dismembered and decomposing. As Usha walked out she saw the injured by the roadside, wrapped in filthy, blood-soaked rags. 'They begged us to help,' she remembers. '"Take us, Take us!" they called out in that terrible stench. They couldn't walk and we didn't have the strength to carry them.'

Usha crossed the emerald-green lagoon into the army-controlled area, walking across a long bridge of earth built up over drainage pipes. On either side was chest-high water, home now to human remains. There was no time to think about defeat; their survival still hung in the balance. Exhausted as they were, everyone walked at an unusually brisk pace, keen to get away from the explosions and gunfire. Barbed wire and sandbags greeted them. As they passed the helmeted soldiers, some Tamil refugees looked up into their faces, wondering how they were going to be treated. They'd been told by the Tigers not to trust the army and were frightened. Usha didn't want to look the enemy in the eye, she just wanted to melt into the crowd.

In the tropical heat, they were soon desperate for drinking water. Through the barbed wire, Usha saw a small pond, but the soldiers warned the civilians: 'Some of your people died in there – do you want to drink that?' There were people so parched that they went and drank from the pond anyway, just as Lokeesan was forced to drink from the corpse-polluted lagoon.

Usha's elderly mother was hardly able to remain upright, she was so weak. Supporting her and the children and carrying their tiny bag was not easy as they walked for two kilometres along a narrow barbed-wire corridor under the watchful eye of armed soldiers, posted every few metres to prevent them escaping. The line of bedraggled, skeletal Tamil refugees came to a crowded field and the army poured drinking water for them into two small fishing boats. Usha gave her children a small polythene shopping bag and they managed to beg a little water from someone else who'd collected some in the scrum.

They spent two nights sleeping on the bare ground in that field crammed with bodies. People who were normally extremely shy just went to the toilet where they were standing. There were faeces and urine everywhere. The soldiers came and threw food parcels over the barbed wire. Those who could catch them ate; those who couldn't had to watch the others eat.

On the second night, Usha recognised some well-known figures from the Tiger movement surrendering. They were with a Catholic priest in his seventies, still wearing his white clerical robes, Father Joseph Francis. The Tigers thought the priest's presence meant they'd be safe. They were wrong: all of them disappeared without trace.

After two days, buses arrived to transport the refugees. Only the elderly and children were allowed to leave; those of fighting age, like Usha, had to stay back. Usha's mother started to lead the girls away. The children screamed so much that a kind policeman took pity and allowed them to go back to fetch their mother – he probably assumed a mother couldn't be a terrorist. Usha was standing with a friend when her children rushed back, and automatically one girl grabbed Usha and the other seized Usha's friend, pretending she was her mother. 'How smart they were,' she marvelled later, impressed by their quick thinking in saving the other woman as well.

They were put onto a bus so crowded that people stood packed in the aisle, drenched with sweat. The journey should have taken two or three hours but the bus kept stopping, making it an ordeal that lasted a day and a night. Finally they reached the military checkpoint, where a loudspeaker announcement in Tamil told people to dismount and sit on the roadside. A voice said, 'If you spent even one day with the Tigers, go over to the right-hand-side queue. Own up now, or if we find out later it will be much worse for you!'[1]

Usha and her family joined the Tamil Tiger line, along with large numbers of people who feared being caught out later on. They were fighters, family members and civilians who'd worked in the rebel admin-istration. Masked Tamil rebels who'd switched sides were scouring the lines for familiar faces. Stinking, dirty and thin after months of no food,

Usha was hard to recognise as a rebel. When she later came to buy a new pair of jeans in London, she found she'd dropped six sizes.

'Why are you in this queue?' snapped the unfriendly Sinhalese policewoman in her heavy khaki twill uniform. Usha explained her husband had been a Tiger but was martyred. She failed to mention she was also in the movement. 'You don't need to be in this queue. Go over there!' the policewoman ordered. Usha was strip-searched and registered as a civilian. Soon she was one of 282,000 Tamils detained in what was then the largest refugee camp in the world, Manik Farm.

Trained to be observant in enemy territory, Usha remembered every detail of the camp. Each of the zones was sandwiched between the road on one side and a little river, adjoining a forest. Women found it difficult to bathe because the wells were in full view of the male soldiers. Some went to wash early in the morning in the river at the back of the camp. Usha heard stories of rape. Sometimes she says the single girls clubbed together, thinking there was safety in numbers, but that only made them more vulnerable: if a tent or shed contained only young women, it drew attention to the fact that they had no male protectors, and also suggested to the authorities that they could be female fighters. The tin sheds used to house some refugees at least had a string to tie the door shut at night, but the tents were open to anyone.

Asked by a foreign journalist about the allegations of sexual abuse, Professor Rajiva Wijesinha, then Secretary of the Sri Lankan Ministry of Disaster Management, replied whimsically, 'We have received a report that a soldier went into a tent at eleven p.m. and came out at three in the morning. It could have been sex for favours, or it could have been a discussion on Ancient Greek philosophy, we don't know.'[2] It was clear the government wasn't too bothered by the allegations of sexual abuse, which had been levelled since the very start of the war. On another occasion, the same professor blamed aid workers, or NGOs as they're called, saying: 'There are a few blue-eyed children in that camp so you will know that some of the NGOs have had a jolly good time.'[3] While government officials joked about allegations of rape, international aid agencies such as the United Nations had severely restricted access and were not allowed to do refugee-protection work. The handful of local charities allowed in to Manik Farm were not permitted to take vehicles inside the hundred-acre site, severely hampering their work. Journalists were barred except on occasional guided tours. Few Tamil inmates dared speak out about what they saw, fearful they would simply disappear.

As Manik Farm filled up, thousands of Tamils from all over Sri Lanka arrived in the heavily fortified garrison town of Vavuniya, thirty-three kilometres away, searching for their relatives from the war zone. They had no idea who was alive and who dead. Visitors were only allowed to stand outside the fence of the camp, separated by two fences of barbed wire a metre apart.

The camp was divided into different zones as more people arrived, but those suspected of being rebels tended to be put in Zone 4, where security was tighter. Usha was detained in Zone 2, where it was just possible to touch the person on the other side and pass food and even mobile phones across. The phones had to be hidden, sometimes buried underground, to keep them from the army. The soldiers, though, would happily rent out their own phones for a price and even take money to charge handsets. On her second day in the camp, Usha paid to get a call through to her brother in London – the same brother who so narrowly escaped during the 1983 riots. He thought her only option was to go abroad. He telephoned relatives in Sri Lanka, who made plans to smuggle Usha out of the camp.

Meanwhile former rebels like Usha were being identified by pro-government Tamil paramilitaries and taken away for questioning. Some Tamil civilians were also turning the Tigers in to the military, in revenge for their children having been forcibly recruited during the war. One of Usha's friends escaped by bribing the police to ignore her climbing out through the barbed wire at the crowded visitors' area. 'Without paying there was no escape unless it was your dead body going out of the camp,' Usha says, adding that every day at least thirty people in each of the five zones were escaping, hidden in the rubbish trucks, the water tankers, the ambulances and even the mortuary van.

Tamils were detained by the military as a potential security threat, but the soldiers made huge profits by letting them escape. They knew family members outside would sell gold or property to save their lives. Some who escaped were caught and jailed, others were blackmailed by the smugglers to pay even more money.

After a while the camp authorities released anyone over sixty, so Usha got her mother to leave. Then she found a group happy to include her in their escape plan because it meant they got a discount on the price. Usha needed to move fast because her elder daughter was sick, loosing weight rapidly after jaundice and severe vomiting.

'One by one, so as not to be too obvious, we deposited the children in a hut near the river at the back of the camp. It was night. They told us to bring a bottle of water, some biscuits and some new clothes to change into before we reached town so we wouldn't arrive looking like refugees. My mother brought us smart new clothes and sandals with heels.'

While they were waiting one of the smugglers, a drunken Tamil construction worker, summoned a pretty girl to follow him to a toolshed. Usha volunteered to go in her place. The man hoped to extort some extra money from Usha's relatives outside the camp, but she pretended to have forgotten their telephone number.

At two in the morning the smugglers, one of whom was very drunk, led them to the back perimeter fence. In total there were fifteen refugees breaking out of the camp. Usha's children were absolutely silent, gripping her hands so tightly they went numb. Everyone got down on their bellies to crawl under the barbed wire and then along the ground for ten metres to reach the riverbank. Just as they were on their hands and knees, a guard dog started barking. It looked as if the game was up. The soldier on night watch, who had been paid off in advance, calmly walked out of the sentry box, switched off the light and took the noisy dog away.

Usha struggled across the river, carrying her children, slipping on the rocks in the chest-high water. She didn't know the other people in the group at all. On the other side, sopping wet, they walked along the riverbank in the dark for a while and then sat down for a rest. That was when they heard a wild elephant crashing about in the jungle behind them. Luckily it went off in another direction.

The guide took them on a detour through the trees, which turned out to be a mistake. Soon they were lost. For the next two days they walked round and round in circles, unable to find their way, all the while being devoured by mosquitoes. They climbed trees to try and get their bearings and listened for the sound of traffic. All the water and biscuits were finished and the children were crying for food.

Eventually they traced their way to a road, where they hid, waiting for the smuggler to fetch transport to take them to town. The next morning he returned with several auto-rickshaws. As soon as Usha got into one, the driver started pestering her for the names of her relatives in town, hoping to make a little extra money from blackmail. It saddened Usha that her fellow-Tamils wanted to exploit her when she'd sacrificed so much to fight for their rights.

Reaching Vavuniya, Usha asked the driver to drop her off in a busy public place. Her cousin brought the money sent by her brother to pay the smugglers.[4] He arrived wearing his motorbike helmet with the visor down to hide his face. Usha waited a while to make sure he wasn't followed. She bought her starving daughters ice cream to pass the time. Then she got in a taxi, drove past her cousin's house and only then got out and walked back, checking nobody was watching.

Vavuniya is a dusty, dry town with a frontier feel, the last place you'd fill up the petrol tank before heading into rebel territory. Predominately Tamil, it's crammed with Sinhalese soldiers and fortified army camps surrounded by barbed wire and sandbagged watchtowers. When Usha arrived the President's portrait was plastered all over roundabouts, bill-boards and buses: the hero who'd crushed the terrorists.

For five days Usha hid, spending each night with a different family to avoid detection. A friendly doctor wrote a letter saying Usha's daughter had to travel to the capital for urgent medical treatment. They bribed a local official to issue a certificate saying she was a permanent resident of Vavuniya; without this, it would be impossible to travel through all the army checkpoints to the capital.

Usha, her girls, her mother and an aunt made their way to Colombo. They had plenty of relatives in the capital but didn't stay with them because family members would be obliged to file a police report, informing the authorities that Tamils from the north were staying in their homes. Even in a hotel they had to register with the police and pay bribes to extend the registration.

Usha already had a joint passport with her children and went straight to the British High Commission to apply for a visa. Knowing how hard it was for Tamils to get visas to the UK, even though she'd been there once before, she decided to try the Indian High Commission as well, but they wanted separate passports for each of the children.

The Sri Lankan passport office is a shabby building on the seafront, normally crowded with nervous young Sinhalese women applying for papers to work abroad as housemaids. By August 2009, the government knew that Tamils hoping to escape the country desperately needed passports, and planted informants to spot former rebels. Usha immediately noticed a senior Tiger fighter, known as Yogi, working with the police there. It was unnerving, as they'd known each other well. 'I think he knew me even in that dilapidated condition,' she said, 'but he didn't point me out to them.' She couldn't help wondering what they had done to Yogi to induce him to cooperate. That day Usha saw two rebels applying for passports. 'One of the boys I knew really well but he didn't even look me in the eye, as if he was scared of me.' Former comrades could no longer trust one another; anyone could be betrayed by anyone else.

Usha was eventually granted a six-month visitor visa for the United Kingdom. First her mother went to India: if Usha was caught at the airport on the way out, her mother didn't want to be in Sri Lanka to be arrested too. Just before boarding her flight, Usha borrowed a mobile phone and called her family to confirm she'd made it through immigration. She was lucky: at that point the authorities hadn't yet posted rebel informers at the airport.

Once the plane took off and she saw the ocean underneath, Usha started to breathe again. Her relief didn't last long: now she was terrified of immigration in London. The anxiety was catching; even the children didn't speak much during the eleven-hour flight.

At Heathrow, Usha was pulled aside for questioning for an hour. Why had her return flight to Sri Lanka been booked for a date three days after her six-month visa ran out? The immigration officer also didn't understand why Usha had taken her children on a trip during the school term. She tried to explain she wasn't planning to return to Sri Lanka, but she didn't know the word for asylum. It was ten at night and there was no translator available. Usha's brother, waiting outside, started to panic.

After being bombed and starved, leading two children out of a war zone though rotting corpses and crawling under barbed wire, it looked like Usha was about to fall at the very last hurdle, undone by a wrongly booked air ticket. Suddenly the immigration officer had a change of heart. It was the end of his shift and he wanted to go home. He told Usha to go and sort out the ticket once she was inside the country. After months of hell, she was finally safe.

Usha calls this her *Great Escape* story, referring to the epic Second World War film. The first time we met, she compared the end of the war to an Xbox video game, with gratuitous shooting and explosions. It was a simile purely for my benefit because nobody had Xboxes in northern Sri Lanka. Over warm drinks and shortbread biscuits in a Costa Coffee shop we talked with the help of a translator, a retired teacher whose father had been assassinated – probably by the Tigers in their early days, but that didn't stop her clasping Usha in a huge hug. We swapped news about who was alive or dead. Every time the Indian waitress came to collect detritus from the tables, Usha and the translator lowered their voices and looked over their shoulders, worried about who was listening. It has taken Usha a long time to feel safe in London.

Adjusting has been hard. She was horrified to see some Tamil families give their children pocket money that would feed an entire family in Sri Lanka. Extravagant birthday parties, saris worn only once for a wedding, new cars – all of them shocked her, knowing the desperate poverty of Tamils affected by war. Perhaps the worst surprise was seeing young Tamil boys involved in gang violence, fighting each other and committing crimes with no sense of unity or political purpose.

Defeat has been a bitter disappointment to swallow. 'I went into the rebel movement with the conviction of doing something meaningful. Day and night I worked, and now I am really sad all this effort has gone to waste,' she says. 'It's unbearable, there were no results. Some of these Tamils here don't realise how hard those cadres worked and put up with being away from home for long periods. Those working here in London are not united even now. There are so many differences between these groups,' she continues, referring to the splits in the diaspora groups now fighting each other for political control and the Tigers' considerable financial assets abroad. 'They were all united before the war ended, but now there are so many factions and all of them say, "I am right – do this." Differences, corruption and struggle for power are ruining our community.'

Usha does not accept the Tigers' own role in their downfall: the assassinations, the child recruitment, the human shields, the suicide attacks on civilians in the south. They are still shining freedom fighters for her and she seems to have no regret about her role in producing rebel propaganda. Instead she blames Tiger supporters abroad for giving the rebel leaders bad political advice, encouraging them to think that the international community would intervene and prevent their annihilation.

At her spartan, impersonal home in south London, Usha cuts a lonely figure. She struggles to live in the present. 'Only my body is here; my mind is still there,' she tries to explain. 'I don't want to be where people are laughing and having fun.' On New Year's Eve, Usha's eldest daughter woke up screaming when she heard the fireworks. It was the same way she'd screamed in panic when they'd been shelled.

Over the course of several days Usha told me her story, never once shedding a tear. At the end I asked if there was anything she wanted to add. She started talking about the worldwide uproar over a woman who was caught on film putting her neighbour's pet cat inside a rubbish bin. The video had gone viral on the Internet. 'Human beings have been slaughtered in the thousands in Sri Lanka,' she said, 'and nothing has happened at all, nothing.' The contrast between the outrage over the mistreated cat and the indifference to Tamils was more than she could cope with, and she broke down in tears for the first time.

Widows

Government Figures

Female-headed Households[1]

Vavuniya	3,989
Mullaitivu	3,364
Kilinochchi	6,044
Jaffna	2,451
Mannar	3,233
Batticoloa	26,965
Ampara	235
Trincomalee	14,435
Total:	60,716

Children in Orphanages[2]

Vavuniya	1,095
Mullaitivu	80
Mannar	309
Kilinochchi	343
Total:	1,827

Figures from the Deputy Minister of Women's Affairs of the Provincial Council of the East

East:	46,000 widows
North:	40,000 widows
Total:	86,000 widows[3]

Figures from Child Development and Women's Affairs Minister of
Sri Lanka, Tissa Karalliyadda

East: 42,565 widows (though not all due to war)
North: 19,936 widows
Total: 59,000+ widows[4]

United Nations Figures[5]

29,742 widows in the Jaffna Peninsula, of whom:

89	less than 20 years old
1,190	21–30 years old
2,945	31–40 years old
4,506	41–50 years old
7,034	51–60 years old
13,978	60+ years old

The Centre for Women and Development, Jaffna Survey

North: 40,000 female-headed households. Over half are single parents under 30 years supporting their own and extended families.

The Volunteer

Difficult times bring to the fore people's strengths, their quirks and weaknesses. Sitting in his wheelchair, Korben observed the oddities of human behaviour from the vantage point of a man being escorted by others through the stampede of misery. Where some in his situation might have despaired, he used humour to get through the ordeal.

'You needed something to laugh about,' says Korben, who has a knack for relating how ordinary people talked and behaved in the bunkers. There were comic moments even as hundreds of thousands camped outdoors under daily bombardment. Like the woman who bought a fridge very cheaply in the chaos of the last few weeks, thinking she'd snapped up a wonderful bargain. Later she was injured and Korben remembers seeing her in the refugee camp, constantly on the lookout for a better wheelchair. 'She was just that type of person,' he says.

People had lost everything in the war but that didn't stop some trying to profit as prices skyrocketed. Korben met a man selling Maliban biscuits, the cheapest cream crackers in Sri Lanka and a favourite with children. 'He was asking sixteen hundred rupees [£8] for a packet that's normally eighty rupees,' he says. 'I just laughed. I couldn't possibly afford that price. I told him to keep it for himself!' However he did find himself willing to pay a ridiculous price for unripe green bananas that were normally just plucked from any tree. Now he laughs at himself for leaving home with live chickens tied to his vehicle that he never ate because they'd been reared in his garden and were like pets.

Some people held on to their prized possessions like their laptops and television sets till the very end, even though food was the only currency with value. There was a woman who pushed her precious motorbike out of the war zone on the last day, holding up thousands behind her as they all tried to escape under fire. 'Do you want to ride around on your motorbike in Colombo?' they teased, until she finally saw sense and abandoned it at the edge of the path.

By contrast there were those who were selfless and generous with what little they had left – people who shared their homes or last meals with strangers or risked their lives to build shelters for the disabled like Korben, without charging for their labour. Fishermen spent hours struggling to get a catch, and then gave half the fish to the injured, who badly needed protein to recover, without expecting money even though prices had trebled.

Polio had confined Korben to a wheelchair from an early age. In war his disability became even more incapacitating. Even the mundane aspects of life, like going to the toilet, became a challenge. Surviving at all was a miracle for a man who couldn't run for cover. Paralysed from the waist down, Korben needed a sitting-style toilet, rather than an Asian squat toilet. As he fled, this became increasingly hard to find. If he did locate one, sitting on it was risky and stressful because he couldn't move fast enough if an attack began. 'Even while I was on the toilet they fired artillery and I couldn't manage to do it. You need peace to go to the bathroom. You can wash your face in a hurry but *that* needs some time and peace of mind!' he says.

A thirty-eight-year-old engineer, with a round, youthful face and animated expression, Korben is scrupulously precise. I went to see him in Europe nearly two years after the war, but I can't tell you which country he lives in because Korben, which is not his real name, was one of a handful of expatriate Tamils from Britain, Australia, Holland, Germany and New Zealand caught up in the fighting, and that makes it easy for the authorities in Sri Lanka to identify his family, still living in Colombo. Although born in Sri Lanka, Korben was sent abroad alone at the age of fourteen in the late 1980s, when the technical college in Jaffna where he studied was closed as the civil war started to engulf the north. Korben's mother desperately wanted to give him a good education so he could support himself, but had no idea when he left Sri Lanka that it would be thirteen long, painful years before they'd meet again. Korben has spent half his life abroad, which meant he saw the war with the eyes of an outsider.

He is meticulous and cautious. As he puts it, if the speed limit on a road is fifty kilometres an hour, he will only ever drive at forty-five. He's adamant that it's his duty to do charity work for those less fortunate than himself and is confident telling his life story in English, which is his third or fourth language.

Taking time off work, Korben brought his family to meet me at the tiny provincial airport. I knew he'd be in a wheelchair but I wasn't prepared for the fact that his beautiful, stern wife, her long black hair tied in a bun at the nape of her neck, was also injured, having lost a kneecap in an early phase of the war. It meant she couldn't bend her leg, and had to drag it completely straight as she walked, pushing his wheelchair with well-practised, speedy determination. After only a few months abroad she still looked uncomfortable in her pink thermal fleece and slim jeans, unused to wrapping up against the cold. On Korben's lap sat a gorgeous, bouncy three-and-a-half-year-old boy, who thought it perfectly normal that neither of his parents could run after him. He was a child who, when he first came to Europe, asked anxiously if 'they' were going to come and take away his new toys.

Today they live in a one-bedroom rented flat in a nondescript tower block on the outskirts of an industrial town. High up on one wall of the sitting room, as in many expatriate households, is a small photo of the dead Tiger leader. The photo carries a range of nuanced meanings – from general solidarity with the Tamil nationalist struggle to uncritical adoration of the Leader, as he's called. Privately Sri Lankan Tamils are still in turmoil, working out where they stand in relation to the Tigers after the bloodbath of 2009, caused in part by the Leader's adamant refusal to surrender or release civilians. For Korben there seemed to be no contradiction in sitting under Velupillai Prabhakaran's photo while talking about how the Tigers forced teenagers to fight, cruelly ripping families apart.

Until his first trip home, Korben had little to do with the rebels. It was 2003 when he stopped off in rebel territory on the way back from a trip to Jaffna, curious to learn how disabled people there lived. He was astonished to discover that his wheelchair afforded him respect, not social stigma. In 2004 he gave up his job abroad and returned to Sri Lanka to teach disabled and orphaned children. He married a local nursery teacher and they built a house, planting neem, jackfruit, mango and passionfruit trees as well as a vegetable garden, literally putting down roots for the future. In 2007 baby Suben was born.

By mid-2008, tractorloads of bedraggled refugees were streaming into Kilinochchi, fleeing the fighting. When shells started to fall just a hundred metres away from Korben's house they left to stay with friends, blithely assuming they'd be back within a month. They packed their belongings into Korben's specially designed auto-rickshaw, adapted so he could operate it with his hands rather than his feet. 'We took all the child's toys and two of everything – plates, cups, cooking pots – like Noah's Ark!' he says. Even his wife's special wedding sari went with them. By the end they'd discarded everything except a thermos flask and a few baby clothes.

It was as a refugee that little Suben learned to walk. Korben and his family were constantly on the move, on one occasion missing shells that fell just 500 metres away from a food queue. In January they fled at three in the morning in the pitch dark after hearing from the neighbours that the army could overrun the area at any minute. Finding a suitable toilet was a nightmare and for a while Korben had to separate from his family and stay with a group of disabled Tigers because they were the only ones with a toilet he could use. They'd paid fifty times the normal price for a bag of cement to build it. A boy blind in both eyes and another with no arms below the elbows insisted on drawing water from the well so Korben could wash. Unable to do it himself, he was forced again and again to accept the kindness of strangers. Now in exile, Korben wonders what happened to all those people who risked their lives for him.

At the end of January 2009, as the Sri Lankan Army made a major push to capture the main road running along the coast, a shell hit the corner of the house where Korben and twenty-five other people were sheltering. The soldiers were in the jungle on the other side of the road and for two nights running fought hard to advance, using artillery and then rifle fire. Spent cartridges were falling on the ground close by, and Korben realised the soldiers were firing in the air to frighten civilians into leaving. Terrified of getting trapped, he fled across a shallow river in his auto-rickshaw with what felt like hundreds of thousands of people. By the path were dead, bloated cattle left rotting in the sun. One small child asked his father what kind of animal lay there, unable to recognise the massively swollen carcass as a cow, and his father told him it was an elephant, trying to convert grotesque abnormality into something friendly.

The resonating *boom* of a bomb hitting the earth greeted them in the next village. 'I wondered what kind of place this was that we were all so keen to reach. I saw a bomb blast close by but everyone just ignored it. It had become part of normal life here too. This place was no safer than the last, but it was so crowded with people that it was hard to find a place even to park my auto-rickshaw.' They spent the night in an abandoned bunker but the next day a friendly rebel advised them to move on.

They were lucky to get out. People fleeing down the same road the following day were attacked. Korben met the survivors later on, among them a mother who had lost three children there and couldn't even spend two minutes with their bodies because she still had two more children to save. 'Others just grabbed a hole and put the remains in it. You couldn't call them bodies any more – they were pieces of meat or flesh. Then they'd plant a cross on top, hoping one day they'd be able to come back and see the spot where their loved one was buried.'

Korben always tried to move as far away from the fighting as possible, paying labourers to build him a reinforced bunker. If he'd known the village he was in, Iranapalai, would soon fall to the Sri Lankan Army he wouldn't have bothered. 'We never thought it would end the way it did; everyone thought the international community would not allow such a massacre,' he says.

In early February their experience of the fighting was still just in the form of news from other refugees. Then one morning as they emerged from their bunker a little girl ran up and showed them the plastic chair Korben's wife had been sitting on the previous day. It had a huge hole made by a piece of shrapnel. It was too unsafe to stay. Korben saw an old man weep as he left behind the only photograph he had of his dead son, who'd been a Tiger. He couldn't take it with him because if he was caught with the photo the army would suspect his other sons of being rebels too. Little did he know that all his sons were to die in the coming months.

Now the shelling continued day and night. People talked about who had died, but no longer bothered to mention the injured, who thought themselves lucky if they could be evacuated on a Red Cross ship. One day Korben bent forward and a piece of shrapnel the size of an orange whizzed past just centimetres away, narrowly missing him. Even the toilet was hit by shrapnel. The simple functions of daily life, like washing, took him much longer than an able-bodied person and now involved dicing with death.

They moved along a street lined with mud, upon which hundreds of people had pitched tents. 'It was so dirty you wouldn't even go to the toilet there; I was shocked to see people living there.' Along the way they met a lady whose husband was a Sea Tiger, a member of the rebel naval wing. She promised to ask her husband to help them build a new shelter.

The tiny coastal villages were so crowded with tents it was impossible to see the ocean from thirty metres away. 'People gathered along the shore, hoping the United Nations would come and save them by sea,' says Korben. The place in which he settled didn't even have a name until thousands of refugees arrived and named it 'Twin Palms'. Every spot was already reserved; they had to sleep in the auto-rickshaw, sitting up.

Unable to find somewhere safe to settle with the baby, they were already losing hope and it was only February. Death was breathing down the backs of their necks. They just couldn't imagine how much worse it would get in the coming months. 'My wife said let's commit suicide at this point. Even with the baby, she felt hopeless,' he recounts in a matter-of-fact tone.

Just as they were at the end of their tether, the Sea Tiger arrived, sent by his wife to help find a space, build them a bunker and rig up a mobile toilet.

They moved right down to Mullivaikkal, the last rebel village to fall to the army at the end of the war. 'We were early settlers,' Korben quips. Over the next few months their life fell into a surreal routine. Korben read the children nursery stories and families living in tents just metres apart would pay social calls on one another.

At this point, still hopeful of returning to his old life, Korben was transporting his solar-power panel and television with him in the auto rickshaw. He found a call centre run by the Tigers and grabbed the opportunity to telephone his sister, now married and living in Denmark. He didn't dare call his mother in Colombo directly, lest it land her into trouble with the authorities. Korben told his sister every-thing was fine. There was no point in alarming her as she couldn't do anything.

In the bunker he listened to the radio avidly, even though the price of batteries had increased tenfold. The hope was that the Indian elections, a few weeks away, might bring changes that would help Tamils, if politicians came to power who were less implacably opposed to the Tigers. President Obama had just come into office in America, and Korben thought that might strengthen the European Union, which he believed had tried to confront Sri Lanka over its human-rights record but had been blocked by China and India.

'I didn't believe Obama was going to send a ship convoy to save us, as others did, but I was still hoping the international community wouldn't allow such a massacre. The Tigers talked about how heavy the army casualties had been and I thought the Sinhalese government wouldn't be able to sustain this…We thought if the Tigers held the army back, they wouldn't need to free all the land. If they could just keep the army bogged down, then the world would eventually react and we would have a peace process again.'

Korben tuned in to Indian radio, the BBC and the rebel station Voice of Tigers. In mid-April, listening to the shortwave radio while under very heavy fire, he heard the BBC Tamil Service announcer say there was a forty-eight-hour ceasefire for the Sri Lankan new year. It was surreal listening to the UN Secretary-General praising the Sri Lankan government for observing a temporary truce while they could hear incoming shells.[1] The reporting on the war was so divorced from reality that the Sri Lankan government could assert there was no fighting just when it was heaviest. The issue of the Tigers releasing the civilian population during the ceasefire never arose because the fighting never let up long enough for anyone to get out of the bunkers. By now the army were just three or four kilometres away.

Living by the sea, they survived off rice and a little fish, cooking on outdoor fires, digging up roots for fuel when wood ran short. Korben was impressed by the fishermen who shared out their catch with everyone in the queue, so nobody was left out. 'They were very friendly, not like the Tamils in town,' he says. Food prices had gone crazy. Coconut powder was now Rs. 12,000 a packet (£60), roughly what it would cost for a person to escape from the detention camp after the war. Soon it became impossible to find milk powder at all. Korben knew a couple who'd been killed, leaving four children behind. He met their relative desperately searching for milk to keep the seven-month-old baby alive.[2]

In mid-April, mothers of young children were queuing for milk powder when they came under artillery fire just 700 metres from the army's forward defence line. According to other accounts, at least forty pregnant women and children were among the dead.[3] Korben was in his auto-rickshaw looking for impromptu food stalls when he saw Dr Niron's crowded makeshift hospital suddenly overwhelmed by the influx of patients. The injured were mixed in with the dead as they arrived on tractors: 'The hardest thing for me was a mother there. I didn't know if she was dead but she was just lying, propped up against a tree, motionless. There was a small child next to her, the same age as mine, who tried to remove her blouse and feed from her breast. I could see she was injured and to me she looked dead, though I couldn't be sure. It was very, very shocking.'

Amid the abnormality and horror, civilians tried to adjust to the routine of the nightly onslaught. First the military would illuminate the sky with flares, a sure sign that an attack was about to start. After an hour of pounding artillery strikes, there would be an interval in which they'd try to catch some sleep, and then at 2 a.m. another hour of incoming shells, followed by a further bout at 5 a.m. Korben says that in just a week more than forty-five people died in a 300-metre area around his tent. One night the family who'd moved in next to them were sheltering in their half-built bunker when a shell hit a nearby coconut tree, spraying sand, small leaves and dust into Korben's bunker. In the morning they found all eight members of that family dead, and pieces of their flesh spread around the entrance to their bunker. Some days it was too dangerous even to go to the shore because the Sri Lankan Navy attacked from the sea. People started crossing over to the army areas, willing to risk being shot by the rebels, who wanted to stop them escaping at any cost. Military defeat was guaranteed now, but the Tiger leader still tried to use his own people as a bargaining chip with the international community to extract political concessions.

'The Tigers didn't allow people to use the coast to escape. They said, "If we keep together there will be some international intervention. Otherwise there will be no more ethnic conflict, just refugee camps where food and water will be the only issues for Tamils." They stopped people crossing the front lines but one time the people gave the Tigers a thousand rupees and said, "If you can buy milk powder for our children we will stay with you; we don't want to see them starve." The Tigers had no answer. I heard they allowed some to cross that time.'

Korben knew the Tigers were shooting at civilians who tried to flee to the government side, but he believed they just fired at the ground or above people's heads rather than aiming to kill. However, he remembers people were furious with the rebels for losing so much territory so fast: 'Everyone was very hopeful they would repel the Sri Lankan

Army, but they saw the army always moving forwards and the rebel area getting smaller and smaller and they were very angry. They even used swear words about the Tigers, which they wouldn't normally do. They were totally fed up and needed someone to blame.'

In a queue for the meagre rations sent in by the World Food Programme that stretched for more than a kilometre, Korben saw an old lady waiting patiently. When she received just fifty grams of sugar and 250 grams of rice, patently not enough to feed a family, she was outraged and said out loud: 'I had better go over to the army side and sell my body to get enough to eat.' Korben was shocked to see a respectable Tamil grandmother say such a thing in public; it was a sign of utter desperation.

He also witnessed livid parents screaming at the Tigers for snatching their children away to fight. 'The Tigers tried to explain how important it was, but the mothers would never accept it. They took them by force.' When families were arranging marriages to protect their children from being recruited, 'They did it without any proper checks first,' says Korben. 'Normally Tamils spend ages doing horoscopes but in those days they didn't even find out if the boy had a past or had been married before; without any questions, they just married them off.' One girl he knew wore her mother's gold wedding chain to fool the rebel recruiters into thinking she was married, but they soon discovered the deception.

Some learned to accept their fate, like the teenage sniper who used to stop for a chat and play with Korben's baby son. In the mass recruitment drive of 2007, her family had been ordered to give one child to the movement. As the eldest she'd been selected, though her mother tried hard to save her. She would hide the girl in a large travelling bag whenever Tigers came to the neighbourhood, but her legs were too long and stuck out. The 'travelling-bag girl', as he dubbed her, told Korben her story, laughing as if it were a joke and not a tragedy.

The Tiger camps were just across the main road but it was too crowded for them to move their artillery guns around, so Korben says there wasn't much outgoing fire. A family of five was killed near him and every day from inside the bunker he heard shrapnel and aerial bombs hitting the earth.

As everyone else inched down the coast to Mullivaikkal, Korben met friends from earlier bouts of displacement who recognised his wheelchair, including the Sea Tiger's wife, who'd lost absolutely everything in an attack. The area was so packed that she was forced to camp in a stinking corner that had been the communal toilet. She gave her old saris to a woman tailor to stitch into sandbags overnight, only to return the next day and find her dead body sprawled on the ground, blood all over her sewing machine. This is the same tailor whom Uma saw being blown to pieces.

Korben's wife managed to buy some prawns, and they were just about to tuck into them when they saw an exhausted mother with a small baby the same age as theirs arriving. On an impulse, she invited the total stranger into their bunker to share the meal with them. 'My wife was smiling at me,' Korben remembers, 'On the one hand she was happy to be able to share the food and on the other hand she was so delighted to be eating prawns again after so many months.'

Food was running out, even for someone like Korben who had money. His savings were in the rebel Bank of Tamil Eelam, which continued to function in a hut in the improvised shanty town that had sprung up along the beach. Korben drove his auto-rickshaw right up to the door of the bank – a structure made of sandbags and coconut-tree trunks – handed over his savings book to withdraw cash and saw that the clerks had printed out the computerised lists of all the customer accounts and balances. They disbursed the money very quickly. 'It was withdrawals only,' jokes Korben, aware that nobody would be depositing funds in the soon-to-be-defunct bank of a non-existent state.

By May the shell attacks were heavier than they'd seen before; the Sri Lankan Army was just one and a half kilometres away now. 'I don't know if I was just not thinking about it or I was a fool or what. I was still heaping up hope that this was not the end. There was a belief among the people that if the civilian casualties reached a certain amount, then the United Nations would step in and do something. The Tigers had lost a lot of fighters, but I did not think it was the end of our people. I thought all we had lost would have some meaning and the world would do something.'

There was no intervention, just another attack that sent blood pouring through the roof of their bunker. Nine people were killed and more injured. They tried to give first aid, but there was too much rifle fire to take survivors to the hospital, by now hardly functioning. For days they were unable to leave the bunker because of the constant barrage. People who still had food started bartering; Korben swapped some rice for fish for his baby, who hadn't eaten protein for a fortnight. When his wife was away, he discreetly handed the family in the next-door bunker a slip of paper with the telephone number of his sister in Denmark. He asked them to inform her if they were killed in one of the nightly attacks.

The swarming flies and sickly-sweet smell suggested the bodies had been lying there for some days. There was mud on the ground, and, if you looked closely, body parts too. Leaning back in his broken wheel-chair, Korben gripped his two-year-old son, who was perched on top of the overnight bag on his lap. His disabled wife jolted the wheelchair forward, tilting it on its back two wheels because the front ones wouldn't move any more. As she struggled to push his heavy weight along the rutted path, Korben covered his toddler's eyes so he wouldn't see the pieces of human flesh. Shells were crashing down behind them.

It was 16 May 2009. Thousands of Tamil civilians, desperate to get out of the war zone, gambled with gunfire and explosions to cross over to the army area. Korben passed an elderly lady on the side of the road who'd collapsed with sheer exhaustion and hunger, her body giving up on her at the last stage. A man was shouting, 'If you can't walk then we will leave you here. I've lost enough people in my family, so stand up and walk if you want to come with us!' There was no respect any more; it was an ugly, undignified struggle for survival. Korben was lucky to have his wife to look after him.

A small group who'd gone ahead had been fired on. Korben thought it safer to use the main road because the Sri Lankan soldiers would be able to see them clearly as they tried to escape. On the first attempt they gave up, returning to the bunker. Then they tried another route, a muddy gravel path. On the way they had to duck for cover from the bullets and lie on the ground, waiting for a lull. If Korben got down on the floor, it needed several men to lift him back into the wheelchair. For about a kilometre they followed the immense crowd.

There were a lot of injured fighters lying around. They had 'injuries of all kinds, eyes, legs, things you have never seen before', he says. Knowing how well they'd been treated in the past, Korben was shocked to see wounded rebels abandoned. The rudimentary hospital had stopped functioning and all the Tigers could do was move their injured forward and then leave them by the roadside with an attendant.

At this point, so late in the day, the rebels had finally allowed everyone to leave. Korben spotted many Tiger leaders escaping with their families. As he was going, he caught sight of 'the travelling-bag girl' who'd played with his son. Still wearing her uniform, she was saying goodbye to her mother and father. It was hard to watch because he knew she'd been forced to join the rebels, but had now decided to stay on and fight to the end. She spotted Korben and understood he was leaving. 'Normally we would have said goodbye but at that moment I didn't have any words. I can still remember her eyes. It was terrible: someone so young choosing death.'

Later he often thought of her, when he saw the pictures of half-naked dead women fighters on the Internet. The disturbing videos, taken by the victorious soldiers, strongly suggested sexual abuse and Korben found it hard to see the women, some of whom he'd seen alive and walking around in their uniforms, sprawled dead in the mud, stripped of their uniforms, their breasts exposed, cold eyes staring out. The lewd commentary by the soldiers left little to the imagination and they could be seen kicking the corpses as they dumped them unceremoniously onto the back of tractors.

As they moved on through the jungle, there was rifle fire to one side of the crowd but Korben felt safe in the middle of thousands of people. 'It was selfish but it was the reality,' he explains. The army fired over their heads and for many hours they repeatedly took cover. Korben got out of the wheelchair and lay on the ground under a burnt-out tractor. 'We thought we were safe, but it was an illusion,' he says. He saw a young rebel he knew, a bright boy who'd excelled at school, getting straight As in his A levels. He was saying goodbye to his parents and came up to Korben to ask if he knew about the rumour of a Red Cross ship coming to save them. Korben told him about the Indian election results instead – something he'd heard on his transistor radio. 'After that I realised we had to keep moving with the rest of the people and I said, "See you later," knowing that he was going to stay back and fight to the end. I don't know why I said that; what had happened to my brain? I was so upset I just said that without thinking.' Much later, Korben made contact with the boy's brother, who lived in Europe, and heard that his parents had stayed two more days, waiting for him to leave with them. Then they said goodbye, knowing he would die there.

People near Korben helped to lift him back into his wheelchair and that was when he saw two dead bodies on the other side of the tractor. They'd been there the whole time but he hadn't even noticed.

Their first glimpse of the Sri Lankan military was a small group of special forces, weighed down Rambo-style with heavy weaponry and sophisticated rifles, each wearing three or four gold necklaces – the *thalis* or gold wedding medallions of married Tamil women. It was an ominous indication of rape and plunder that struck fear deep in Korben, who had his young wife walking just behind him. He wondered what had happened to the women who'd once worn those necklaces.

On both sides of the path the coconut trees were severed in half, their stumps blackened. Flies buzzed around the corpse of an old lady whose bandages showed she'd been wounded before dying. In the jungle, parallel to the line of weary fleeing civilians, another posse of Sri Lankan soldiers passed. One showed his middle finger to them and said 'Arsehole' in Tamil. Some welcome, Korben thought, wondering why the soldier's only Tamil was swear words. He was careful not to look the man in the eye lest he sense his seething anger.

They hurried across the long narrow earthen bridge at the south of the lagoon to reach the army area. Floating in the water were three dead bodies, half-naked girls dressed like civilians.

Korben was so tired that his foot had slipped off the footrest of the wheelchair and he didn't have the energy to lift it back on. He wanted to stop and adjust it with his wife's help but the soldiers wouldn't allow them to halt even briefly. His foot dragged along the ground, painfully scraping off the skin.

In the *mêlée* they met a boy they knew, who'd lost his parents to an artillery attack some months earlier. Scared to enter the army area alone, the boy asked if he could join Korben's family, offering to push the wheelchair for them. They were grateful for the help.

Waiting in a dried-up paddy field to be counted and searched, Korben looked back at the land they'd escaped and saw artillery fire hit the bunkers they'd just abandoned at twenty-metre intervals. He spotted some soldiers carrying a few injured Tamils out, all the while being filmed, rushing as if in an action movie. They could have saved many more, he thought bitterly, if they'd genuinely wanted to help.

An army officer with countless medals adorning his chest came over and asked if the boy pushing Korben's wheelchair was from the Jeyantan Regiment, a Tiger fighting unit from the east of the island. The boy said no, but the soldiers were suspicious because he was young. Then the officer asked Korben, who told him the boy ran a grocery shop and wasn't a fighter.

'Do you really know or don't you?' snapped the army officer rudely.

'If he was a Tiger I would have told you, but he's not. There's no reason for me to tell you a lie,' replied Korben confidently, wanting to add that the boy's Jaffna Tamil accent clearly showed he couldn't be from the east of the island.

'I will pull you down to the ground and you will have to crawl to move. Get lost!' said the officer, slapping Korben hard in the face.

Is this why we entered this bloody area? We could have died there in dignity, thought Korben, understanding how intensely the officer disliked him because he was Tamil. 'For them we were all suspects because we stayed so long in rebel areas; it was one more reason to hate us. Maybe he wanted me to say the boy was a Tiger, but even if he was, I wouldn't have told them.'

The soldiers took the boy away and he vanished, one more of Sri Lanka's thousands of disappeared. Korben has found no trace of him. The military searched the civilians, confiscating batteries from radios and electric shavers. At first Korben assumed it was some security rule, but then he discovered it was just that the soldiers were short of these things.

As they waited for a bus to take them to the refugee camp, another soldier started talking to Korben in English, asking what he did in the rebel areas.

'I was a teacher giving extra tuition classes,' he replied, which was half true.

'Did you help the Tigers?' asked the soldier.

'No, no. We just had to supply them with items during Heroes' Week. We had to collect flowers for the tombstones and make snacks.'

'No. All you people from there are Tigers.'

'It's not true,' replied Korben, trying hard to smile at the man.

'Then why did you stay in that area so long?' asked the soldier.

Korben was shocked at the question and had no answer because he never tried to escape rebel areas, always believing that there would be a political deal to end the misery. 'The Tigers wouldn't give me a travel pass to leave,' he lied.

They spent all night on a crowded bus which stopped every few kilometres. In the morning they arrived at the main checkpoint which used to mark the border between the government and rebel territory. Loudspeaker announcements warned anyone who'd had anything to do with the rebels to present themselves to the authorities. Mixed with the instructions were swear words in Tamil. For Korben it was a novel experience to hear such words broadcast on a public-announcement system.

As thousands sat on the ground waiting, a female soldier came and threw packets of Maliban biscuits at the crowd. Little children who hadn't seen such luxury for six months were running here and there trying to catch a packet. 'They are like flies running after fish,' the woman soldier said in Sinhala, laughing disparagingly.

Korben was aghast: 'They thought they were being kind, giving the poor Tamil people food, but the manner in which they handled us was not human. My son also tried to stretch out his little hand to get a biscuit packet. I cried at that time, seeing it. I will never allow my son – or any child – to beg on the street. Not all the soldiers were racist, but they didn't know about Tamils and didn't understand that we once had a good life but had suffered for many years. They didn't realise what they had done to us. They were not curious to find these things out.'

An international aid worker from the Red Cross was present at the screening; Korben asked her if he could get help repairing or replacing his wheelchair. She was friendly but told Korben a broken one was better than none at all.

At first he wondered about telling the Sri Lankan authorities about his foreign passport, but then decided against it, fearing he might be separated from his wife and child. The refugees spent the night on the ground in the compound of a school, lying amid dried-out dog faeces. Korben didn't dare eat much, for fear of not being able to find a toilet he could use. He explained his problem to a soldier, who reassured him that in the refugee camp he'd have a toilet all to himself. For some reason Korben believed him.

At Manik Farm they were assigned a tent, two by four metres, to share with twenty-one people. Initially the ration was two litres of water a day per person. Korben's wife found an old Coca-Cola bottle and some plastic bags in which to collect the water. With all the trees felled to clear space for tents, the area was scorching. They tried to bathe in the river but the slope was virtually a ninety-degree drop – impossible in a wheelchair. For a while Korben didn't eat more than one meal a day for fear of having to go to the bathroom. His wife walked one and a half kilometres to find the nearest toilet, only to return saying it was too dirty to use. Laughing in extreme embarrassment, he explains that after a week he was forced to remove the back panel of his wheelchair and defecate in a corner of the camp, in full view of everyone.

'Even women and girls had no choice but to choose a corner and go. You can't compromise on your toilet needs. They were all like the cat who when drinking milk closes his eyes and pretends not to be seen by his owner! Before we had a respectable life. Yes, we lacked some things but we had dignity. We had covered toilets, with nothing to be ashamed of, even during the displacement. This was a new degradation.'

It was a week before they managed to get a cup of tea. Five times Korben's wife queued from early morning outside the camp's cooperative shop to buy a pan in which to boil water. She never reached the front of the line. The sixth time, she started crying and shouting, which was completely out of character for a woman so stoical. They allowed her to buy a pan and she was delighted, even though one corner was chipped and broken. Korben remembered the Red Cross lady who'd told him it was better to have something broken than nothing at all.

One day the United Nations Secretary-General's special representative, Vijay Nambiar, visited the camp. A senior Indian diplomat, Nambiar's impartiality has been questioned because his brother once advised the Sri Lankan Army. Korben says he watched the UN official drive straight through in his air-conditioned car, never once opening the window to take in the stench, let alone get out. So much for the international community, he thought to himself.

In the corner of the camp a policeman charged refugees to make calls on his mobile phone. Korben informed his family he was still alive and they contacted his embassy. Weeks later, two UN officers came to visit, a Swedish lady and a Kosovan man, whom many remember for his kindness, but there wasn't much they could do to help. Aided by a kind Tamil construction worker in the camp, Korben acquired his own mobile phone. At first there was no way to charge its battery, but later the refugees figured out how to tap into the power lines to the kitchens without anyone noticing.

The food was disgusting: the vegetables rotten and even the soya 'meat' full of weevils and bugs. After a few weeks baby Suben's vertebrae started showing because he'd lost so much weight. Soon the child was too weak to stand up alone and his underpants started falling off his body. Korben became so sick that he started talking incoherently and his wife thought he was going to die. At first the doctor gave him paracetamol but, after losing twenty kilos, he was finally hospitalised. When he returned to the camp, he was so weak he had to be propped up against a tree or wall or he would fall over. His mother came from Colombo to visit and hardly recognised him. Though she was meeting her daughter-in-law and grandson for the first time, she was only allowed to see them for five minutes, tossing food and money across the barbed wire.

Korben was questioned before being released; he told the authorities about his foreign passport but they didn't care. All they wanted to know was whether his father had been in the Tiger or the government police. Once free, Korben paid an agent to sort out his expired visa with a bribe so he could leave the country.

It took a year for his wife and son to join him in Europe, where Korben met unexpected kindness. An employer with many Tamil staff heard of his story and offered him a job out of the blue. 'I had lost everything in the last year and then suddenly some man helps,' he says in awe.

By contrast, back in Sri Lanka his wife had regular visits from naval officers, who showed her pictures of women rebels in the detention camp and threatened that if she didn't pay up she too would end up there. Twice she paid; the third time she gave them the baby's gold chain because that was all she had left. 'They didn't care that she had a child. They knew she would sell something to pay; it wasn't their problem,' he says bitterly.

Today Korben saves and sends money to charities back home, doing what he can to help those left behind. He has Sinhalese friends but no longer feels they all belong to one nation. Unable to return to Sri Lanka, he is exiled for the second time in his life. 'It's as if you cannot love your mother because she somehow hates you. You wish to love her, but she doesn't love you back,' he says, feeling rejected by his own country.

Sitting in his wheelchair high up in the grey tower block, he loves to remember the days before the war when he would drive his autorickshaw along the coastal road, with its windswept palms and paddy fields, and stop to watch the magnificent sunset. But then his memories turn sour. 'It is no longer the wonderful place I have loved,' he complains, 'it is tainted. I can't reconcile the beautiful nature with what I saw in 2009 – the abandoned houses and people carrying the dead and injured in tractors. I prefer to live in the past but I can't filter out the bad times.'

Nine months after I visited Korben, he sent me a message saying his wife had given birth to a beautiful baby girl.

Disabled in the North-East of Sri Lanka

Source: Sri Lankan Government's Lessons Learnt and Reconciliation
Commission

Vavuniya	1,255
Mullaitivu	1,561
Kilinochchi	2,436
Jaffna	4,432
Mannar	1,337
Batticoloa	1,797
Ampara	163
Trincomalee	3,375
Total:	16,326

2010   14,324 soldiers disabled due to war,
according to Sri Lankan Army
Commander.[1]

The Fighter

He thought that as long as he had his rifle he'd be all right, even though the Sri Lankan soldiers were just a few hundred metres away. The adrenalin rush from fighting on the front line for months had all but removed his sense of fear. It was the second week of May 2009, the temperature a scorching thirty-five degrees. Black smoke and the smell of burning rubber filled the air; the sound of gunfire and explosions was all around. Neriyen was trapped in a bunker on a small stretch of squalid beach where the Tamil Tiger rebels were making their last stand. Behind him were tens of thousands of people caught between the two sides, the civilians who had served as a human shield for the Tigers. Still bandaged in the neck and stomach after being shot by army snipers two months earlier, Neriyen was starving and frenzied. He hadn't washed for weeks, defecating in the bunker where he lived. Raw sugar and candy bars had given him the energy to stay awake at the front line; now the food had run out.

Neriyen had no idea what was going on but he could sense that the war was reaching its end; the dream of a separate Tamil nation was well and truly over. He'd watched the Black Tigers, the feared suicide cadres, move towards the enemy lines and blow themselves up. Time and again he saw them go over the top and rush towards the army positions. He'd once wanted to be a Black Tiger himself, but they'd rejected him. It was the elite corps – hardened fighters whose training was tougher than anything he'd endured, hundreds of young men and women honoured for blowing up presidents, prime ministers and innocent civilians. Normally the suicide squad covered their faces, even from other rebels, to hide their identity for secret missions. Now the end had come, there was no need for secrecy.

He particularly remembers one girl fighter. She was slim and pretty, with short hair, wearing what looked like an ammunition jacket – but it was packed with explosives and had a button for detonation. Neriyen thought the girl seemed very happy in those last moments of her life; she was smiling. 'We will meet again in the future,' she said to him. They were her last words before moving forward – there wasn't even time to ask her name. Not long after, he heard the explosion and saw the smoke in the distance. He had witnessed her last moments on earth.

Neriyen is the *nom de guerre* he chose when, just twenty-two years old, this Norwegian Tamil travelled to Sri Lanka to join the Tigers.

'We had no chance of survival in those last days of war,' he says, back home in Oslo, sipping coffee from a Nespresso machine in my hotel room. He's taken time off work to talk to me. Tall and sturdy, he looks like a Tamil football player, with bushy eyebrows and close-cropped hair, dressed in an electric-blue fleece jacket and well-used white sneakers. Nervous, he had brought a friend to translate and provide support.

Brought up in Oslo from the age of four, Neriyen hardly spoke Tamil when he first arrived in rebel territory in 2005. Unable to find his way in Europe, armed struggle seemed to offer the meaning he was looking for in his life. He had no idea where it would lead him.

It's only when he peels up his sleeve that you see that Neriyen's left arm is peppered with tiny round wounds – the result of an accident while manufacturing hand grenades. When he opens his jacket collar you can see the bullet wound in his neck given to him by a Sri Lankan Army sniper. Later he shows me the scar on the joint of his ring finger, where, after he surrendered at the end of the war, the torturer cut him to the bone.

You don't want to know what they did with the wire cutters.

Physically fit, Neriyen coped well during his six months of training in the secret rebel camp in the jungle. The routine was punishing. Up at 4 a.m., he would wash and drink a quick cup of tea before lining up on the parade ground, saluting the red Tamil Tiger flag and pledging allegiance to the Leader. Then there'd be a six-kilometre run before breakfast. After shooting practice, another run, then two hours of marching were followed by classes in politics and weapons before lunch and a rest.

The afternoon would involve more parade training, a little football or volleyball, and then, after a glass of milk at teatime, a shower and more classes, during which one of the boys would read aloud from the newspaper and they'd be taught about politics and equal rights for women. In the evening the generator would be switched on for two hours so they had electricity. Once a week they had a video screening – normally an action movie or a documentary dubbed into Tamil. Neriyen remembers watching a film about his hero, Che Guevara, as well as Second World War movies, Cold War dramas and Clint Eastwood Westerns, the latter a particular favourite of Velupillai Prabhakaran.

At ten o'clock it was lights-out. If the day wasn't gruelling enough, there was also night-time sentry duty, securing the camp perimeter in teams of ten, in rotating half-hour slots. The punishment for falling asleep on sentry duty was dire: standing on an empty artillery shell filled with sand for half a day in the sun, holding up a heavy rifle. Neriyen was careful not to get into trouble and quickly felt at home.

Hidden deep inside dense forest, the training camp was surrounded by tall trees and anti-aircraft guns in the very heart of the Tigers' territory. Ten recruits shared a dormitory: cement huts with palm-thatch roofing, covered in green camouflage cloth to hide them from the Sri Lankan planes flying overhead. There was a jogging track around the base, a kilometre long. The only open ground was a small jungle clearing about 150 metres wide, used as the parade and sports ground. There was no contact with the surrounding civilian population, no shops or telephones. The area was tightly guarded by sentries from a separate rebel unit to prevent anyone getting in or out.

Neriyen was one of several diaspora Tamils – from Britain, France, Germany, Canada and Norway – who'd come back to fight for the rebels. 'They showed me respect because I came from abroad, but I told them not to give me special treatment, to treat me as an equal, but they always had it in mind to take good care of me,' he explains.

After training, he graduated to a special unit that researched new

weapons and machinery on the Internet, translating the technical specifications into Tamil. They wrote the shopping lists for the Tiger arms
dealers and experimented with new grenades, mines and scopes for
weapons. The rebels had a sophisticated procurement network: smugglers obtained weapons from Eastern Europe and the Far East and
shipped them to the island's east coast in Merchant Navy vessels. The
Tigers had the dubious distinction of transporting more arms around
the world than any other insurgent group.

There were four arms workshops in the jungle where Neriyen
worked, staffed by seventy men and women. One room was always
air-conditioned to keep the imported machinery cool: the Tigers
used computer-aided design to manufacture explosive devices, and
the computers could malfunction in the tropical heat and humidity.
The workshops, classrooms, dormitories and offices were completely
hidden by trees, draped in camouflage and off-limits to civilians. It's
only now that the Tigers no longer exist that a few insiders are slowly
beginning to talk about how they operated as a guerrilla force, but
secrecy is still second nature to most.

In April 2007 Neriyen was manufacturing and testing a home-made
grenade with a French Tamil man when the plastic overheated and
accidentally detonated the mix of TNT and RDX explosives. Seventeen hot metal ball-bearings flew through his left arm, the workshop
filled with smoke and there was blood all over the table. The other man
fell to the ground, pierced in the neck by the ball-bearings. Horrified
and unsure how to react, Neriyen ran outside before collapsing. For
three days he was unconscious; when he came round he discovered
that his colleague's funeral had already taken place.

As the fighting drew closer during 2008, the arms workshop was
moved to avoid the advancing army. Neriyen taught new recruits how
to make grenades, careful not to repeat his lethal mistake, and designed
prototypes for parts of landmines, anti-tank mines and 81mm mortar
shells. He didn't go out much or mix with the local population but, like
them, had to shelter from the bombs and shells that now landed daily.

★

By January 2009 the Tigers were engaged in a last-ditch struggle for survival. Well equipped and with 200,000 men, the Sri Lankan Army had been shelling its way across the island, recapturing thousands of square kilometres step by step, taking on a few thousand guerrillas who knew the dense shrubs and trees like the back of their hands. They had finally succeeded in capturing Kilinochchi, now a ghost town abandoned by its people. The rebels were on the run, short of supplies after several ammunition dumps had been hit by shells. The army's artillery had a range of forty kilometres and by now there was no town beyond its reach. The attacks came from the south, the north and the west. Casualties were piling up on both sides and hundreds of thousands of refugees were moving away from the advancing army towards the eastern shore, which was still controlled by the rebels. The chaos was beginning to affect the Tigers, with signs emerging of a breakdown in the command structure. Infiltration and desertion eroded the rebel ranks even further.

As an experienced fighter who'd been through extensive training, Neriyen could man the front-line positions. In a big jacket he carried ten kilos of weapons: RPG's, a grenade launcher, 300 rounds of ammunition and eight grenades. Most rebels wore civilian dress but because he was on the front line Neriyen had stripy green camouflage uniform and rubber slippers, which were easier in the jungle heat than combat boots. He never had a helmet; nobody in his unit did. They were issued with a small water bottle, some tins of tuna, sugar and Kit-Kat bars for a quick energy rush. Some female fighters cooked rice and dahl for everyone if they found an abandoned house, but the men had no time to cook. (It seems the Tigers' creed of equality didn't work 100 per cent on the battlefield – as well as fighting, the women still had to shoulder domestic duties.)

Three rebels manned each position – they dug a series of bunkers on the front line, careful to choose a spot their own forces could overlook from the vantage point of a building. The idea was that if the Sri Lankan Army overran the trenches, the Tigers would still be able to pick them off from above. A girl Tiger was posted as a sniper 300 metres behind their position. The Sri Lankan Army also built little treehouses high up in the palms for their sharp-shooters to use.

The rebels dug twice as many bunkers as they could man, to give the enemy the impression that their numbers were much larger than they were. Every alternate bunker was a dummy one; sometimes they'd fire from it. Seven bunkers away was the commanding officer, who communicated by walkie-talkie. Neriyen placed weapons fifty metres forward of his position and booby-trapped them with mines, burying the tripwires underground so they'd be forewarned if the soldiers advanced.

Neriyen was given two young conscripts to manage. The Tigers were notorious for recruiting underage soldiers but he says the boys were eighteen and only looked younger because they were so malnourished. Weak and frail, the recruits hardly knew how to cock their rifles. 'They'd been forced to join and spent their whole time complaining,' Neriyen says. 'They were very afraid of the army but they were also terrified of our commander, who would fire into the sky from behind to force them to move forward.' Neriyen had little time or sympathy for the boys, although his life depended on keeping them with him. When one of the new recruits was injured, a reinforcement would be sent; there was very little time to get to know them.

Occasionally they would listen to the radio, with the sound turned very low so the army wouldn't hear them, but mostly they had no idea what was going on in the outside world.

By the end of February, civilians were desperate to leave, but many parents were unwilling to abandon children who'd been drafted. Neriyen now thinks it would have been better to have allowed Tamil civilians out of the war zone, to save their lives, but he's not sure they'd have left. 'The families stayed for their children,' he claims, adding implausibly that the Tigers never shot at civilians to prevent them escaping. Instead he says it was pro-government Tamil paramilitaries who infiltrated the rebel forces in order to discredit them.

Tiger fighters lived in filthy, rain-sodden bunkers, heads always down so the snipers wouldn't get them. The smell was dreadful and sometimes they slept in water. All the rebels – male and female – had ringworm and lice from not washing, and they'd long given up brushing their teeth. Neriyen survived for months with no sleep, just taking a ten-minute nap every two hours.

At night the Sri Lankan Army fired flares to light up the battlefield, constantly pushing forward. 'I was not frightened at all,' he says. 'I was mentally very strong inside the killing zone. It was only afterwards when I crossed over to the army side that I was so afraid because I had nothing to fight with.'

Neriyen would throw a grenade at the army side and then, under the cover of the smoke, stand up and shoot, diving back down into the trench once the smoke abated. 'The army were walking against us through the jungle,' he says. 'They fought in a different way from us because they had shellpower and they were good at defending territory; we also used shells but we were short of weapons.' The Tigers had lost several arms shipments to the Sri Lankan Navy, which received tip-offs from the Indians, whose satellites watched the ocean from above.

On 10 March, the day started well, with breakfast in the bunker brought to him by a girl Tiger. She was a new recruit, a teenager dressed in an oversized shirt belted around the waist over jeans, but with no protective clothing to save her from the shrapnel and shells. 'Be careful!' had been her parting words before she returned to her bunker. Just as she reached her position a shell landed, spraying shrapnel that ripped her head open. Neriyen heard the screaming. Three other women fighters also died in that attack.

There was no time to think; danger was all around. Their commanding officer had already been killed in the shelling and Neriyen hadn't managed to make contact with his deputy, who was far away. 'We were left to make the decisions on our own,' he says; 'only one guy on a motorbike came by once to see what was going on.'

One of Neriyen's team had already deserted and the remaining combatant was a twenty-four-year-old recent recruit with only a month's training who didn't want to fight. Throughout the day Neriyen kept on shooting from the forwardmost trench. Just after three o'clock in the afternoon he looked back at the bunker behind him and realised he was all alone; the second recruit had also bolted. Without ammunition or grenades, there was no option but to retreat. As he was getting out of the bunker, a sniper shot Neriyen in the base of his neck and a second sniper hit him in the left upper arm. A third bullet went in and out of his stomach. The snipers probably thought they'd bagged a top rebel commander because Neriyen was six foot tall and in uniform.

'I saw the blood. A lot of Tigers when they saw blood like that would just take their cyanide capsule and kill themselves, but as I was running I took out a field compress from my jacket. I couldn't scream because of the wound in my neck but I saw a rebel and signalled for help and told him to call the medical corps to pick me up.' Suddenly Neriyen realised he'd left behind his Norwegian passport and a large sum of cash in his kitbag, and he asked the man to run and fetch it for him before the medics carried him away.

The Tigers' front-line medical unit was a tiny cement house surrounded by tall palm and coconut trees. Inside were two rooms buttressed with piles of sturdy tree trunks and on the floor were badly injured fighters, bleeding. Three female medics trained for battlefield first aid ran around cleaning up wounds and depositing corpses in the room next door. They quickly removed the bullet from Neriyen's neck and cleaned and dressed the wounds before putting him in a jeep to be taken to the civilian Puttumatalan Hospital on the coast. They sent him first, knowing he wouldn't survive the open stomach wound, covered with only a field compress, unless he got treatment fast. Years of war had forced the Tigers to train doctors in battlefield surgery and build up a sophisticated front-line medical corps. 'They were the best doctors in the world,' says Neriyen, who owes them his life.

He arrived at the makeshift hospital, formerly a school, still clutching his rifle. The Tigers were now so short of weapons that he had to hand it over for someone else to use. Using a local anaesthetic that didn't make much impact, a doctor stitched up Neriyen's stomach, taking special care of him because he was an expatriate.

For weeks he lay on a mat on the floor of the hospital without any antibiotics, repeatedly coming under shell and air attack. He could hear the army's big guns getting closer. Shrapnel would pepper the building even if the bomb fell a hundred metres away. When the hospital was displaced further down the coast Neriyen moved with it. 'The doctor told us to take cover behind the walls. RPGs and rifle rounds were coming from everywhere. The attacks were continuous. Kfir fighter jets dropped bombs and shells came from all directions. Every day people were injured inside the hospital while the injured arrived from outside too. Patients and their relatives were lying in the compound of the building in the open air.'

In April Neriyen was discharged and sent on foot to a rebel camp in the care of another Tiger. He found walking painful and had to slow down but the other man rushed on ahead for a couple of minutes. 'I took a little break because I had trouble breathing. Then I heard rounds of rifle fire everywhere. A bullet hit my friend's cheek, going right in and out. He was still alive so I lifted him and carried him until I found a vehicle that could take him to hospital. It was painful for me to carry him but I had to do that. I was mentally strong at least. He survived and now he's in India, alive!'

In the rebel camp, a German Tamil called Vettrichelvan cared for Neriyen, changing dressings and fetching him food. They were close friends, having worked together in the arms workshop. 'Vettrichelvan was like a real brother to me. He was four years older than me, a little plump, handsome and jokey but deadly serious in the field. He joined two months before me. We had spent a lot of time together.'

It was only now that Neriyen managed to call his family in Oslo, on a satellite phone, to tell them he was still alive. He didn't tell his mother he'd been injured because she objected to him fighting; he only told his father a little of the truth, but not how seriously he'd been injured.

In early May he visited another 'hospital' for further treatment. It was a single-storey building of yellowing cement with red terracotta roof tiles, fenced in with corrugated iron. This too had been a school, and some of the classroom walls still had toy cars and letters of the alphabet painted on them in bright colours. Many of the rooms had walls only to waist height and were open for more ventilation in the tropical climate. The structure offered little protection from flying metal. The injured and dying lay in rags on the verandahs and out in the open on the hard sandy rubble next to open drains, flies buzzing around them. Some had a blue plastic cloth for shade, or a tent, but others were left lying on stretchers on the ground. Volunteers in ancient tractors arrived periodically to remove the piles of corpses and bury them in mass graves.

While in the hospital, Neriyen had a narrow escape. Hearing the incoming shells, he instinctively leapt into a trench to take shelter. One shell landed just twenty metres away, on top of three elderly patients who were hiding in another trench. 'I saw their bones on the ground. They were literally blown to pieces. I collected the body parts and buried them inside the trench,' he says numbly, his dark eyes delving into an abyss of horror. 'After that burial I realised the situation was becoming hopeless.' Surrender still didn't cross his mind. It was simply not part of the rebel ideology. He had no inkling that Norway had tried to broker a mediated surrender with an amnesty for fighters like himself.

During the final weeks of the war Neriyen and Vettrichelvan fought together in small groups, defending the shrinking perimeter of the tiny rebel enclave. Once invincible, in just three years the Tigers had lost 8,000 square kilometres of territory in the north and 6,000 in the east. The mood was one of utter desperation. Now it pains Neriyen to remember how he watched so many young suicide bombers willingly embrace death. There was something terrible about well-trained fighters' sense of self-sacrifice overpowering their will to live. The human instinct to survive should have been paramount but they went to their deaths smiling. And it was all for nothing in the end.

On 15 May a message came down the ranks from the rebel leader, Velupillai Prabhakaran. He ordered them to lay down their weapons and throw away their cyanide capsules and metal dog tags.

'It was very hard to hear; we were proud to be Tigers and wanted to fight to the death. I was depressed and sad. Going across to the army, I knew I would either die or be tortured. Sometimes I considered disobeying the order and taking cyanide, but then I thought: we have to bring out the truth, and it's enough if one person gets out of the war zone alive.'

It was two in the afternoon of 17 May and searingly hot when Neriyen and Vettrichelvan finally decided to give up. The rebel movement had totally disintegrated. Its top military figures were nowhere to be seen and its political leaders were feverishly negotiating their own surrender. Discarding their weapons and uniforms, they joined thousands of people who grabbing the last chance to flee. Seventy thousand people had walked out in just two days. Bent forwards to shelter from the staccato crackle of automatic-rifle fire, whole families dashed towards safety, carrying small children, the elderly and injured as well as their last pathetic belongings. Exhausted and starving, they rushed to save their lives, not knowing what awaited them on the other side, the terror visible on many of their gaunt faces.

Neriyen and Vettrichelvan mingled with the civilians moving towards the muddy stretch of grey water that separated them from the Sri Lankan Army. They were terrified about what lay ahead.

As they reached the shore of the lagoon they saw about thirty decomposing bodies lying on the sand, people who had been shot as they were trying to escape. Unable to swim because of his injuries, Neriyen waded through the water, which reached his chin at its deepest point. Over his head he carried a small bag that contained his Norwegian passport and the money – about £500 worth of Sri Lankan rupees – that he'd stashed away for an emergency. Underfoot he could feel the corpses. 'The blood from the dead people was in the water and it tasted like hell, not like fresh water.' He was full of dread about what would happen to him on the other side. 'When I saw the army it was as if I was stepping into purgatory. I will never forget the face of the first soldier I saw, as long as I live.'

The Sri Lankan military instantly guessed the tall and muscular Neriyen was a fighter. Military police separated him and Vettrichelvan from the civilians. They were taken to a jungle clearing and blindfolded. Neriyen's hands were bound behind his back and, kneeling on the ground, he was tied to a tree with rope. He couldn't see the army boots that kicked him as he knelt, utterly petrified.

In the darkness, with his senses on high alert, he says he heard several women's voices screaming in the distance, 'Older brother, help us, save us!' Neriyen says he is sure it was the female Tigers being raped. 'It was chilling,' he says. 'This is the first time I've told anyone about it.' Recalling that sound, he looks utterly frozen with fear.

Neriyen thinks there were seven or eight Sri Lankan soldiers who tortured him and his friend. 'They used the tip of some wire cutters to drag the skin off,' he says, and when I ask where on his body, he just says, 'Down there,' pointing to his genitals.

The soldiers wanted to know his rank and the whereabouts of Prabhakaran, who hadn't been captured at this point. 'I told them I was a Tamil who came from abroad and that the Tigers had taken my passport away in 2008 and forced me to fight against my will. They didn't believe me.'

For two days he was kept tied to the tree, bleeding with no food or water. Knowing he had money hidden in his bag, he waited to get one of his Tamil captors alone to see if he could bribe his way out. The man he selected was a rebel who'd secretly switched sides towards the end of the war. Neriyen knew him slightly and they even had a friend in common. After taking the money, the man told the soldiers that he could vouch for Neriyen having been forced to fight. They flatly refused to release Vettrichelvan as well, but escorted Neriyen back to the area where civilians were being screened. The money had saved his life.

'I tried very hard to get my friend out. I feel guilty today to have escaped and come here. I have no idea what happened to him. I think he is dead. I asked many people later on if they had seen him anywhere and I wasn't lucky,' he says, anxiously fiddling with his fingernail. 'He was my best friend. I speak to his parents and I always tell them he is alive because he surrendered. I am still waiting for his call.'

Neriyen himself was still not safe; rebel informers were pointing out their erstwhile colleagues to the army. Again he was spotted as a fighter, but this time sent to the checkpoint where fighters were separated from civilians and processed. A United Nations representative was stationed at this checkpoint to observe proceedings but wasn't allowed to speak to any of the detainees. His presence didn't seem to deter abuse.[1]

Having taken him to a small room for questioning, an intelligence officer put a knife to Neriyen's throat and snapped: 'Where is your leader? What kind of work did you do there? How long have you been a Tiger?' Neriyen was frightened. He thought they were going to kill him. Showing his foreign passport, he lied that he'd been forced to fight for the rebels.

Neriyen was detained with 3,000 other men in a school building transformed into a temporary jail, with extra tents pitched in the compound and surrounded by electrified barbed wire.[2] A few individual soldiers treated the prisoners well. Every evening after dinner, some Tamils would be blindfolded and taken away for questioning. Neriyen could smell alcohol on the interrogators' breath. He says he was repeatedly beaten with bamboo poles on the soles of his feet and his lower back. The military wanted to know where the top rebel commanders were and what route they'd used to escape. Again Neriyen told them he was a Norwegian citizen, but it didn't help.

'One time a soldier took his pistol, cocked it, put it in my mouth and fired it. He wanted to frighten me. Then he punched me,' he recounts numbly.

Over ten months he was held in a series of five different detention camps.[3] His account is consistent with other testimony documented by human-rights groups. 'I was put in a chair and given electric shocks, but they didn't use the electric current every day. They used the wire cutters in the same way as before. They also took a knife and cut my finger joint right to the bone.'

Neriyen says he never saw the faces of his interrogators because it was dark and he was blindfolded, but a few days after they'd tortured him, two men came to speak to him during the daytime and he knew them instantly from their voices.

'It was a big shock for me that Tamils from the north of Sri Lanka were among those who did the torture, although most of the torture was done by Sinhalese. Sometimes I wished to die. I thought of killing myself,' he says, fidgeting with his fingers and struggling to hold back tears.

Desperate to tell his parents he was alive, Neriyen tossed a scrap of paper across the fence to a Catholic nun working in the school next door. She passed on the message. During his months of detention representatives from the Red Cross, the Norwegian embassy, a Sri Lankan aunt and eventually his mother came to visit Neriyen. He was repeatedly warned he'd be killed if he mentioned the torture during these visits. He didn't even dare tell his mother, who travelled alone from Norway to see him.

'My father didn't come to Sri Lanka because he didn't think it was safe. My mother took a chance. I was very happy to see her but I couldn't tell her I'd been tortured. I think maybe she knew when she saw me.' It was the first time Neriyen had seen his mother for six years and he wept when she put her arms around him. She stayed for a fortnight, during which she was allowed to visit twice a week for ten minutes each time.

In 2010 Neriyen was sent to Colombo and locked in a cell on the notorious fourth floor of the Criminal Investigation Department, a dark, nondescript building in the commercial centre of the city. It's so infamous as a place of torture that Sri Lankans now talk of being 'sent to the fourth floor' as a shorthand for being abused.

'The torture here was very hard – more intense. On those days we were interrogated they didn't give any food. They used electric current on different places of my body at different times and the wire cutters again.'

It's hard to imagine what function the torture served, nine months after the end of the war, except ritual humiliation. It's doubtful Neriyen had much useful intelligence to spill and despite the torture he never let on that he'd worked in the Tigers' weapons factory.

After he'd managed to smuggle out another message, a Norwegian official came and told Neriyen his case was now before the courts. Two weeks later he found himself in the dock, charged with being a member of a proscribed organisation. The judge declared Neriyen not guilty, even though he'd repeatedly confessed to being a Tiger. Norwegian pressure had secured his release.

Although he stayed in the safety of the white-stucco residence of the Norweigian Ambassador before flying out, Neriyen never breathed a word about the torture, terrified he might be stopped from leaving or his relatives harmed. Only when he reached Oslo did he go to a doctor, who saw the marks on his body. 'In one way I think I am proud of myself because I am telling someone else what I have been through,' he says. 'I don't talk with my dad or mother. I can't tell them like this, because it would cause them pain.'

Neriyen now lives with his parents and works in a courier company. Seemingly confused about his identity, he thinks of himself as an exile in the very country where he grew up, saying Sri Lanka is where he really belongs.

'So long as I am breathing I will do something for my country. The Tigers are not yet finished. For the time being we will fight the political way, without arms. Who knows, someday it might start again – there will be armed struggle again and I will fight and die if necessary,' he says defiantly, putting on a brave show to signal that he's not crushed.

I saw Neriyen several months later, in a Tamil restaurant in north London. He was wearing jeans and a heavy black winter jacket. The first thing he asked was whether I remembered what he'd told me before, about his willingness to die for the Tamil cause. He was keen to project the image of a hard-line rebel with unswerving commitment to the struggle. But he is a young man full of contradictions. For all the talk of dying for his people, he's on the brink of a new life, full of hope for the future.

This time he was with his fiancée, a diminutive former Tamil Tiger nurse whom he had met just three weeks earlier, a refugee living in London. With extraordinarily long black hair in a ponytail, she wore make-up, high-heeled black suede boots and skin-tight jeans and carried a patent-black handbag – a quick adaptation to street fashion. She clasped Neriyen's arm and snuggled up to him, excited and slightly awed by the marriage just arranged by their families. Neriyen explained that his bride understood him because she suffered in the war and lost her mother to a shell attack in 2009. 'We are both traumatised,' she told me in a matter-of-fact tone, as if that made them compatible.

Neriyen himself is surprised at how fast his life seems to be changing, proudly telling me how he now prays at the Hindu temple every week, thanks to his fiancée. Then he admits that it's a major step forward for him to visit a restaurant and that this is only the second time he's done it since he returned from Sri Lanka. He never goes out in Oslo because he is petrified of what people on the street might think of him if they knew his past. 'I am afraid people will look at me as a terrorist,' he says.

Tactfully waiting for the moment when his fiancée goes to the bathroom, I broach the question of how many people he killed during the war. Neriyen says he never saw the dead bodies but he thinks the number is twenty-eight, judging by how many soldiers were firing at him before he threw grenades into their bunkers. Does he feel any remorse?

'I feel guilty when I think about their parents; it's very difficult. But what can I do? We were fighting for our freedom, while the Sinhalese soldiers were fighting for money.' He tries to rationalise it. 'I had to do good things and bad things,' he says, then corrects himself to say they weren't bad things because he was serving his nation. There's clearly confusion in his mind. A little later he acknowledges that the raw grief is the same on the Tamil and the Sinhalese sides.

Embarking on a new phase of his life, there's a part of Neriyen that still misses the thrill of armed struggle. 'Ordinary life seems so tame and pointless. I earn and I spend money. It's so normal and unexciting,' he complains, but then walks off arm in arm with his fiancée, looking very much part of a couple and quite delighted with the domestic adventure ahead.

Tiger Equipment According to Sri Lankan Military Estimates

Microlight aircraft	2
Light aircraft ZLIN 143	5
Helicopters	2
Unmanned aerial vehicles/remote-control planes	2
T55 Tank	1
130mm Cannon type 59-1	12
152mm Howitzer gun type 66	9
122mm gun	2
107mm rocket artillery	2
140mm mortar	4
120mm mortar	150+
Cargo boars	25+
Fast attack craft	20–30
Transport boats	20+
Suicide boats	23
Submarines (locally manufactured)	6
Underwater scooters	20+
Remote-control boats	1
Fibreglass boats	76
Fibreglass dinghies	115
Outboard motors	'large quantity'
Various radars	50+
GPS and other navigation equipment	'large quantity'
Electronic remote-control systems	'unknown quantity'

1985–2009	Attacks on civilian targets by Tigers	137
1972–2009	Number of civilians killed by Tigers	9,878[1]

The Shopkeeper

Villawood Immigration Detention Centre in Australia is a modern building, surrounded by barbed wire and high metal fencing, in an unremarkable Sydney suburb. It's clean and neat and impersonal, with a picnic area and a children's playground for visitors. Inside the dormitories there are Internet facilities and plenty of bland food. The Sri Lankans, who've known far greater hardship, don't complain about the conditions, only the lack of freedom and the delays in processing their cases. It's similar to a medium-security prison: visitors are X-rayed, and escorted in and out by a guard, and they are not allowed to go inside with phones, tape recorders or cameras. Food can be taken in but no chillis or anything in a glass jar, for fear they could be used as weapons in the periodic riots that have erupted at this facility.

Detention centres like this house what Australians call 'boat people': asylum seekers and migrants who risk their lives to reach their shores, including survivors of the final carnage in northern Sri Lanka. They're generally not welcome and their stories are rarely told. Sitting outdoors at a plastic garden table in the family detention area[1] at Villawood is a Tamil couple who have gone through hell to get here. Their curly-haired two-year-old daughter, whom I shall call Puni, noisily scrapes plastic chairs along the floor, trying to attract attention, unwilling to be pacified by the sweets and biscuits I've brought.

She is a very precious baby for her parents, the first after five years of trying for a child. Born in a bunker, Puni has known more suffering in two years than most people experience in a lifetime. She's been bombed, starved, imprisoned and threatened with death, she's been in detention for more than a year. She smelled death and heard explosions before she even had the words to describe them.

Puni's father Karu (not his real name) was a shopkeeper in the rebel areas of northern Sri Lanka. He is a fragile man who looks older than his thirty-eight years: already half bald, with a moustache and a large mole on his left cheek. He wears an Australia Cricket T-shirt, as if to say he belongs to this country. I can't help noticing as we talk of starving babies that the T-shirt advertises Milo, a soothing bedtime milk drink.

This worn-out, vulnerable man starts weeping even before he begins to tell his story. The mere prospect of reliving his odyssey of death, torture and escape causes him to break down.

His wife, Gowri, is the opposite. A large, tough-looking woman in a beige and white striped cotton shirt, with all her hair scraped back in a ponytail to reveal tiny gold ear studs, she comes and goes, attending to Puni, describing the war, starvation, sexual abuse, disappearances, death threats and the horrendous boat journey almost casually, showing no emotion whatsoever.

Accompanying me is an off-duty Tamil translator from the Immigration Department, familiar with interviewing Sri Lankans in the notorious Christmas Island detention centre, where asylum seekers are held offshore. She's never heard a story like this one. Normally immigration interviews focus on specific threats to security, not people's feelings. As I wait for her to listen to the Tamil version and convey it in English, I can read the horror and shock in her face. It seems that every time his suffering must surely finish, something worse is around the corner. Once Karu reaches the end of his story, I know why he'd cried at the outset.

He is a simple man who wanted nothing more than to be left to get on with his life in peace. There is no hatred or bitterness in him, even after all he's been through, and he never mentions ethnicity or politics. He shows none of the keen ideological sense of a rebel. Gentle and passive, he took the beatings and abuse just as he took the kindness of strangers who saved his life – stretcher bearers, a nurse, a policeman, an elderly refugee. He hasn't yet attempted to make sense of it all. He is still trying to survive.

Karu was born in eastern Sri Lanka, at the start of an ethnic conflict that shaped his whole life. He lost his father when he was only nine, shot by the army. His teenage years were spent in four different refugee camps because of the fighting. Aged seventeen, he fled to the rebel-held north of the island, repeatedly displaced by shifting front lines in the intermittent battles of the civil war. Finally he settled and married in the heart of rebel territory, hoping to steal some calm in which to be a farmer. When the final phase of the war arrived, he'd recently started a small grocery shop in PTK, the sleepy town that was the rebels' last stronghold.

During one unusually intense bout of shelling in late January 2009 Karu and Gowri finally abandoned their home, something they'd hoped to avoid, and they found themselves running for their lives, following the crowd on foot. There was no time to collect any luggage – just one bag of important documents, later destroyed in an attack, and another of biscuits and packets of instant noodles. It was chaos. People were fleeing in different directions, nobody knew which way was safe. Karu and Gowri took short-cuts and small lanes because the main road was blocked with thousands of people fleeing and their vehicles. As they ran they heard the crackle of gunfire amid the explosions of incoming shells, which meant the army were near. They headed for the government-declared 'safe zone' they'd heard about on the radio.

Gowri worried desperately about her baby, due in three months, on 27 April. For the next few months she lived in constant terror of miscarrying her first child. They moved repeatedly, from one shelter to another, one night spent sleeping in a shed, the next in a bunker with a plastic sheet on top. What Gowri saw around her only made her more fearful. A neighbour miscarried out of sheer stress and she heard of babies dying inside their mothers' wombs because of all the noise and fear. First-time mothers are naturally apprehensive, but in the war many feared they simply wouldn't live till the delivery date or that their bodies wouldn't be able to stand the pressure of the conflict and would reject the baby.

In March she passed a heavily pregnant woman on the roadside, who'd been badly injured and was begging a group of rebel medics to deliver her by Caesarean section, knowing she herself might not survive but wanting to give her unborn baby a chance of life. The doctors, who were in the middle of shifting a hospital to a new location, had all their equipment with them; they reluctantly stopped and erected a plastic curtain by the road to deliver the baby right there and then. 'I saw it while I was walking but I don't know what happened to the woman afterwards. The doctors couldn't cope – they had hundreds of dying people on their hands daily and without any drugs they couldn't save many people.'

On one day in March, while cooking on a little fire outdoors, Gowri heard bullets whizzing past her ear, looked back and saw the person who'd been standing behind her lying dead on the ground. On another day, fifteen people died while cooking, strewn around the pathetic wood fires. Gowri visited a community hall being used as a hospital, only to find it filled with what she describes as 'heaps' of wounded women and children, after an attack on a queue for milk powder. 'There was nobody to look after the injured; if anyone was still alive, they just ran for their lives,' she says.

With his wife more than seven months pregnant, Karu was the one who had to queue for rations – the tiny portions of dry food, given away by the cooperative shops from the limited international aid allowed into rebel territory. On 11 March Karu and his mother, who had now joined them, got up very early to stand in line, knowing as many as 1,500 people would already be there before them. Bedraggled and thin, Karu stood next to his mother for hours, holding pots and pans in the hope of receiving rice and sugar, with no idea that this would be a day he'd never forget.

Without warning a shell smashed into the waiting people. Karu says he managed to make out his mother being killed right in front of him before passing out himself. 'I couldn't feel anything below the hip. One leg was broken by the shell. It was bent completely backwards. The other had the veins severed and there was a lot of blood. I felt the bleeding as I lost consciousness. My mother fell in front of me and I knew she'd died, but I was unable to move or do anything. While they carried me, I vaguely felt what was happening, but I wasn't fully conscious. I was taken to hospital with a broken bone poking out of my leg and they put two sticks as a splint and ripped up part of my clothes to stop the bleeding. They didn't operate on me; they just tied my sarong round the legs, one of which kept on bleeding anyway.'

A few hours later Karu woke up, finding he was unable to move. He saw blood all over the floor around him. 'Yes, I thought I would die,' he says, laughing nervously. 'Injured people next to me had bled to death and nobody came for them, so I thought the same would happen to me.' He noticed people gathering up the dead using white sarongs as improvised shrouds. Ten people died in that attack.

Then a drone flew overhead, he remembers, signalling that another attack was imminent. With both legs injured and lying on the ground in a house full of injured people adjacent to the makeshift hospital, Karu couldn't run away. A plane screeched overhead, dropping a bomb which hit the corner of the one-storey building where he lay. It was a sturdy house with a roof of robust palm trunks, but the roof caved in and Karu was buried in rubble. He survived only because he happened to have been placed on the floor under a cement shelf, which protected him from the collapsing masonry.

'I was lucky I wasn't in the corner which was hit. I just lay there, buried, praying for help, my face covered in rubble. It was two hours before they dug me out. People didn't come immediately because they were scared for their own lives, fearing a second attack. I really thought I would die. After the jet went away, the shelling continued. I couldn't hear anyone else there. I think they were all dead. I was so weak I couldn't even raise my voice to call out. I just tried to move my arms.'

At the memory of being buried alive, Karu starts to cry again. He remembers being dug out and laid on the ground by the roadside, occasionally tended to by volunteers from the hospital, which was overflowing and unable to do anything for him.

Gowri, meanwhile, received news that her husband was injured, but it was three days before the attacks let up and she could find someone who would take her to visit him. She had no money and there was nowhere for her to stay by the hospital, which she believed was being targeted. Twice she managed to get a lift and travel the few kilometres to see Karu. The last time was a week before Puni was born.

By mid-April, Gowri was convinced she couldn't wait another fortnight to give birth naturally: she thought the baby might not survive the terror and stress she was experiencing. She persuaded a government doctor to perform a Caesarean section, and on 12 April she was operated on inside a sandbagged bunker in one of the rooms of the two-storey school building that had been turned into a hospital in Mullivaikkal, just five minutes' walk from where she was sheltering. The doctor gave her an injection, removed her baby and stitched her up before sending her back to her bunker. She walked home completely alone, carrying her newborn, hardly noticing the pain from her stitches. The baby's safety was uppermost in her mind and that kept her going.

'This was normal in those days. Thirteen other women gave birth the same day as me; it was the same situation for the others,' she says, uncomplaining. A surprising number of women were pregnant when the war intensified. The Sri Lankan government had banned the import of contraceptives into rebel territory for more than a year.

Gowri cowered in the bunker by the beach. Every time an attack began, the others would run into the sea for safety. 'If you wanted to run, the question was where to run. There was no space there. It was hopeless. You needed to build a toilet, a bunker, and prepare food and have a well for water but all that needed energy. Everyone was too tired to do it, so they ran into the sea to avoid having to build a bunker. It wasn't their first time being displaced. After April I decided not to run any more. I thought if I am going to die, let me die. I just leaned over and protected the baby with my body.'

The instinct to save the child was paramount. For the first two days Gowri breastfed Puni, but then she found she was too malnourished to produce milk. Some neighbours gave her tiny amounts of precious milk powder they'd saved for themselves, but soon she was forced to climb out of the bunker and walk back to the hospital to line up for handouts. 'I had to feed my kid,' she says. Every ten or fifteen minutes more injured patients would be brought in to the hospital.

There wasn't any baby milk available, let alone something suitable for the delicate stomach of a newborn. All they had was Anchor milk, the powdered milk Sri Lankans put in their tea or coffee, and even that had to be watered down because it was so expensive by now. Gowri had no money left once she'd sold her last gold bangle for a mere tenth of its worth: sixteen grams of gold bought just two kilos of rice, which didn't last long. Baby Puni spent her first few months constantly hungry and sick, with viral infections and high fevers.

'I had a baby, not knowing if it had a father,' says Gowri. Nor did frail, thin Karu know what had happened to his pregnant wife. The makeshift hospital had to keep on moving and could provide only very basic medical care – once a week somebody would change his bandages, using strips of old sarongs.[2] He was fed one meal a day of rice porridge, if he was lucky and they were not under attack. Somehow Karu survived the two months until the end of the war.

On 16 May he begged two Red Cross volunteers whom he knew slightly to help him cross over to army-controlled territory. Exhausted as they were, the men fashioned an improvised stretcher from two sticks and a sarong and carried Karu out, saving his life.

Tens of thousands of people were on the move and many families became separated in the panic. Little did Karu know that on the same day his wife was also walking out of the war zone. It would be almost a year before he discovered she was alive and that they had a baby girl.

Dark smoke hung over the beach as Karu, carried on a stretcher by ICRC volunteers, and Gowri, who had no idea where her husband was, fled; the rebels had blown up one of their naval boats and countless motorbikes had caught fire because of the pounding rockets. Once they'd crossed the earthen bridge over the lagoon into the army-controlled area, the frightened refugees were channelled into the narrow barbed-wire path mentioned by other interviewees, where only two people could walk abreast, to be sorted, screened and strip-searched.

Exhausted from carrying her one-month-old baby and numb

with fear, Gowri filed along, hardly daring to raise her head to look. At intervals on both sides of the barbed-wire path she noticed army sentry posts reinforced with sandbags, and she could hear the Sinhalese soldiers taunting the Tamil women.

'All the time that we walked the soldiers were talking about us, saying, "These girls are ideal to satisfy our needs." They spoke in broken Tamil because they wanted us to know what they were up to and to frighten us,' she says. She saw soldiers summoning pretty young girls out of the line at gunpoint, holding the two lines of barbed wire apart so that they could step through.

'I saw one girl going away and then heard screaming. I feared she had been raped behind the sentry post. I just kept on walking and didn't look because I was so scared. She was about eighteen or nineteen years old. I saw her taken out of the line in front of me and step through the barbed wire and be led away. I was afraid to turn back and look in case they saw me but when the path turned a corner I could see the girl behind the sentry post, crying, half naked, with all her clothes badly ripped. It was dreadful. I was very angry and disappointed. I felt helpless and afraid but I had to survive myself. Then in the shed where we were searched, another person asked if I'd also seen all the girls being taken away and raped.' It was an atmosphere of mass terror; everyone wanted to stay alive and nobody dared speak out, bitterly ashamed of their fear and silence.

In Manik Farm camp, where she was taken along with thousands of others, Gowri was too exhausted to walk the long distance with her newborn baby to the washing area. She knew women feared going there. The showers were next to an army post and there were rumours of dead female bodies and rape.

The baby had a constant high fever and diarrhoea. Soon Gowri and Puni were transferred to hospital, where Tamil refugees were guarded by the army to prevent escape. They spent two months there, during which Gowri says she suffered a kind of mental breakdown from the stress of not knowing where her husband was and the terror of repeated interrogations and threats to her baby's life if she didn't cooperate.

She managed to get a message to her family in Jaffna, who scraped together the money to bribe the security forces to take her to the capital in an ambulance and obtain a passport and visa for India. When Gowri and Puni boarded the flight for Tamil Nadu, she still had no idea if her husband was alive or dead.

The couple had been among tens of thousands of Tamils who fled the war zone on 16 May, but Karu had been loaded onto a truck for the injured. Even if he'd been fit, he would probably not have found Gowri in the pandemonium of the escape. He was taken to hospital in Polonnaruwa, a predominately Sinhalese city, with a medieval heritage site that tourists visit. For a month Karu says he just lay on the floor of the overcrowded hospital, unable to stand, with no treatment.

'We were dumped on the floor next to the wards where normal people were treated, or left on the grass outside. A lot of elderly people and children died and their bodies were taken to the mortuary. The Sinhalese people who came to visit the normal patients would look at us on the floor and see the infected wounds, which had maggots crawling out of them, and they would get angry and cover their noses. I think the army told them we were all Tigers, because there was so much hatred in their faces. Even the doctors looked at us with racist eyes.'

The hospital was full of soldiers and Tamil paramilitaries. Every day Karu noticed that they took away seven or eight Tamils for questioning, who never returned. One day his turn came.

He was still on his stretcher but the other six injured men could walk. He says they were driven somewhere in the jungle where an interrogator, fluent in Tamil, asked the men if they'd worked for the rebel administration or were fighters.

'Some said they were not rebels but had worked for the Tigers, but they didn't bother to find out what jobs they'd done. I said no, I was doing business. They made everyone lie face-down on the ground and they shot them one by one. They shot them all right in front of me. They were wearing black civilian clothes and had covered their faces with monkey masks like party masks that only showed their eyes. They still didn't believe me when I said I wasn't a Tiger, so they beat me up on the stretcher. Then they took me to a room next door and kept on beating me until I couldn't feel anything and passed out.'

The next day Karu woke up bruised and battered in a training centre that had been turned into a detention centre for the injured. Two or three groups came to interrogate him, urging him to confess that he'd worked for the Tigers or knew others who had. In a swathe of Sri Lanka that had been under rebel administration for two decades, civilians had little choice but to work in the Tigers' banks, cooperative shops, agricultural institutes, colleges and law courts. It didn't mean they were fighters who'd undergone military training. Karu, who was not a rebel, was constantly harassed by the interrogators. 'Even if you told the truth, still they would return to ask more questions,' he says.

Over the next months Karu was transferred to a series of hospitals for treatment of his fractured legs. Some nights the security forces would come and question the patients as they lay in their beds. He saw others taken away for interrogation who never returned. Immobilised, he couldn't even go and find a telephone to tell anyone he was still alive.

In Colombo General Hospital a metal plate was inserted in his leg. Karu and one other Tamil were put in a ward with injured Sinhalese soldiers, who made their lives a misery: 'They called us Tigers all the time. We didn't have a change of clothes, so they opened up a hot-water bottle and mixed chilli powder and water and urine inside and then threw it on us, knowing we had no way of cleaning ourselves afterwards.'

Fearing for his life, Karu managed to bribe a nurse to move him, offering her his wedding ring and gold chain. She refused to help the other Tamil man in the hospital ward and it haunts Karu to think that he abandoned him.

Transferred to Vavuniya Hospital, the interrogations started all over again, usually at night, when the foreign doctors from Médecins Sans Frontières had gone home. Here help came from an unexpected quarter. A friendly local police sergeant who'd had enough of the killing came to Karu's rescue, hiding him in the hospital and then putting him on a bus to Manik Farm. 'If they notice you, then you will end up dead,' he warned. 'Do not sleep in the tent where you are registered; they will come for you!'

Karu doesn't know whether the policeman who saved his life was Sinhalese or Tamil – he couldn't tell from his accent – all he saw was a figure of power and authority, not a member of a particular ethnic group, he says, anxiously fidgeting with the white tissue he used to blot his tears, folding it into a tiny triangle and squeezing it with his fingers.

While others were desperately breaking out of Manik Farm, Karu escaped *into* the camp, hoping he'd be safer there. For a month he hid in a tent that housed a group of elderly people, not even daring to come out to go to the toilet, urinating in a bottle and defecating in a plastic bag. When the authorities started resettling Tamils from Jaffna, one of the old men registered Karu as his son so that he could be released. It was a stranger's defiant act of altruism, made more extraordinary because it occurred at a time when friends were betraying one another.

In Jaffna Karu contacted his father-in-law, who hid him with a relative in a remote village and told him his wife was alive and had given birth to a baby girl. Once a week Karu had to visit Jaffna Hospital to have his leg treated because it was only just beginning to heal. On the fourth visit he walked out of the sprawling ochre-coloured building to find himself dragged into a waiting white van. As everyone in Sri Lanka knew that 'white-van culture' means abduction by shadowy paramilitaries or death squads, Karu had no doubt his life was in peril once again. For an hour they drove around while a masked man in uniform beat him and asked questions.

'Then they took me to a place with blood all over. I was tied by my legs and hung upside-down, despite the metal plate in my injured leg. They beat me so badly I was crying. I had no idea what would happen to me, whether I would live or die.'

The next day the same masked man came back, along with a

Muslim who said to Karu in Tamil: 'The people who come here don't ever leave. I can take you out if you are willing to pay'. Karu didn't even ask the price. 'Yes,' he replied, 'take me out alive.'

Hidden in the back of a car with tinted windows, Karu was driven hundreds of kilometres to the capital along a highway that was still off-limits to all except the military. When they reached Colombo, Karu was smuggled around town in a van full of biscuit boxes, hidden between the crates in case anyone stopped to search. For two months he lived in one room, never once coming out, with no idea where he was. The same Muslim man brought him food and kept on demanding more money. The only person Karu could ask for help was his father-in-law, who sold land to pay the smugglers to get him a passport and visa so he could join Gowri in India. Extorting money from Tamil survivors had become an industry on a scale simply not possible in such a militarised environment without official complicity.

In the southern Indian state of Tamil Nadu, Karu was reunited with Gowri and saw his baby daughter for the first time. It was March 2010 and the child was almost one year old. He doesn't speak of his joy at being together again. Their story was not over yet.

Karu heard of a neighbour who was also a Tamil refugee in India who had disappeared and then been found dead in Sri Lanka. He began to feel very unsafe, fearing he too might be caught and sent back. A rickshaw driver told him about a boat leaving for Australia that was smuggling Sri Lankans. With help from his father-in-law, Karu paid the £10,000 for himself and his wife, and the smugglers threw in the baby's passage for free.

When the tiny, rickety boat set off from the Indian coast it was packed with people. There were seventeen children on board; Puni was the youngest. The journey would be a twenty-seven-day life-and-death struggle.

After many days at sea they ran out of fuel. The engine stopped and they drifted. The food was finished and they were getting desperate. Aware that the Australian Navy destroys these boats if they capture them, the people smugglers economise by using unseaworthy craft.

Karu finds it difficult to say what happened next and breaks down again. After seven days of their bobbing hopelessly up and down on the ocean, a big ship came past. They put on their lights to call for help. With difficulty the ship steered alongside them and threw down food, but only enough for one day. By now they were starving. When help still didn't come, five boys decided everyone would die unless they tried to swim to shore for help. They could see a light far away in the distance and hoped it might be land. Four more days passed. Another ship was spotted and they signalled to it but it didn't even stop. The five boys never returned. They wouldn't have stood a chance in the icy, shark-ridden waters.

The ship that failed to stop did at least pass on information about the stranded boat full of starving women and children, because the refugees noticed a plane flying overhead. A few days later a Russian ship stopped to give them food and towed them for two nights and two days to the Cocos Islands, tiny atolls 2,000 kilometres from the Australian mainland. Everyone on board was detained and sent to the offshore asylum detention centre at Christmas Island, 1,000 kilometres to the east. After some months the Australian authorities transferred Karu's family to Sydney so that he could have medical treatment for his leg.

As witnesses to repeated war crimes and human-rights violations – the bombing of hospitals, rape, summary execution, abduction and torture – I assumed Karu and Gowri wouldn't have too much trouble being granted asylum in Australia. Their experience after the war was almost worse than what they went through in the bunkers. It was a tale that lurched from one disaster to the next, a story that never seemed to end. Just when I thought it had, Karu explained that Australia had rejected their asylum application. The reason he'd been given was that both he and his wife were born in towns controlled by Sri Lankan government forces, so it was assumed they'd be safe to return to them. To his horror, Karu says he was told, 'There is no problem in your country. You can go back.'

Six months after I interviewed Karu and Gowri, they sent me a message saying their case had been accepted on appeal but they had not been released from Villawood. Australia has a system of vetting approved refugees to ensure they don't pose a security risk. Immigration lawyers believe the process mainly involves checking with the Sri Lankan government that there are no criminal cases pending – consulting the very country from which they fled. Baby Puni isn't free, but at least she's safe for the first time in her life.

Asylum Seekers

Australia

AS OF 30 NOVEMBER 2011   355 Sri Lankans in detention (including 6 children);
242 in the community (including 89 children)[1]

European Union

2010   6,480 asylum applications from Sri Lankans

2011 FIRST QUARTER   1,915 applications from Sri Lankans (1,395 rejected) of which 990 (52 per cent) in France (625 rejected), 565 in UK (470 rejected), 140 Germany, 60 Netherlands, 50 Belgium, 110 other[2]

UK

Sri Lanka is among the top ten countries of origin of asylum seekers.

2007	990
2008	1,475[3]
2010	1,357
2011	1,758 (1,289 refusals)[4]
IN DETENTION END 2011	71

Canada

Refugee claimants of Sri Lankan origin

2008	3,297
2009	2,758
2010	2,778

Permanent residents of Sri Lankan origin accepted

2008	4,509[5]
2009	4,269
2010	4,181

As of 2001, 87,305 Canadians were born in Sri Lanka, compared to less than 150 in 1983 before the civil war escalated. It is estimated that 200,000 Sri Lankan Tamils live in Canada, making it the largest Sri Lankan diaspora in the world, with Toronto the largest diaspora city.

Sri Lanka

JANUARY 2012   156,000 internally displaced persons inside Sri Lanka (source: UN High Commission for Refugees)

The Wife

Manimolly's mouth had gone dry with fear as she waited alone in an empty villa in the room lit by a single bulb. There was no furniture other than one small table and a chair. It was the early hours of the morning; outside was pitch dark and quiet. The young Tamil housewife didn't know where she was. In the next-door room she could hear the policemen getting more and more drunk and singing loudly in Sinhala.

A pretty Tamil girl originally from the tea estates in central Sri Lanka, she'd been brought up in a middle-class family in Colombo. Throughout her whole life, Sri Lanka had been embroiled in a vicious civil war, but it wasn't really her struggle. She was as apolitical as it was possible to be. Her husband, though, was much more involved. He came from the north of Sri Lanka and his mother and sister had died in the fighting at the end of the conflict in 2009. The first time Manimolly met her father-in-law and other relatives was when they arrived half-starved at Manik Farm. She was introduced to them across the barbed wire. Manimolly was shocked to see all those exhausted, emaciated people but her focus was her newborn baby. She only visited the camp twice, preferring the reassuring comfort of home.

Over their two years of marriage, Manimolly had gradually realised that her husband had secrets. 'Every day there were problems. He was not at home and I didn't know where he went. Something was not right. I didn't ask and he didn't tell.' It had been an arranged marriage – the groom a stranger who, to her parents' relief, didn't demand a dowry. Manimolly had only seen his photo the day before the ceremony. She wasn't keen but decided to make the best of it.

Slowly it dawned on her that she had married into a Tamil Tiger family. Her husband wasn't a rebel but his brothers and sisters were and he was happy to run errands for them. After the war he travelled to India frequently but she didn't know why. He was on one of those trips when there was a knock at the door of their home in Vavuniya. Manimolly's uneventful domestic life was about to descend into a long, lonely, personal hell.

She remembers it was about three or four in the afternoon on 1 May 2010, almost a full year after the guns had fallen silent. She was at home with her sixteen-month-old baby girl and her mother, who was staying to keep her company while her husband was away. Five uniformed policemen from the Criminal Investigation Department stood outside the house. They showed their identity cards and demanded to come in.

'Where is your husband?' they asked. 'We are from CID and we have to talk to you and take down some details.' Three officers pushed their way inside the house and began firing off questions.

'Why has he gone to India? Have you received any unusual parcels at this address? Have strangers been coming to stay here?'

Manimolly was scared. She didn't tell them anything about her husband's family. 'My husband is a photographer; he's gone to India for business,' she repeated several times.

'You are lying,' they replied.

Then they insisted she come to the police station to make a statement. 'It won't be for long, then we will release you,' they promised, 'just half an hour and you can go home.' Manimolly put up a struggle. No Tamil woman in Sri Lanka would voluntarily walk into a police station alone. She told them she couldn't leave her baby because she was still breastfeeding. They took no notice. She shouted, she cried, she screamed; her mother said she would come with her to the police station. It was to no avail.

'You must come!' they said. Her heart was pounding as she was dragged outside and into a vehicle.

At the police station she was put on a seat and left to wait for two hours, ignored almost. Then two policewomen asked her to follow them. Before she knew what was happening, Manimolly was pushed into a cell and locked inside. 'Your husband has to come, then we will release you,' they said.

Unknown to Manimolly, her mother had come to the police station, demanding to see her, desperate with worry about what could happen to a twenty-nine-year-old Tamil woman in such a place. Everyone knew there had been plenty of cases of women being raped in custody, and few members of the security forces were ever punished. 'Tell your son-in-law to come to Sri Lanka and then we will release your daughter,' she was told.

A couple of hours went by before three Sinhalese policewomen arrived and ordered Manimolly to follow them for questioning. She was led to a dirty room with a chair and table. 'I was really terrified. There were two male police and three women. They asked questions about my husband, accusing him of being a Tiger. They said, "He has been involved in bomb blasts. You've been hiding people in your house. We have an album with a picture of your husband in rebel uniform."' Then they took a length of wire and a wooden stick and beat her on the legs through her thin cotton trousers. The marks remain to this day.

When Manimolly was returned to the cell the wounds burned but there was no blood, just swelling. She was exhausted – hours had gone by in the heat with no water and she was desperately worried about her baby at home. Two girls in the cell, much younger and unmarried, said they'd been through the same treatment, but Manimolly had no time to take an interest in others. Anyway she suspected they might be Tigers, because they had short hair, and she wanted nothing to do with them.

After midnight a policewoman came again, calling for Manimolly. 'Why do you want me now?' she asked suspiciously. 'It's night-time; the police station is closed and there's no sound at all. Why can't you ask your questions tomorrow?'

The policewoman insisted, saying the officers wanted to take her to see if she could identify two captives they thought were her husband's friends. Manimolly was escorted outside and put into a van. There were three Sinhalese men in plain clothes who spoke Tamil and said they were from the Criminal Investigation Department. They drove around town but she had no idea where they were going. The van stopped and Manimolly was taken inside a villa; upstairs she was shown two blindfolded young Tamil men.

'Do you recognise them?' they asked, removing the blindfolds.

'I don't know them,' she replied truthfully.

'You wait in that room,' the men ordered, taking her to the ground floor and locking the door behind them. She could smell the alcohol on their breath and hear them drunkenly singing next door.

After what felt like a very long time one of the CID officers came into the room, so inebriated he could hardly stand up and swearing badly. He was in his early forties and naked from the waist up. 'He was like a giant; he came close to me and I moved back. "Actually you are very beautiful," he said. I tried to save myself. I moved back and he came after me. I was terrified. He pulled at my cotton scarf but I didn't let him take it. I moved back again. Then he slapped me so hard on my face that I fell on the floor. I was dizzy and weak and I couldn't stand up. Before I knew it he took a pair of handcuffs and he snapped one round my wrist and the other round the chair so I couldn't escape.'

Manimolly screamed, hoping that someone would hear and save her. 'The sound of the singing was too loud,' she said. 'I tried to fight with him. I was just conscious. But he slapped me three or four more times and removed my trousers.'

Manimolly was raped; just when she thought it was over, another CID man came and raped her too. 'They were like animals. I was crying. At that time I was forty days pregnant and I started to bleed, having a miscarriage.'

At four in the morning the policemen put her back in the vehicle. 'If you say anything or tell anyone we will kill your husband and kill you. Nothing happened here. Do you understand?' they warned as they drove her back to the police station. Unable to walk properly, her trousers covered in blood, she staggered back into the cell. Three policewomen came and offered Manimolly water and she asked them if they could bring her some sanitary towels to stem the bleeding. Another woman helped her make it to the toilet to clean herself.

The two other girls in the cell talked about suicide, hinting that they'd been raped as well. Manimolly was in no state to engage with their suffering, though now she admits she's better off because a single girl who was raped would have no chance of ever marrying. She also says she was lucky she wasn't burned because someone else she knew was arrested, raped and burned with cigarette butts on her breast.

Three days later her husband arrived to hand himself in at the police station to secure the release of his wife. She promptly tried to kill herself with an overdose of sleeping pills. In the following months she lost weight, suffered memory loss, sank into depression and could no longer care for her daughter. She never told her mother and sister explicitly what had happened, just that the men had not treated her with respect. She refused even to go to a doctor after the miscarriage, fearing the shame associated with the rape. She tried to kill herself again, jumping out of an auto-rickshaw into the path of an oncoming bus, which luckily stopped before it ran her over. Her mother had to remind her of the need to survive for her child's sake.

It was double torment: dealing with the stigma and trauma of the rape while worrying about her husband being tortured in detention. After two months they raised Rs. 800,000 (nearly £4,000) as a bribe to get him out of jail, offering their house deeds to the bank as surety and selling Manimolly's gold jewellery.

Being reunited with her husband wasn't much comfort. They still haven't openly discussed the rape, though the suicide attempts were a way of telling him what really happened. 'I blamed him for what they did to me. I constantly fought with him and could find no peace,' Manimolly says, adding that she often shouts at him.

All the while, the police were visiting their house and calling her husband for questioning. To escape the shame and fear, they decided to go abroad. They managed to obtain student visas for the UK. Manimolly went to college in London for a few months to study to be a beautician before claiming asylum. 'At least in the UK it's better because I don't keep seeing the police and army. In Sri Lanka, every time I saw them it would all come back to me and I would panic.'

Since they left Sri Lanka the police have continued to visit their house. Unable to find Manimolly's husband, they once arrested his seventy-year-old father instead, keeping him in jail for three months in lieu of his son.

I went to interview Manimolly in her suburban terrace house in east London, an area full of new immigrants. While we spoke her husband pottered about in the background, keeping the child amused, taking her to the local shop on her tricycle to buy sweets.

I went alone to visit Manimolly because she refused to allow any Tamil to come with me to translate. Her English is fluent, but I still don't know her full name because of the need for security. 'They just gossip,' she says of the neighbourhood Tamils, convinced that her life wouldn't be worth living if her own community found out what she'd been through. It's a lonely life — apart from the immigration officer and her trauma counsellor she's never really talked to anyone about the rape, even her own mother. Manimolly says it's something she doesn't want to relive, but then explains that it's with her all the time anyway. 'I am not alive,' she says, still scared of every man that walks past her in the street, even of her own husband. She knows he is a good man — he doesn't smoke, drink or womanise, and he's kind, often reassuring her that he will stay with her. He supports Manimolly in her decision to speak out. He knows she's telling me, a total stranger, all about something they can never name between themselves.

There is very little first-hand testimony of rape from this war because of the extraordinary stigma in Tamil society against women who've survived sexual abuse. The cultural prejudice against rape survivors is tantamount to a second form of abuse. Suicide is often considered the only honourable way out.

Manimolly's rare first-hand testimony suggests that the rape of Tamil women in custody continues with impunity. Throughout the decades of war, there were sporadic reports of rape by the security forces at checkpoints or in detention. At the end of 2006 the Refugee

Council in London conducted a study of rape among asylum seekers in the UK in which half the 153 women were Sri Lankan Tamils. It discovered that the Tamil community assumed that if a young woman was detained she would be raped almost automatically. Many women had been burned with cigarettes so as to mark them out as former detainees to their families and the security forces.[1]

Manimolly is lucky that she escaped abroad, but Human Rights Watch has alleged that asylum seekers deported from Britain have been raped in custody after being sent back to Sri Lanka – something the UK government rejected. HRW's case studies include gang-rape of men as well as women.[2]

What's not clear is whether the rape at the end of the war was a continuation of the opportunistic attacks perpetrated by individual security officials, encouraged by the idea that they can get away with it, or more organised and officially condoned.

In late 2009 the US Secretary of State, Hillary Clinton, referred in passing to Sri Lanka as a country where rape had been used as a tactic of war. It was a deliberate warning to the Sri Lankan government, a carefully thought-out statement based on confidential information collected by aid workers as well as the videos of dead female fighters filmed by Sri Lankan soldiers chatting lewdly about naked female bodies. The UN's expert advisory panel said that in the videos there was a 'strong inference that rape or sexual violence may have occurred'. There is even reported to be a video of a gang rape of a Tamil woman, filmed by soldiers. Ms Clinton's remark suggested the United States believed there was a degree of official sanction for the abuse of Tamil women. However, after fierce protests by the Sri Lankan government, the US State Department qualified its remarks to say rape wasn't used as a tool of war in Sri Lanka in the same way as in other conflicts.[3]

Other human-rights groups have discovered evidence of sexual abuse by the Sri Lankan military at the end of the war.[4] A middle-aged Tamil woman appeared on Channel 4 saying she had been raped in a forest clearing after surrendering to the army during the spring of 2009. She is the only woman to have spoken out publicly, albeit with her identity disguised. She gave this written statement: 'The soldiers made all the men and women remove our clothes completely in front of the children. The women were forced to go around the army in a circle, while they laughed. All the women were then raped in front of everyone, irrespective of their age. Myself and my daughter were raped in front of her children.' An anonymous male soldier also told Channel 4 that he'd witnessed a group of six soldiers raping a young Tamil girl.[5]

Gowri's testimony above suggests that at the end of the war girls were being raped more or less in full view of tens of thousands of Tamils too cowed to protest. It is possible under extreme stress that she genuinely believed she saw something that didn't actually happen, but she mentions that other women commented on the incident. Other survivors have not spoken of this sort of attack; one explanation could be collective shame at their passivity. It was 'everyone for himself' by the end, and that is not easy to admit. Clerics say that in the final weeks there was a social and moral collapse, young boys and girls having sex outside marriage while sheltering in the church building in what they described as an 'end of days' scenario.

A Tamil girl whom I shall call Selvy says she was groped by an armed soldier on a bus packed with surrendering civilians. No Tamil man came to her defence; only an elderly lady who bravely rose from her seat and placed herself between the soldier and Selvy to block his unwanted attentions. The atmosphere was so tense that Selvy says she didn't dare scream or resist when the soldier touched her for fear she'd just be taken off the bus, raped in the bushes and shot. Afterwards she didn't dare say a word of thanks to the old lady, only giving her a grateful look with her eyes. There was an atmosphere of terror where few came to the aid of strangers.

Every Tamil woman detained in Manik Farm feared rape, and absolutely nothing was done by the authorities to calm their fears. Some say there were empty tents for rape in certain areas of the camp where the lights were switched off at night to hide what went on. There were reports from aid workers of buses rounding up attractive young women to be taken away for sexual abuse and, when that became too obvious, the women were summoned for 'questioning' one by one and then removed. Among them was the wife of a UN employee. I have also heard of women who've escaped abroad but are too destroyed by repeated sexual abuse to speak of their ordeal to journalists.

Although the international media raised the issue of rape in the refugee camps in 2009, [6] no Sri Lankan official or civil group came out with a clear condemnation to send a message to the security forces that this sort of behaviour would not be tolerated. The *Australian* newspaper even reported that Sri Lankan officials were running a prostitution racket using women from one refugee camp. The authorities' response was blanket denial. Sri Lanka's Foreign Secretary, Palitha Kohona, now permanent representative to the UN, had this to say about the military: 'These are the guys who were winning the war – they could have raped every single woman on the way if they wanted to. Not one single woman was raped.'[7]

Worse still, some Sri Lankan government officials made light of rape, as explained in Usha's story. The Defence Secretary mentioned the case of a young British Tamil woman who was not raped, bizarrely arguing that this proved all other attractive women must have been safe too: 'Now she is one person who will get attracted by the people… (haha), soldiers…So, I want to know whether SHE was raped…Now she was talking about the rape. How can she talk about the rape when she…a person so attractive…safely came into this area?'[8]

As one writer commented, inordinate delays in court cases and the lack of witness protection mean few rape cases are ever prosecuted in Sri Lanka, with the result that there is a perception that rape is not really a crime.[9]

Very little is known about the fate of female combatants held in army-run detention centres, as opposed to refugee camps for civilians. Religious figures have met mothers who tell them their daughters have been enduring nightly rape in detention centres. There are stories of young unmarried women in secret camps committing suicide after becoming pregnant as a result of repeated gang rapes. Discarded women's clothes and bloodstained handprints on the walls were discovered by a Tamil cleaner sent into the rebels' main district hospital, a building occupied by the army at the height of the war. One Sri Lankan newspaper reported that former rebels working at a garment factory as part of their rehabilitation programme had been raped by the managers.[10] A former parliamentarian said he'd met a Tamil Tiger woman who worked as a prostitute after being released from detention because she saw no other way to survive economically. Women are too afraid to confront the military and many ex-combatants are routinely visited in their homes by the security forces to check up on them after release. So tainted are the women who've spent time in the camps for former combatants that few Tamil men will marry them.

Extraordinarily, in comparison to other conflicts, there have never been allegations of rape levelled against the rebels. The Tigers' use of women fighters and their avowed feminist ideology may be one reason. However, this emancipation had unforeseen consequences. For the male Sri Lankan soldiers, the realisation that they were fighting young girls was horrifying; the dead bodies of the early women Tiger fighters were routinely mutilated, their breasts chopped off. The new-found equality for Tamil women on the battlefield had the effect of blurring the distinction between civilians and combatants, transforming all females into potential enemies.

Conclusion

Two years after the end of the war, I received an email from a young Tamil Tiger asking me to give evidence at his asylum hearing in London. He needed someone to confirm his identity because the name on his passport was different from his *nom de guerre*. I've called him Bala, though it's not his real name. He'd been my Tiger minder during the 2004 tsunami, a young apparatchik in the political wing charged with escorting me around the marshes where his traumatised comrades were still pulling out rotting human limbs and decomposing animal carcasses. We were moving in the coastal areas that were the Tigers' heartland and foreign journalists were not allowed to wander about on their own. Bala watched my response to the terrible suffering we saw everywhere, constantly quizzing me on what I thought of the political situation in Sri Lanka. None of us could imagine the people who survived the tsunami would experience something even worse. After 2009 I wondered if this eager, inquisitive young man had survived. I went to meet him full of expectation, keen to hear the story of someone I knew before the war.

We met in a café at a mainline railway station, with his lawyer, who did most of the talking while Bala sipped hot chocolate and smiled. I don't know if it was the surprise of a face resurfacing from the past, or relief that I remembered him and could testify in his case. His lawyer said it was the first time he'd seen him smile. Thoughtlessly I asked after his parents, only to discover they were still missing, perhaps somewhere in a government refugee camp. An uncle was looking for them and, if they were alive, they had no idea their son was in England.

The man seated before me was utterly broken. He was physically recognisable as the same person but completely changed in character. His lawyer told me he'd been very badly tortured, and I later heard at the asylum tribunal that his body bore torture scars that would

226

be obvious if he was returned to Sri Lanka and strip-searched at the airport. Two psychiatrists testified that he was too badly damaged to give evidence, even in his own appeal. He still understood English but hardly spoke in any language. Childlike, he allowed others to talk for him – that was when he wasn't trying to harm himself.

I never discovered what happened to Bala, and I am not sure I want to find out. It's different when you know what a person was like before torture. To many he was just a terrorist, but he was also a human being who paid an enormous price for his political choices. Most of his colleagues are dead: only a few made it abroad, missing limbs and/or deeply traumatised. They want nothing more to do with politics or armed struggle; it's been kicked and trampled out of them. All they want is to find somewhere quiet to live in obscurity – as far away as possible from their fellow-Tamils because of the fear of betrayal. There is no appetite for revenge. Not one single survivor I met in the course of this book really wanted to take up arms again.

This of course presents an extraordinary opportunity for resolving the conflict – a rare moment that is unfortunately being squandered. The Tamil Tigers have been totally eliminated but that hasn't made the victors any more willing to share their beautiful island.

The Sri Lankan military has actually expanded since the end of the war, adding 100,000 men to its ranks. The army has taken over land and businesses in the north of the island, settling Sinhalese in traditionally Tamil areas. The Tigers' dream of a Tamil homeland is now impractical because concentrations of Tamil populations are being diluted.

Many survivors of the war live in extreme poverty, with barely any shelter, sleeping under tarpaulin. At the time of writing almost 50,000 of the survivors of the final stage of the war were still displaced and another 20,000 staying temporarily with friends and relatives.[1] One survey, by the US Agency for International Development, found 89 per cent of families didn't have a single member with a job or income. In the north of Sri Lanka more than half the population lives below the poverty line; in Kilinochchi a quarter of families live on less than half the official poverty line.

Worse still is the lack of security. At the time of writing, human-rights groups know of at least seven secret detention sites in northern Sri Lanka. Torture and rape have persisted and Sri Lanka has the dubious distinction of being second in the world in terms of the number of disappearances. Human-rights activists and journalists have continued to disappear well after the war ended – not only Tamils but Sinhalese too.[2]

On the political front there has been a deathly silence about minority rights or devolution of power for Tamils. Even commemorations for the dead have been banned from taking place lest they become oppor-tunities for espousing nationalism. The official rhetoric is that it's better not to dig up the past, rather everyone should concentrate on the future. That simply fails to acknowledge the extent of the indescribable suffering inflicted on Tamil civilians by both sides in 2009.

Since the defeat of the Tigers there's been no attempt to address the underlying causes of the conflict. Sri Lanka is a small country but according to some accounts there are now 200,000 internally displaced Tamils, 40,000 war widows in the northern town of Jaffna alone and possibly as many as 165,000 war-disabled in the north of the country.[3] Yet in 2011 Sri Lanka's military budget was the biggest in the country's history. In the north there is one Sri Lankan soldier for every eleven citizens. Millions of pounds of government money were spent on a UK public-relations company, Bell Pottinger, to deflect war-crimes charges.

Many Western countries tacitly supported Sri Lanka's 'little war on terror'. It's the lack of democracy, not war crimes, that embar-rasses them now. Privately, politicians express disappointment with what they call the 'family dynasty' that runs the island. At the time of writing, Mahinda Rajapaksa is not just President but also Minister of Defence, Finance, Planning, Ports and Aviation, and Highways. Another Rajapaksa brother is the all-powerful Defence Secretary, controlling the army, police, coastguard and immigration. A third is Economic Development Minister and heads a task force to develop the war zone. A fourth Rajapaksa is Speaker of Parliament; while the President's sister is his private secretary and his son a Member of Parliament. Corruption and nepotism are rampant, while censorship has increased. The atmosphere has not been conducive to justice. It's hard to discuss the present, let alone the past.

Experienced aid workers who could have helped were thrown out of Sri Lanka in record numbers immediately after the war (see page 31). The government refused to renew the visa of any foreign aid worker who'd been in the country more than three years, in a deliberate attempt to eliminate anyone with access to information and contacts in the conflict areas. After two decades the International Red Cross was told to close its offices in the north and east, even though Sri Lanka had conducted what was then the largest mass detention without trial anywhere in the world, and family members were still desperately trying to locate missing children and spouses from the war. The Sri Lankan government had accused the International Red Cross of spreading panic when it spoke of a 'humanitarian catastrophe' at the end of the war.[4]

Speaking out about war crimes has been deterred inside Sri Lanka, with even civil and peace groups saying it's better to leave alone. The few international parliamentarians, human-rights lawyers, aid workers or journalists who've asked questions have been automatically branded as terrorist sympathisers. I have been called wicked, mendacious, melodramatic and with no regard for the truth or consistency – and that was all in just one article. When I lived in Sri Lanka I wallpapered my small radio studio with abusive newspaper articles and emails, as a reminder to be careful on air. My predecessor and successor as BBC correspondent both had death threats as well as hate mail.

Yet Tamils still look to the United Nations and the International Criminal Court for justice – the same system that failed them so utterly in 2009.

The UN has dragged its feet on accountability. Under pressure from human-rights groups, in June 2010 Ban Ki-moon commissioned a panel of three independent legal experts to look into allegations of war crimes. It was a thorough and balanced report but the Secretary-General's office delayed making it public, allowing the Sri Lankan government time to leak the document with its own spin. Then they delayed transferring the report to the UN Human Rights Council for follow-up action.

All the Human Rights Council delivered for the first two years after the war was an embarrassing travesty of justice. In 2009 the agenda was hijacked by Sri Lanka's new friends, China and some of the Non-Aligned Movement nations opposed to Western interference in their internal affairs, who passed a resolution actually praising Colombo's actions in the war. Only in March 2012 did the US and India finally support a watered-down resolution, calling on Sri Lanka to ensure accountability, with the UN providing advice 'in consultation with, and with the concurrence of the Government of Sri Lanka'. There was absolutely no mention of the term 'war crimes'. Sri Lankan human-rights activists and journalists who campaigned for the vote in Geneva received death threats and abuse while still inside the UN building, while one Sri Lankan minister in Colombo threatened to break their legs if they returned home. A shocked UN High Commissioner for Human Rights had to issue a statement complaining of 'an unprecedented and totally unacceptable level of threats, harrassment and intimidation', including, she said, by members of the seventy-one-strong government delegation.[5]

Ban Ki-moon, however, has remained silent even though the independent experts he commissioned concluded in 2011 that war crimes and crimes against humanity were committed in Sri Lanka. They said:

> The Panel's determination of credible allegations reveals a very different version of the final stages of the war than that maintained to this day by the Government of Sri Lanka. The Government says it pursued a 'humanitarian rescue operation' with a policy of 'zero civilian casualties'. In start contrast, the Panel found credible allegations, which if proven, indicate that a wide range of serious violations of international humanitarian

law and itnernational human rights law was committed both by the Government of Sri Lanka and the LTTE [Liberation Tigers of Tamil Eelam], some of which would amount to war crimes and crimes against humanity. Indeed, the conduct of the war represented a grave assault on the entire regime of international law designed to protect individual dignity during both war and peace.

The experts recommended that Ban Ki-moon review the actions of the United Nations during the war in the light of its humanitarian and protection mandates. They also said the Secretary-General should immediately establish an independent international mechanism to monitor accountability inside Sri Lanka and conduct its own independent investigations – neither of which has he done so far. Sri Lanka's actions had emboldened 'some to believe the rules could be disregarded when fighting terrorism', they said.

The UN has quickly rebuilt relations with the Sri Lankan military, despite the allegations of war crimes. The commander of one of the brigades active in the final war front, Major-General Shavendra Silva, was posted as Deputy Ambassador to the UN, giving him immunity from prosecution. A civil lawsuit filed against him by two Tamils in New York complaining of torture was thrown out because of this diplomatic immunity.

Some of Sri Lanka's troops who were at the front are now deployed around the world as UN peacekeepers, and the plan is to expand the army's involvement with the UN.[6] Major-General Silva managed to get himself appointed to a ten-member UN peacekeeping committee, until his presence there caused uproar. The UN human-rights chief, Navi Pillay, complained to Ban Ki-moon that it was reasonable to conclude there was 'at the very least, the appearance of a case of inter-national crimes to answer by Mr Silva'.[7] However, other controversial Sri Lankan brigadiers and generals have been posted as ambassadors around the world and few governments have objected.

Meanwhile, some Tamils who worked for the UN have been

cruelly abandoned by the organisation, forced to flee for their lives unsupported. Thousands of survivors of the war escaped to southern India and Singapore, and then on to Kuala Lumpur and Bangkok. They are too frightened to go home to Sri Lanka but often unable to get asylum in the West through legal channels. Those who make it to Europe, Canada or Australia tend to be the ones with friends abroad who can pay the people smugglers. The law-abiding and those without money have few options. They have been left in limbo. Hundreds of traumatised and desperate men and women with military training from a proscribed terrorist organisation are now at large, desperate for liveli-hoods and without access to any rehabilitation programme. It would not be surprising if some turned to crime.

Many Western countries that preach human rights turned their back on Sri Lanka during 2009, and continue to do so. They waited for the Sri Lankans themselves to conduct a drawn-out internal inquiry – the Lessons Learned and Reconciliation Commission, or LLRC – even though they knew it was flawed in its composition and remit.[8] The commission included government officials who'd publicly defended Sri Lanka against accusations of war crimes – a serious conflict of interest. During the first hearing the chairman told survivors to forget the past and focus on problems in accessing education, medical care and housing.

The Sri Lankan inquiry did however acknowledge for the first time that the casualties were considerable, and that some hospitals were shelled, but it exonerated the military of deliberately targeting civilians and appeared to blame the rebels for all the deaths:

> …the Commission is satisfied that the military strategy that was adopted to secure the LTTE areas was one that was carefully conceived, in which the protection of the civilian population was given the highest priority…the Commission concludes that the Security Forces had not deliberately targeted the civilians in the NFZs, although civilian casualties had in fact occurred in the course of crossfire.

The report failed to address the issue of sexual violence or the incident in which the Tiger political wing leaders Puli and Nadesan were killed while surrendering with a white flag. Nobody – Tiger or soldier – has been held accountable for any of the war crimes, even in the most symbolic, non-punitive way.

The army's commander at the time of the war, General Sarath Fonseka, has been court-martialled and jailed, but it was not for anything he did on the battlefield. In 2010 he challenged Mahinda Rajapaksa for the post of president. After losing the election he faced a variety of charges, including 'spreading disaffection' for allegedly telling a newspaper that the President's brother had ordered the shooting of Puli and Nadesan. The decorated war hero who'd narrowly escaped a Tiger suicide bomber found himself stripped of his rank and at the time of writing languishes in a jail cell with a bucket collecting the rainwater that drips through the leaking roof.[9]

Eleven thousand suspected rebels were detained for years without trial.[10] By the government's own admission, some had very tenuous links to the Tigers. One such man was detained for 435 days simply because he'd been forced to join the rebels for a brief spell fifteen years earlier.[11] Gradually almost all of the rebel suspects have been released. Three years after the end of the war, not one has been put on public trial as part of the accountability process.

Tamils in the diaspora champion an international war-crimes trial because almost all the senior rebels are dead and they have little to lose. Tamil nationalist groups conveniently overlook the fact that the Tiger leaders deliberately exposed their own people to slaughter and refused to surrender, even when all was plainly lost. Suicide bombing of innocents is still glorified as the ultimate sacrifice, while the extreme cruelty of the rebels to their own people is largely denied. There's little public discussion of what went wrong over decades of armed struggle, except to look for scapegoats and traitors. At a personal level many Tamils who experienced the last phase of the war have been preoccupied with survival and escape and it's unrealistic to expect a process of reassessment of the past so soon. For them it's still very much a work in progress.

Impunity for Sri Lankan war crimes sends a clear signal to other repressive states that this model of fighting internal rebellion can be replicated. It also leaves the Tamil Tigers' dangerous ideology of martyrdom and sacrifice unchallenged, preventing any soul-searching on the Tamil side. In short, it sets the stage for a repeat.

Psychologists argue that trauma, especially in conflicts, can be transmitted from one generation to another, storing up trouble for the future. It is said that Velupillai Prabhakaran was radicalised by hearing tales of the anti-Tamil riots in the 1950s. Thousands of young Tamils took up arms after the traumatic 1983 pogrom that fuelled decades of fighting. How much worse will it be next time, when the children who survived the atrocities of 2009 grow up and want revenge? As International Crisis Group puts it:

> The international community has particular reasons to be concerned about any resurgence of violence that might be fed by the defeat of the LTTE and the humiliation of Tamil civilians. Most of the drivers of Sri Lanka's conflict have not been resolved and some new sources of resentment have emerged. While the government's security apparatus is powerful and pervasive enough to suppress any rapid re-emergence of violent resistance, it will not be able to do so indefinitely so long as legitimate grievances are not addressed. A quarter of the Sri Lankan Tamil population lives abroad. This million-strong diaspora is a reservoir of separatist aspirations and has been willing to fund violence in the past. A new generation has been politicised by the final months of the conflict. The defeat of the LTTE has left many shocked and directionless; as yet it is unclear whether the inchoate fury and sense of humiliation will coalesce into a renewed support for violence. If it did, it would only take a small portion of the diaspora to fund and propagate a new insurgency.[12]

One aid worker, himself a refugee from the break-up of Yugoslavia, is haunted by the memory of a tiny malnourished twelve-year-old

Tamil boy whom he found alone in the refugee camp, sleeping rough and separated from his mother, after having watched his father and siblings literally blown to pieces in front of him.

'After all he went through, will that twelve-year-old ever grow up thinking, this is my government?' he asked. 'The war is not over in Sri Lanka; you don't solve these kinds of problems on the battlefield.'

Humiliation was heaped on top of unimaginable suffering, so that Tamils experienced extreme loss, shame and helplessness. Yes, there were many unsung heroes in the final phase of the war. But there were also plenty of Tamils who abandoned their friends to save themselves and are now haunted by that choice. Denied space in which to assert themselves politically or socially, they are now part of what psychologists term a 'massively traumatised group'.

After Iraq, Afghanistan and Darfur, Sri Lanka probably has the highest number of casualties of any conflict this century, and yet few have heard of it.

It's unrealistic to expect survivors just to put the war behind them, forget the past and move on. Without acknowledging the truth it will be easy for radical politicians to exploit the collective rage. The risk is that next time it won't just be the Sinhalese they hate, but also the international community that abandoned them.

Appendix One

Casualties

Death Toll

One way to gauge the scale of casualties is to subtract the number of survivors in the government refugee camps from the total population figures for rebel territory before the war. We know that every Tamil who came out of the war zone alive was enumerated, irrespective of whether they were a civilian or a combatant. The registration occurred twice – once at the point of surrender and once at Omanthai checkpoint.

The Sri Lankan government says it killed 22,247 Tigers over the last three years of the war.[1] In late December 2008 Lieutenant-General Sarath Fonseka said they'd killed 15,000 rebels in the past three years. It's not clear how many were killed in the final phase of the war, and whether this figure could account for some of the missing civilians.

Survivors
It's known that between 282,380 and 289,915 Tamils were counted at the end of the war.[2] There were 14,000 evacuated by Red Cross ships and possibly a few hundred who escaped on fishing boats, but most of these would have been put in refugee camps.[3] The army detained 11,954 alleged Tigers after the end of the war but these appear to have been screened from among the surrendering civilian population.

Population before the War
For decades there had been no national census conducted in rebel areas. However the last head count there[4] was in June 2006 and recorded 432,262 people. This was a count conducted jointly with government officials. It's unlikely more than a few thousand left after this date

because the Tigers operated such strict controls over population move-ment. In fact, the population may well have grown because of the babies born during this time.

There had also been a UNICEF census of schoolchildren, but it was less reliable because it used indirectly collected data from local organisations.

The Sri Lankan civil service used a population estimate for rebel areas of 429,059 people in October 2008. This is very close to the 2006 number which was based on a head count.

The UN, which had international staff living in rebel areas until this point, used a figure of 420,000 in September 2008. These estimates were important because they were used to determine food aid and other humanitarian assistance.

A senior Tamil administrative officer testified to a government inquiry that on 22 January 2009 there were nearly 350,000 people still in rebel areas. Another official testified in early February that there were 330,000 people, based on a survey of village officials and ration cards, but UN staff say this would not have included rebels and their families as they were not issued with ration cards.[5] When this popula-tion figure of 330,000 was first given during the war, the government in Colombo threatened its representative on the ground with disci-plinary action for providing what it said was 'wrong information', but he has consistently stuck to this figure.

The Sri Lankan government initially said in January 2009 there were between 150,000 and 250,000[6] people inside rebel areas, and a few weeks later abruptly revised that figure down to 75,000–100,000. Their figure was proved to be a gross underestimate. Many more people emerged from rebel territory as refugees at the end of the war. Politicians never explained how they'd got the numbers so wrong; their critics believe they deliberately reduced the population numbers to justify sending in less food. We know from WikiLeaks cables that American diplomats became quite cynical about the Sri Lankan refusal to allow the UN to go into rebel areas to assess population numbers, commenting in telexes that Colombo wanted to provide just enough food to ensure Tamil civilians didn't starve but still had an incentive to flee the war zone.

Disappeared, Presumed Dead

Simple mathematics leaves anywhere from 26,000 to 146,679 people unaccounted for, presumed dead. Analysing the available population figures, International Crisis Group wrote: 'While some inflation in the figures is possible, it is unlikely to have been large enough to explain all, or even most, of the discrepancies. There is also some corroborating evidence that argues for taking seriously even large estimates of the missing and demanding a full and independent accounting.'[7]

Other Concerns

A survey in Manik Farm in early May 2009 – before the worst casualties – found 22 per cent of refugees had a close family member who'd been killed in the fighting. Extrapolating for the entire population, this would suggest 18,000 deaths before the final weeks. However this is a very rough calculation.

The government said in 2010 it had a list of 40,000 war widows in the north, but then in 2011 reduced this to 16,936 without explanation.

The UN's *Report of the Secretary-General's Panel of Experts on Accountability in Sri Lanka* said that estimates based on the number of operations (40,000 surgical procedures and 5,000 amputations) could point to higher casualty figures.

Sri Lankan Government Casualty Data

Throughout the 2009 war the government claimed it operated a 'zero civilian casualty policy'. Only much later, in August 2011, did a government report, the *Humanitarian Operation Factual Analysis*, concede that there were unavoidable civilian casualties. In December 2011 the government-appointed inquiry known as the Lessons Learnt and Reconciliation Commission (LLRC) finally accepted there were considerable civilian casualties. It said there were some incidents in which civilians were killed in the crossfire and suggested that in a few cases possible wrongdoing by the security forces should be investigated. This has not been done at the time of writing. The commission also called for 'a professionally designed household survey covering all affected families in all parts of the island to ascertain first-hand the scale and the circumstances of death and injury to civilians'.

In February 2012 the government released a report called *Enumeration of Vital Events*, based on a survey conducted in the north of the island from June to August 2011. It found fewer than 7,000 war casualties, with another 2,500 missing, but it didn't differentiate between civilians and combatants, nor assign responsibility.

A group of anonymous civil-society activists alleged the forms used to collect information in this government census did not contain a category for 'died in the war', and complained that the military was heavily involved in the process.

Worryingly, this document also reduced the population for the two main towns in Tiger-held areas, Kilinochchi and Mullaitivu, by 100,000 people, giving no explanation for the drop.

Appendix Two

Alleged War Crimes

(as defined by the *Report of the Secretary-General's*
Panel of Experts on Accountability in Sri Lanka)

War Crimes

By the Sri Lankan Government

1. Killing of civilians through widespread shelling (including indiscriminate or disproportionate attacks)
2. Murder, mutilation, cruel treatment, torture including rape, outrages on personal dignity, humiliating and degrading treatment, failure to collect and care for the wounded and sick
3. Intentional attacks on civilians
4. Shelling of hospitals and humanitarian objects, including humanitarian convoys and Red Cross-designated facilities
5. Denial of humanitarian assistance and starvation
6. Enforced disappearances

Indiscriminate shelling on the final UN food convoy that entered rebel territory in January 2009 was documented by two international aid workers. They repeatedly informed the Sri Lankan military that its shells were killing civilians in the safe area but the attacks did not stop. The UN workers concluded that the shelling was intentional.

A fifteen-strong Indian military medical team was based near the war zone from March 2009 to treat casualties; they are also witnesses to the types of injuries inflicted on civilians.[1]

The repeated use of weapons like multi-barrelled rocket launchers in densely populated areas must also constitute an indiscriminate attack. Witnesses in this book testify to coming under heavy fire even when the Sri Lankan government maintained, in February and then again in late April, that it had stopped using heavy weaponry.[2]

The Sri Lankan President announced an end to the use of heavy weapons on 27 April 2009, but several witnesses to the government's own flawed inquiry testified that shells were fired by both the government and rebels in May.[3] US Embassy cables in May also repeatedly referred to heavy shelling and requests to the government to uphold its commitment not to use heavy weapons.[4]

Diplomats were aware that the Sri Lankan government was shelling civilians. A leaked US Embassy cable from mid-March 2009 complains that despite repeated assurances that it would not use heavy weapons or shell the safe zone, the Sri Lankan Army continued to do so on an almost daily basis, killing hundreds of civilians.[5]

On 4 May 2009, US diplomats showed the Sri Lankan Foreign Minister two 'before and after' declassified satellite images taken on 26 and 28 April to prove artillery shelling of the safe zone had taken place.[6] The Foreign Minister reportedly responded by implying that the Tigers had shelled their own positions. According to the diplomatic cables, the same pictures were then shown to the President, who offered no credible explanation and even denied reports of a shell attack on 2 May 2009 on the makeshift hospital, on the grounds that the facility simply didn't exist.

Human Rights Watch and Amnesty USA commissioned an analysis of commercial satellite imagery of the war zone and found shocking evidence of shell craters and burned dwellings visible in areas where civilians were settled.[7] The analysis noted that the images didn't pick up damage from air-burst munitions, which were reportedly being used as well.

Both sides appear to have recklessly endangered thousands of civilians fleeing the war zone in May by continuing to fire at one another from across opposite sides of the lagoon. Several witnesses to the government's own inquiry referred to the Tigers and army shooting while they tried to cross, even though the large mass of thousands of civilians would have been visible to both warring parties.

At what point does an indiscriminate attack become intentional? The Sri Lankan military was not firing into a black hole. It made heavy use of drones, which gave the commanders a good idea of where civilians were concentrated. The Tigers did wear sarongs over their uniforms to confuse the drones and exploited civilians as a human buffer. However the military admits it had informers behind Tiger lines.[8] It was easy to infiltrate rebel ranks once the Tigers' recruitment drive became chaotic and desperate and central control started to break down. Many witnesses report seeing Tamils who they'd thought were Tigers working with the army when they left the war zone in May.

By the Rebels

1. Violence to life and person, in particular murder, mutilation, cruel treatment (including forced labour) and torture and taking of hostages
2. Forcible recruitment of children

The entire civilian population was kept by the rebels inside the war zone, large numbers of them against their will. Many had little choice but to stay because their children or husbands were fighting and they couldn't bear to abandon them. Others remained because they believed the reassuring statements from the rebels that international help was on its way. Lack of reliable information meant even Tigers like Usha didn't seem to realise the end was nigh until it was too late.

The nun's story explains how strict the Tigers' 'pass system' was that controlled all movement out of their territory, inflicting penalties such as loss of property on those who left illegally. Local UN staff were also held hostage in the war zone.

Most Tigers and civilians who were interrogated at the end of the war about why they were in rebel territory claimed that they'd been forced to stay by the rebels. In many cases they'd been there voluntarily, but were aware there was no freedom of movement for others who wanted to leave.

★

The use of child soldiers by the Tigers has been documented not just in 2009 but throughout the course of the civil war. I have personally met such children in rehabilitation centres in Sri Lanka and seen them manning sensitive checkpoints and marching in Tiger parades.

Aid workers witnessed the ruthless efficiency with which the Tigers combed the countryside picking up the young, including staff from international humanitarian organisations. By the spring of 2009 the rebels were forcibly recruiting multiple children from the same family, some of them under-age, and with increasing brutality. Neriyen's story tells of how untrained recruits were sent to the front line as cannon fodder and deserted if they possibly could. The nun hid a deserter, while the clergy witnessed the child catchers at work and parents' desire for revenge afterwards. Tiger brainwashing was so intense that the travelling-bag girl in Korben's story opted to stay on at the end of the war and fight to the death, even though she'd initially been forced to join.

One skeletal farmer's wife from the Tigers' heartland told me her nephew had been forcibly recruited in March. He was the third child to be taken: his parents begged the Tigers to take them instead, but they wouldn't listen. The boy never came back. Physically shaking with the effort of relating the event, the woman said if she'd seen the Tigers who'd taken her nephew she would happily have handed them in to the army. Her desire for revenge was overwhelming.

The US State Department reported eighteen incidents in 2009 of children as young as twelve being forcibly recruited by the Tigers.

Crimes Against Humanity

By the Government

The threshold requirement for 'crimes against humanity' is the existence of a widespread or systematic attack directed against a civilian population. This is irrespective of whether there are combatants among the civilians.

The UN panel of experts found there were credible allegations of crimes against humanity committed by the Sri Lankan government in its widespread shelling, extrajudicial killings and disappearances, deprivation of food and medicine and mass detention. Specifically it pointed to the following:

1. Murder: this can involve reckless disregard for human life
2. Extermination: by creating conditions calculated to bring about the destruction of a significant part of the civilian population
3. Imprisonment: hundreds of thousands of civilians were detained without reasonable grounds in Manik Farm
4. Persecution: on racial or political grounds against the people of rebel areas
5. Disappearances

International law prohibits all violence to life and person, including murder, of armed forces who have laid down their arms or are in detention.

A video clip from Journalists for Democracy in Sri Lanka broadcast on Channel 4 showed the execution of nine bound and naked Tamils by Sri Lankan Army soldiers. Sri Lanka has repeatedly disputed and investigated this film but the UN's special rapporteur on extrajudicial, summary or arbitrary executions concluded it was genuine. Channel 4 also broadcast a documentary called *Sri Lanka's Killing Fields: Unpunished War Crimes*, which used a forensic expert to examine a photograph of the dead body of the rebel leader's twelve-year-old son which indicated the child had been executed at point-blank range.

By the Rebels
(source: *Report of the Secretary-General's Panel of Experts on Accountability in Sri Lanka*)
The UN panel of experts cited the crime of widespread or systematic attacks directed against a civilian population, in so far as the rebels had a consistent practice of holding civilians against their will and killing some who tried to leave, and also deployed suicide bombers against civilians during the war.

A Tiger suicide bomber exploded herself among fleeing refugees at the height of the war, killing women and children. The army says there were three other suicide attacks in the midst of civilians in March 2009.[9] There are also reports of rebels shooting at civilians trying to escape, though there is some disagreement among survivors as to whether there was a policy of shoot-to-kill.

Notes

Introduction

1. This has also been reported by the US government: 'May 16 – An organization's local sources reported that they attempted to escape the NFZ [no-fire zone] with a large group of children, coming out with white flags. The SLA [Sri Lankan Army] started shooting at them and told them to go back to their bunkers. The sources reportedly saw soldiers throw grenades into two bunkers, and saw tanks going over bunkers and destroying everything inside'; 'May 18 – An organization reported accounts from witnesses in the NFZ of SLA soldiers throwing grenades into several civilian bunkers as a precaution against the LTTE attacking them from those bunkers. Some civilians also reported seeing an army truck running over injured people lying on the road. Later in the day, the SLA brought in earth-moving equipment to bury the bodies that had been lying outside for two days or more. Civilians reported seeing among the corpses injured people who were asking for help, and believed that the SLA did not always attempt to separate the injured and the dying from those who had died.' US State Department, *Report to Congress on Incidents During the Recent Conflict in Sri Lanka*, 2009, http://www.state.gov/documents/organization/131025.pdf, p. 44.

2. International Crisis Group, *The Sri Lankan Tamil Diaspora after the LTTE*, 23 Feb 2010, http://www.crisisgroup.org/en/regions/asia/south-asia/sri-lanka/186-the-sri-lankan-tamil-diaspora-after-the-ltte.aspx.

Sri Lankan Government Statements

1. http://www.lankamission.org/content/view/850/.
2. http://www.president.gov.lk/speech_New.php?Id=59.
3. http://abcnews.go.com/Politics/story?id=6769373&page=1.
4. 'Act Responsibly or be Chased Out: SL Tells Foreigners', *Indian Express*, 1 February 2009, http://www.indianexpress.com/news/act-responsibly-or-be-chased-out-sl-tel ls-f/417770/.
5. http://archive.lacnet.org/2009/2009_02_04/.

The War the United Nations Lost

1. *Sri Lankan Tamils Block UN Withdrawal*, 17 September 2008, http://www. dailymotion.com/video/x6s45k_sri-lankan-tamils-block-un-withdraw_news.
2. International Crisis Group complained of the UN's quick acceptance of the order to withdraw, saying. 'UN agencies in Sri Lanka allowed themselves to be bullied

by the government and accepted a reduced role in protecting civilians, most notably with their quick acceptance of the government's September 2008 order to remove all staff from the Vanni' (the Sri Lankan name for the area under rebel control), *War Crimes in Sri Lanka*, Asia Report No. 191, 17 May 2010, p. 29, http://www.crisisgroup.org/~/media/Files/asia/south-asia/sri-lanka/191%20War%20Crimes%20in%20Sri%20Lanka.pdf.

3. The fuel sent by the government for the hospitals in Kilinochchi was normally 15,000 litres a month but was reduced to 6,250 litres in July 2008 and to 2,250 in August. Aid workers commented that 'Reduced fuel allocations are significantly impacting the hospital's ability to maintain its ambulatory services as well as run generators for cold chain maintenance.' Inter-Agency Standing Committee Country Team, Colombo, *Situation Report No. 139*, 7–14 August 2008, http://www.reliefweb.int/rw/rwb.nsf/db900sid/MUMA-7HQ8AB?OpenDocument.

4. United Nations, *Report of the Secretary-General's Panel of Experts on Accountability in Sri Lanka*, 31 March 2011, p. 24.

5. American diplomats knew what was happening but remained silent, reporting in cables: 'We are in indirect contact with one of the two UN expatriate workers still in the Vanni. He reported shelling by the SLA within the no-fire zone, including a significant explosion 8 meters from the UN bunker which killed and injured scores of civilians, and also injured a UN staff member.' WikiLeaks cable 09COLOMBO86, 26 January 2009.

6. Gordon Weiss, *The Cage: The Fight for Sri Lanka and the Last Days of the Tamil Tigers*, London: Bodley Head, 2011.

7. The UN task force talked to priests, civil servants, doctors and local staff from organisations like Oxfam, Care and the Danish Refugee Council on a satellite phone. There were 213 Tamil aid workers left behind and 60 clerics and nuns. UN staff tried to tally the reports, recording where incidents had taken place, what type of weapon was used and where. They found that an overwhelming majority of injuries were caused by artillery.

8. This figure is for the period August 2008–13 May 2009. It didn't include any of the heavy casualties after 21 April, when the army captured a large chunk of rebel territory at Puttumatalan, because there was nobody left to pass information. It is cited in the *Report of the Secretary-General's Panel of Experts on Accountability in Sri Lanka*, p. 40. An American Embassy cable acknowledged the figures as a credible minimum count of casualties and reported that a majority of the deaths occurred inside the successive 'safe zones'. WikiLeaks cable 09COLOMBO402, 7 April 2009.

9. This is an estimate for the period after 10 May 2009: WikiLeaks cable COLOMBO 00000539, 18 May 2009.

10. Letter from Rev. Fr G. A. Francis Joseph, 10 May 2009, given to the author.

11. 'UN Concealed Carnage to Keep Sri Lanka Goodwill', Indymedia UK, 30 May 2009, http://www.indymedia.org.uk/en/2009/05/431282.html.

12. Julian Borger, 'Wikileaks Cables: David Miliband Focused on Sri Lankan War "to Win Votes"', *Guardian*, 1 December 2010, http://www.guardian.co.uk/world/2010/dec/01/wikileaks-david-miliband-sri-lanka.

13. Jonas Lindberg, Camilla Orjuela, Siemon Wezerman and Linda Åkerström, 'Arms Trade with Sri Lanka – Global Business, Local Costs', 2011, http://www.svenskafreds.se/sites/default/files/, p. 75.

14. Jason Burke, 'Adam Werritty and Liam Fox's Sri Lankan Connections', *Guardian*, 13 October 2011, http:/www.guardian.co.ukpolitics/2011/oct/13/adam-werritty-liam-fox-sri-lanka.

15. Only the United States wanted to delay the loan, to pressure Colombo to do more to protect civilians: Louis Charbonneau and Ranga Sirilal, 'UN Council Sees No Need to Punish Sri Lanka', Reuters Alertnet, 1 May 2009, http://reliefweb.int/node/306840.

16. Claire Magone, Fabrice Weissman and Michael Neuman (eds.), *Humanitarian Negotiations Revealed: The MSF Experience*, London: Hurst, 2011, p. 31.

17. A US Embassy telex reported that, in response to a question about his assessment of conditions at Manik Farm, Ban said his visit there had been 'very sobering and very sad'. The telex quoted Ban saying the conditions were worse than those at any other camps, including in Darfur and Goma, that he had visited, and noted he had seen signs of malnutrition. Asked about his flyover of the no-fire zone, Ban described seeing 'complete devastation' and no movement of human beings. '27.05.2009: Sri Lanka: Ban Ki-moon Briefs Co-Chair Ambassadors on Visit', *Aftenposten*, 7 May 2011, http://www.aftenposten.no/spesial/wikileaksdokumenter/article4109583.ece.

18. Médecins Sans Frontières treated 4,000 patients, whom they estimated were 5–10 per cent of the total number from the immediate aftermath of the war. Claire Magone, Fabrice Weissman and Michael Neuman, op. cit., pp. 29–33. A US Embassy cable said: 'The amount of wounded and deceased people is increasing as the situation in the NFZ intensifies, with estimates that some 20 out of every 27 people have at least one injured family member.' WikiLeaks cable 09COLOMBO473, 30 April 2009.

19. Their cable said: 'Patients, including many children and babies, were emaciated and exhibited signs of malnourishment. Many had been separated from their companions. The proportion of patients with amputated hands, feet, and legs is staggering…Post-operative care had virtually ceased with patients being discharged if able to walk.' WikiLeaks cable 09COLOMBO473, 30 April 2009.

Aid Worker Expulsions 2008–9

1. Rohan Abeywardena, 'Berghof Chief Asked to Leave', *Sunday Times* (Sri Lanka), 30 December 2007, http://www.sundaytimes.lk/071230/News/news0001.html.

2. Jeremy Page, 'Aid Workers Forced to Leave Sri Lanka Under Strict New Visa Rules', *The Times*, 3 June 2009.

The Journalist

1. Sri Lankan TV footage proves this. The commentary says: 'This is the Chalai–
   Puttumatalan road,' and points out buildings clearly visible on the other side of the
   lagoon. ITN, A Look at the No Fire Zone from the Defence Front Lines – ITN
   News, 8 April 2009, http://www.youtube.com/watch?v=rM6FLvyUUZA&feature
   =related.
2. Still photos were released by Human Rights Watch of the Puttumatalan Hospital in
   April 2009. *Human Rights Watch Researcher Anna Neistat Says: Srilankan Govt Shelling
   on Tamil Civilians*, http://www.youtube.com/watch?v=B4IVr-j-tXI. A government
   report quotes a nursing officer saying that at Puttumatalan 'patients had to be
   kept on the ground on tarpaulins and it was after 5 days that they had been able
   to get beds'. He also said there were 'no anaesthetics and painkillers'. *Report of the
   Commission of Inquiry on Lessons Learnt and Reconciliation* (LLRC Report), p. 98, para
   4.194. Two other witnesses testified to the government commission about patients
   lying on the hospital floor.
3. The Sri Lankan government has spoken of its infiltrators operating behind Tiger
   lines for reconnaissance. LLRC Report, p. 61, para 4.68.

The Spokesman

1. This is referred to in US Embassy cables: 'The Government of Norway has been
   engaged in quiet efforts to persuade the LTTE to allow civilians in the safe zone
   to leave. (Note: Norwegian efforts must be strictly protected and not referred to
   either publicly or privately by USG [United States government] officials with third
   country nationals.) The LTTE has responded to Norwegian overtures by insisting
   there should be a ceasefire and political negotiations to resolve the conflict. The
   LTTE has also raised numerous procedural and other questions about how the UN
   and ICRC [International Committee of the Red Cross] might evacuate civilians,
   the treatment they would be subjected to in the camps in Vavuniya, and GSL
   [government of Sri Lanka] plans to resettle them. The Norwegians have made clear
   that the time for a ceasefire to pursue political negotiations is now passed; they are
   only responding to LTTE questions regarding the treatment of civilians once they
   leave the North.' WikiLeaks cable 09COLOMBO308, 19 March 2009.
2. 'The Norwegian Ambassador reported to Ambassador over the weekend that he
   had communicated a GSL offer of amnesty for all LTTE fighters except the top
   two (Prabhakaran and Pottu Amman), but had yet to hear back from the LTTE.'
   WikiLeaks, US Embassy cable 09COLOMBO65, 20 January 2009.
3. 'Chargé called Foreign Minister Bogollagama April 24 to convey strong Co-Chair
   interest in working with the GSL to obtain an LTTE surrender through laying
   down arms to a third party (UN or ICRC), amnesty for cadres, and custody with
   international monitoring of the remaining LTTE leadership. Bogollagama was
   non-committal, saying that the GSL is looking at these options. Charge reiterated

support for a UN mission into the safe zone to talk to the LTTE leadership about surrender.' WikiLeaks, US Embassy cable 09COLOMBO459, 24 April 2009.

4. The Tigers wanted US and UK security guarantees and assurances that the 'human and political rights of the Tamil people' would be met.

5. The UN's *Report of the Secretary-General's Panel of Experts on Accountability in Sri Lanka* cites a group of about 300, but sources tell me forty names were on the list of those wanting to surrender.

6. Questions have subsequently been asked about Vijay Nambiar's impartiality, given that his brother was an Indian Army general who'd fought the Tigers in the 1980s and later acted as an unpaid adviser to the Sri Lankan Army. However it's doubtful Nambiar's invitation to witness the surrender would have really materialised. At this stage the Sri Lankan government was adamantly refusing any international presence. There were parallel efforts under way to ensure a team of Sri Lankan religious officials could witness the surrender, but even these failed.

7. Andrew Buncombe, 'Tamil leaders "Killed as They Tried to Surrender"', *Independent*, 20 May 2009, http://www.independent.co.uk/news/world/asia/tamil-leaders-killed-as-they-tried-to-surrender-1687790.html.

8. Nadesan had good contacts with Sinhalese leftists from his days as a policeman in Colombo. One of the advisers to President Rajapaksa was a witness at Nadesan's wedding before he joined the Tigers.

9. Marie Colvin, 'Tigers Begged Me to Broker Surrender', *The Times*, 23 May 2009.

Tamil Tigers

1. Coalition to Stop the Use of Child Soldiers, *Global Report 2008*, http://www.childsoldiersglobalreport.org/content/sri-lanka.

The Doctor

1. *2009 01 24 Udayar Kattu Suthendra Puram Shell Attack*, http://www.youtube.com/watch?v=zNUJ-qUC3Pk&feature=mfu_in_order&list=UL; *2009 02 02 Sri Lanka Hospital Shelled by Army*, http://www.youtube.com/watch?v=Oiq0Fu26X-Q; *Sri Lankan Cluster Bomb Attack on PTK Hospital 07th Feb 2009*, http://www.youtube.com/watch?v=hNGPeEk4p0I; *Wanni Meheuma 2009-03-12 (SL Army Captured Puthukudirippu Hospital)*, http://www.youtube.com/watch?v=IdM8Da3sxzU; *LTTEs Last Hospital (VIP) Captured by SLA After PTK Hospital 2009 Mar 13*, http://www.youtube.com/watch?v=YSrE2RFLphk.

2. Confidential letter from the International Committee of the Red Cross to Lieutenant-General Fonseka, 24 January 2009, referring to Valipunam Hospital being hit by a shell on 21 January; the same hospital being hit by two shells on 22 January, leaving five dead and twenty-two injured; and Uddayarkattu Hospital being hit by a shell and another shell striking its compound, on 24 January, five dead and twenty-seven injured. This was after the coordinates of the hospitals had

been communicated by the ICRC to the Sri Lankan military on 18 and 20 January. The ICRC letter says these were the second structures to be hit in January – referring to an earlier letter of 14 January.

3. Hospitals in Valipunam, Iranapalai and Matalan; a converted house in Valayanmadam; a building near to Mullivaikkal Hospital.

4. *PTK hospital shelling*, 19 February 2009, http://www.youtube.com/watch?v=RFP3UjAwfSY.

5. Confidential letter from ICRC to Lt-Gen Fonseka, February 2009, LLRC Report, Annex 3, regarding PTK Hospital, whose coordinates were communicated on 23 January. The ICRC says a shell hit the building at 1710 hours on 1 February.

6. *Report of the Secretary-General's Panel of Experts on Accountability in Sri Lanka*, p. 36, para 123.

7. Thirteen deaths from starvation in late February 2009, according to Dr Sathiamorthy in 'Situation Report' from Mullaitivu District, a Sri Lankan government document, February 2009, http://www.sangam.org/2009/03/GA_Report.pdf.

8. WikiLeaks cable 09COLOMBO307, 19 March 2009.

9. This death was reported to the US Embassy: 'Reports from a doctor inside the NFZ the morning of April 22 told of deteriorating conditions for civilians there... The doctor saw 600 or more seriously wounded in his location on April 21, with over 100 of them dying after admission. He stated at this point many wounded were not coming to the medical points as they understood there was almost no treatment available. He reported "cluster munitions," likely air bursts, hit the medical facility on April 21, killing Dr. Sivamanoharan, a mental health doctor.' WikiLeaks cable 09COLOMBO454, 22 April 2009.

10. The UN's *Joint Humanitarian Update Report No. 6*, covering the period 1–15 May 2009, quoted in LLRC Report, p. 101, para 4.210.

11. 'Credible local NGO sources have said the families were told the doctors may be released following such confessions and they may have had to videotape individual confessions for the President...Of particular concern is what will happen to the doctors if in fact they are released soon...If the doctors are released, it will be critical for the GSL to take meaningful action to ensure that the doctors are not then "disappeared" in order to prevent them from making any modifications to this press statement.' WikiLeaks cable 09COLOMBO695, 13 July 2009. One of the four government doctors, Dr Shanmugarajah, was injured on 15 May 2009 and later testified that he received inadequate medical treatment before being detained in the notorious 'fourth floor' of the Criminal Investigation Department in Colombo: LLRC Report, p. 82.

12. *Sri Lanka Army Hospital Attack – Ambulance Burned – 13-May-2009*, http://www.youtube.com/watch?v=rye6ZrmC4i4.

The Nun

1. Amantha Perera, 'How the Virgin Mary Survived Sri Lanka's Civil War', *Time*, 17 August 2009, http://www.time.com/time/magazine/article/0,9171,1917716,00. html#ixzz1iEedKYqb.

2. 'Priests and Sisters Stranded', *Daily Mirror* (Colombo), 18 February 2009, http://www.highbeam.com/doc/1P3-1648100861.html; Melani Manel Perera, 'Rajapaksa to Apostolic Nuncio: Get Priests out of Conflict Zone', 2 February 2009, http://www.asianews.it/news-en/Rajapaksa-to-apostolic-nuncio:-get-priests-out-of-conflict-zone-14391.html.

3. Sr Mary Lourdes told reporters afterwards that she'd been shot in the leg by the Tigers while escaping. With her was a seventy-four-year-old nun, Sr Mary Colostica, who confirmed that the Tigers were willing to let the nuns leave, but not the people with them. Fr Sunil de Silva, 'Two Rosarian Sisters Shot by LTTE While Fleeing with People to Safe Zone', Archdiocese Website, 13 February 2009, http://www.archdioceseofcolombo.com/news.php?id=592. A priest also told me his sister was badly beaten by the Tigers for trying to escape and later collapsed and died.

4. *Feb 9th/09: LTTE Female Suicide Bomber Targets Rescue Centre*, http://www.liveleak. com/view?i=c29_1234208416.

5. A member of the clergy giving evidence to the Lessons Learnt and Reconciliation Commission said that on 23 March 575–580 children between the ages of fifteen and eighteen were forcibly taken from St Mary's Church, Valayanmadam. Reports said the Tigers shot the parents who tried to resist, killing one person and injuring others: LLRC Report, p. 176, para 5.85. The US State Department's 2009 *Report to Congress on Incidents During the Recent Conflict in Sri Lanka* also quoted a *New Indian Express* story of 3 May 2009 quoting a woman who'd escaped to the army saying about 600 had been rounded up: http://janamejayan.wordpress.com/2009/05/03/for-better-or-worse-tamils-in-lanka-back-ltte/. However, the priest I spoke to said the above reports were exaggerated. He said nobody was killed and the exact number of children taken was not known but probably not more than 100–150, and some were underage but not all.

6. Fr James Pathinathan, the parish priest of Mullaitivu, was injured in Valayanmadam on 22 April 2009. Fr Sunil de Silva, 23 April 2009, http://www. archdioceseofcolombo.com/news.php?id=648.

7. One source who spoke to the US Embassy at the time estimated that 25,000 civilians were there, and that a casualty figure of 1,000–1,500 killed and 2,000 injured was conservative. He said civilians wanted to escape to the government-controlled areas but couldn't due to intense firing and shelling. He also confirmed that the church was hit by a shell. WikiLeaks cable 09COLOMBO545, 22 April 2009.

8. The UN estimate was of about 130,000 people still left in the war zone at this point, but the numbers were downplayed by the Sri Lankan government, according to the *Report of the Secretary-General's Panel of Experts on Accountability in Sri Lanka*,

p. 37. The US State Department also released two pictures in April that it said showed 100,000 civilians crammed onto a beach in the conflict zone: Jeremy Page, 'Satellite Images of Sri Lanka Conflict Used in War Crimes Inquiry', *The Times*, 22 May 2009. US Embassy cables say that on 16 and 17 May an estimated 72,000 civilians escaped: WikiLeaks cable COLOMBO 00000535, 21 May 2009.

9. On 21 April the UN Humanitarian Coordinator in Sri Lanka, Neil Buhne, told Integrated Regional Information Networks (IRIN): 'Our calculations and reports from government officials still in the area suggest there are at least some tens of thousands, and perhaps as many as 100,000 or more left. We hope it is less, but we must be prepared for more.' The government said there were 10–15,000: 'Sri Lanka: UN Calls for "Maximum Restraint" to Protect Civilians', IRIN, 21 April 2009, http://www.irinnews.org/report.aspx?reportid=84025.

10. The new archbishop was even more sympathetic to the government side. He opposed any action against Sri Lanka at the UN Human Rights Council in 2012 on the grounds that it would be an insult to the intelligence of the Sri Lankan people: 'Catholic Church Oppose UNHRC Resolution', BBC, 27 February 2012. He also warned 'misled' priests abroad who tried to promote 'divisions' in the country: Anto Akkara, 'Church Leaders on Opposite Sides after Report on Sri Lankan War Crimes', Catholic News Service, 29 April 2011, http://www.catholicsun.org/2011/april/29/sri-lanka.html; 'Archbishop Congratulates Armed Forces on the Conclusion of War', 18 May 2009, http://www.lankaweb.com/news/items/2009/05/18/archbishop-congratulates-armed-forces-on-the-conclusion-of-war/; 'Archbishop of Colombo Calls for Forgiveness after Sri Lankan Civil War', Catholic News Agency, 22 May 2009, http://www.catholicnewsagency.com/news/archbishop_of_colombo_calls_for_forgiveness_after_sri_lankan_civil_war/.

Disappearance

1. Report of the UN Working Group on Enforced or Involuntary Disappearances.
2. 'Horrible Rise of Disappearances in Post-war Sri Lanka Continues Unabated', Groundviews, 5 April 2012, http://groundviews.org/2012/04/05/horrible-rise-of-disappearances-in-post-war-sri-lanka-continues-unabated/.
3. 'UN Says Body of Sri Lankan Activist Found', *Wall Street Journal*, 29 July 2009, http://online.wsj.com/article/SB10001424053111904888304576475721525790388.html.
4. Indika Sri Aravinda, 'Missing: Post War Abductions Rise', *Sunday Leader*, 11 December 2011, http://www.thesundayleader.lk/2011/12/11/missing-post-war-abductions-rise/.

The Rebel Mother

1. This is corroborated by testimony to the government's own commission, where a civilian said, 'There had been an announcement saying that if anyone had been in the LTTE even for a day they should surrender.' LLRC Report, p. 108, n. 299.
2. Gethin Chamberlin, 'Sri Lankan Guards "Sexually Abused Girls" in Tamil Refugee Camp', *Observer*, 20 December 2009, http://www.guardian.co.uk/world/2009/dec/20/tamil-tigers-sri-lanka-refugees.
3. *Tamil Tigers Admit Defeat*, ABC Radio Australia, 18 May 2009, http://www.abc.net.au/ra/connectasia/stories/200905/s2573372.htm.
4. She paid half in advance and the other half, an additional Rs. 40,000 (£200), on top of what was already paid.

Widows

1. LLRC Report, Annex 8, November 2011, http://slembassyusa.org/downloads/LLRC-REPORT.pdf.
2. District Secretariats of Vavunyia, Mullativu, Mannar, Kilinochchi.
3. Rajani Iqbal, 'Tragic Plight of the War-Widows in Sri Lanka', 4 July 2011, Transcurrents, http://transcurrents.com/news-views/archives/2002.
4. 'Over 59,000 War Widows in Sri Lanka's North and East', ColomboPage, August 2011, http://www.colombopage.com/archive_11A/Aug13_1313209283JR.php.
5. Status of Widows' Monthly Income, Humanitarian Portal, Sri Lanka, UN Office for the Coordination of Humanitarian Affairs, http://www.hpsl.lk/Catalogues.aspx?catID=23.

The Volunteer

1. Pulidevan also told me there was very heavy fighting then, contrary to news reports.
2. A Catholic priest, Father Reginold, was filmed describing how children were starving. He showed a man whose wife had been killed in shelling who needed milk powder to keep his baby alive: *2009-05-02 Safe Zone Situation Report by Father Reginold*, http://www.youtube.com/watch?v=T1XXIfeRQaU.
3. Korben says the injuries occured in Pokkunai, but the patients were brought to Mullivaikkal makeshift Hospital. The LLRC Report includes testimony (p. 74) that refers to one or possibly two incidents of shelling of queues for milk in Pokkunai in mid-April 2009, where 40–45 pregnant women and children were the casualties. It's not clear if they were two or one incidents and if the women died – the quotations in the report are vague. No explanation is given for how this could have happened or who was responsible for such an atrocity. The witnesses, though, blamed firing by the Sri Lankan military for the deaths. A separate UN report also said a large number of women and children were shelled on 8 April 2009 in Pokkunai while waiting for milk. See also p. 81.

Disabled

1. 'Over 14,000 Sri Lankan Soldiers Disabled in War', Xinhua news agency, quoted on Chinese Radio International website, 19 March 2010, http://english.cri. cn/6966/2010/03/19/189s557666.htm.

The Fighter

1. Testifying to the government's commission in 2010, Major-General Shavendra Silva confirmed there were no NGOs around on 17 and 18 May when combatants first surrendered to the military. He said they 'never kept surrendees or captives in their areas for long periods of time'. LLRC Report, p. 103, para 4.217.
2. Omanthai School.
3. In Omanthai School, another school building in Vavuniya, then Nelikulam and Joint Operations Security Forces Headquarters Camp, and then the 'fourth floor' in Colombo.

Tiger Equipment According to Sri Lankan Military Estimates

1. LLRC Report, Annex 3, November 2011, http://slembassyusa.org/downloads/ LLRC-REPORT.pdf.

The Shopkeeper

1. The place where this family was living is known as an 'Alternative Place of Detention', but it is inside the Villawood compound and there were security checks and paperwork to be filled out before being allowed in.
2. Karu says he was treated by Dr Kamilini, who was killed in an attack not long afterwards.

Asylum Seekers

1. According to Immigration Detention Statistics Summary, 30 November 2011, http://www.immi.gov.au/managing-australias-borders/detention/_pdf/ immigration-detention-statistics-20111130.pdf.
2. Piotr Juchno and Alexandros Bitoulas, 'Population and Social Conditions Statistics in Focus', European Union, Eurostat Statistics in Focus 48/2011, epp.eurostat. ec.europa.eu/cache/ITY...SF.../KS-SF-11-048-EN.PDF.
3. Information Centre About Asylum and Refugees, *Key Statistics about Asylum Seeker Applications in the UK*, http://www.icar.org.uk/9556/statistics/analysis-of-asylum-and-refugee-statistics.html.
4. Refugee Council, briefing on Home Office asylum statistics for 2011, February 2012, http://www.refugeecouncil.org.uk/policy/briefings/2012/asylumstats2011.
5. Citizenship and Immigration Canada, *Facts and Figures: Immigration Overview 2010*, http://www.cic.gc.ca/english/pdf/research-stats/facts2010.pdf.

The Wife

1. Refugee Council, *The Vulnerable Women's Project: Refugee and Asylum Seeking Women Affected by Rape or Sexual Violence*, February 2009, http://www.refugeecouncil. org.uk/Resources/Refugee%20Council/downloads/researchreports/RC%20 VWP-report-web.pdf.

2. 'In December 2010, CB was arrested at the Colombo airport on his return and was detained for a month…He said that during this time he was beaten with metal rods and raped four or five times by two men', Human Rights Watch, 'UK: Halt Deportations of Tamils to Sri Lanka: Credible Allegations of Arrest and Torture upon Return', 25 February 2012, http://www.hrw.org/news/2012/02/24/uk-halt-deportations-tamils-sri-lanka.

3. US Ambassador-at-Large for Global Women's Issues Melanne Verveer said: 'in the most recent phase of the conflict, from 2006–2009, though we remained deeply concerned about reports of extrajudicial killings, disappearances and mistreatment of detainees, we have not received reports that rape and sexual abuse were used as tools of war, as they clearly have in other conflict areas around the world', quoted in International Crisis Group, *Sri Lanka: Women's Insecurity in the North and East*, Asia Report No. 217, 20 December 2011, p. 15.

4. Ibid.

5. 'The Sri Lankan Soldiers "Whose Hearts Turned to Stone"', Channel 4 News, 27 July 2011, http://www.channel4.com/news/the-sri-lankan-soldiers-whose-hearts-turned-to-stone.

6. On 6 May 2009 Channel 4 aired a video reporting that aid workers had found the bodies of at least three dead women at a bathing area in the camp. The incident caused the UN to ask for the soldiers guarding the bathing area to be replaced by twenty female police officers. On 21 May 2009, the UK's Sky News aired a video quoting a woman who asked not to be identified saying there was sexual assault and harassment in the camps. Alex Crawford, 'Claims of Abuse in Sri Lankan Refugee Camps', Sky News Online, 21 May 2009, http://news.sky.com/home/world-news/article/15285938.

7. Amanda Hodge, 'Tamil Refugees Forced into Sex Rackets', *Australian*, 2 July 2009, http://www.theaustralian.com.au/tamil-refugees-forced-into-sex-rackets/story-fna7dq6e-1225744996639.

8. 'Defence Secretary Gotabaya Rajapaksa speaks to "Headlines Today"', Transcurrents. com, 11 August 2011, http://transcurrents.com/news-views/archives/2921.

9. Sofie Rordam, 'Decriminalising Rape Through Immunity for Perpetrators', *Sri Lanka Guardian*, November 2010, http://www.srilankaguardian.org/2010/11/decriminalization-of-rape-through.html.

10. Raisa Wickrematunge, 'The Scars Remain: Sexual Abuse in the North and East', *Sunday Leader*, 15 January 2012, http://www.thesundayleader.lk/2012/01/15/the-scars-remain-sexual-abuse-in-the-north-and-east/.

Conclusion

1. International Crisis Group, *Sri Lanka's North II: Rebuilding under the Military*, Asia Report No. 220, 16 March 2012.

2. Amnesty International cited seven torture detention sites in northern Sri Lanka; five in Vavuniya and two in Mullaitivu. '"Secret Detention Centres" in Sri Lanka', 8 November 2011, http://www.bbc.co.uk/sinhala/news/story/2011/11/111108_torture.shtml; *Sri Lanka: Women's Insecurity in the North and East*, Asia Report No. 217.

3. Melani Manel Perera, 'Tamil Refugees and War Widows in Militarised Jaffna', 14 December 2011, AsiaNews, http://www.asianews.it/news-en/Tamil-refugees-and-war-widows-in-militarised-Jaffna-23440.html. Jaffna has 40,000 war widows according to the government: LLRC Report, p. 183. According to the Sri Lanka Foundation for Rehabilitation of the Disabled, an estimated 10–15 per cent of the over 1.1 million population of the Northern Province is physically handicapped: Amantha Perera, 'Peace Brings Little for the War-Disabled', Inter-Press Service (IPS), 19 December 2011, http://ipsnews.net/news.asp?idnews=106249.

4. International Commission of Jurists, *Beyond Lawful Constraints: Sri Lanka's Mass Detention of LTTE Suspects*, September 2010, http://icj.org/dwn/database/BeyondLawfulConstraints-SLreport-Sept2010.pdf; 'Sri Lanka orders cut in Aid Work, BBC Online, 9 July 2009, http://news.bbc.co.uk/1/hi/8142550.stm.

5. 'Senior UN Official Warns Against Harassing Sri Lankan Human Rights Defenders', UN News Centre, 23 March 2009, http://www.un.org/apps/news/story.asp?NewsID=41617&Cr=Sri.

6. Sri Lanka is currently ranked as the twenty-first-largest contributor of troops and police to UN Peacekeeping operations in several areas in the world, according to the Sri Lankan Ministry of External Affairs. 'At present nearly 1,190 personnel are deployed in many peacekeeping missions in countries such as Haiti, Iraq, Chad, Lebanon, Liberia, Somalia, Burundi, Sierra Leone, Ethiopia, and Cyprus, the Annual Performance Report of the Ministry tabled in Parliament today said', 'SL 21st largest contributor to UNPK ops', *Sunday Times*, 14 December 2011, http://getlocalne.ws/world/sri_lanka_national/sunday_times_news_9526616.

7. 'UN Committee Bars General Linked to Atrocities', Agence France Presse, 23 February 2012, http://www.google.com/hostednews/afp/article/ALeqM5juZmNHf5ybQ2SWe2B28-71CnHrdg?docId=CNG.46afe210f3a4daba53d5421f5e7c7364.1a1.

8. In 2010 the US Ambassador wrote in a cable: 'There are no examples we know of a regime undertaking wholesale investigations of its own troops or senior officials for war crimes while that regime or government remained in power. In Sri Lanka this is further complicated by the fact that responsibility for many of the alleged crimes rests with the country's senior civilian and military leadership, including President Rajapaksa and his brothers and opposition candidate General Fonseka', 'US Embassy Cables: Rajapaksa Shares Responsibility for 2009 Sri Lankan Massacre',

Guardian, 1 December 2010, http://www.guardian.co.uk/world/us-embassy-cables-documents/243811.

9. 'Lankan Court Orders Better Prison Conditions for Fonseka', ZeeNews.com, http://zeenews.india.com/news/south-asia/lankan-court-orders-better-prison-conditions-for-fonseka_668988.html.

10. There were 11,954 ex-combatants in custody after the war, but by September 2011 there were 2,727 left, according to government figures given in the LLRC Report.

11. LLRC Report, p. 106, para 4.229.

12. International Crisis Group, *War Crimes in Sri Lanka*, Asia Report No. 191, 17 May 2010, p. 29.

Appendix One: Casualties

1. LLRC Report, p. 37, para 3.20.

2. The figure of 282,000 comes from the Sri Lankan Ministry of Defence: 'Therapeutic Diet for IDP Children', http://www.defence.lk/new. asp?fname=20100102_03; 290,000 is from International Crisis Group.

3. The ICRC reported on 12 May 2009 that since mid-February it had evacuated nearly 14,000 sick or wounded civilians and their relatives: WikiLeaks cable 09COLOMBO695, 13 July 2009.

4. Conducted jointly by the government's village officials (Grama Sevak) and the Tamil Eelam Administration department of the rebels.

5. The LLRC report quoted civil servant Imelda Sukumar saying nearly 350,000 people were in rebel areas when she left on 22 January 2009. Another government officer said it was 330,000 people, based on a survey of village officials and ration cards. If 296,000 (282,000 in camps and 14,000 ICRC evacuees) emerged from the war by end May, simple subtraction says 40–60,000 people are missing presumed dead. Even if a portion of the government's own estimate of approximately 20,000 dead LTTE from 2006–9 is subtracted, there are still tens of thousands of missing people. However, Tiger families are said not to have had ration cards, which would have led to an underestimate.

6. *Report of the Secretary-General's Panel of Experts on Accountability in Sri Lanka*, 31 March 2011, p. 37.

7. International Crisis Group, 'Sri Lanka's Dead and Missing: The Need for an Accounting', 27 February 2012, http://www.crisisgroupblogs.org/srilanka-lastingpeace/2012/02/27/sri-lanka's-dead-and-missing-the-need-for-an-accounting/#more-78.

Appendix Two: Alleged War Crimes

1. LLRC Report, p. 100, para 4.202.

2. 'Opposition Says Sri Lanka Lied to UN over Heavy Weapons', Agence France Presse, 15 January 2010, http://www.lankabusinessonline.com/fullstory. php?nid=1983239780.

3. LLRC Report, p. 68, para 4.93; also paras 4.91, 4.90.

4. 'Sri Lanka: Embassy Shares Images of Safe Zone with President', WikiLeaks cable 09COLOMBO495, 5 May 2009; 'Northern Sri Lanka SitRep 69', WikiLeaks cable 09COLOMBO514, 11 May 2009; 'Northern Sri Lanka SitRep 70', WikiLeaks cable 09COLOMBO519, 12 May 2009; 'UK: Miliband Discusses Middle East, Iran, Africa and Sri Lanka with Ambassador Rice', WikiLeaks cable 09COLOMBO 0492, 13 May 2009; 'Northern Sri Lanka Sitrep 74', WikiLeaks cable 09COLOMBO535, 17 May 2009.

5. WikiLeaks cable 09COLOMBO308, 19 March 2009.

6. 'Sri Lanka: Embassy Shares Images of Safe Zone with President', WikiLeaks cable 09COLOMBO495, 5 May 2009.

7. Human Rights Watch, *High-Resolution Satellite Imagery and the Conflict in Sri Lanka Summary Report*, 12 May 2009, http://www.hrw.org/sites/default/files/related_material/srilanka_12may2009.pdf.

8. LLRC Report, p. 64, para 4.68.

9. LLRC Report, p. 105, para 4.226.